MOON HAN

SMOKY MOUNTAINS

© JEFF BRADLEY

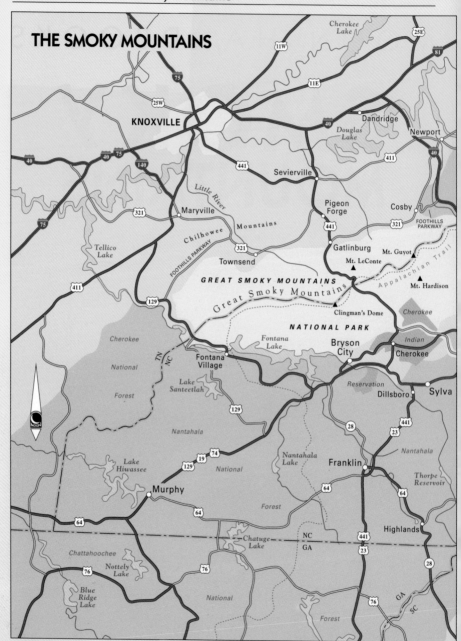

THE SMOKY MOUNTAINS

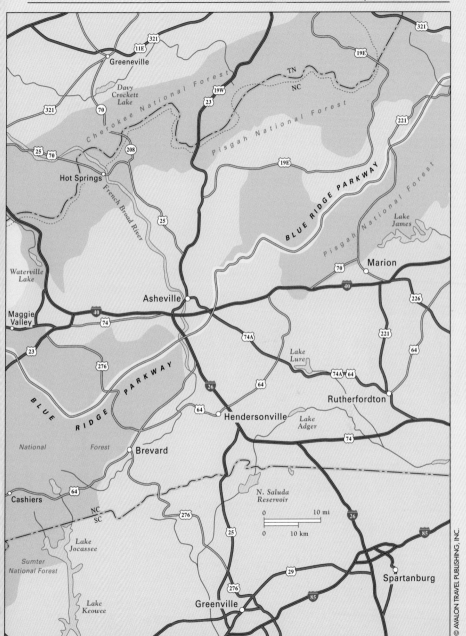

MOON HANDBOOKS

SMOKY MOUNTAINS

FIRST EDITION

MIKE SIGALAS & JEFF BRADLEY

AVALON
TRAVEL

Moon Handbooks: Smoky Mountains
First edition

Mike Sigalas & Jeff Bradley

Published by
Avalon Travel Publishing
5855 Beaudry St.
Emeryville, CA 94608, USA

Please send all comments, corrections,
additions, amendments, and critiques to:

Moon Handbooks: Smoky Mountains
AVALON TRAVEL PUBLISHING
5855 BEAUDRY ST.
EMERYVILLE, CA 94608, USA
email: atpfeedback@avalonpub.com
www.travelmatters.com

Printing History
1st edition—February 2002
5 4 3 2 1

ISBN: 1-56691-366-7
ISSN: 1536-8394

Editor: Ellen Cavalli
Series Manager: Erin Van Rheenen
Copy Editor: Peg Goldstein
Graphics Coordinator: Susan Snyder
Production: Darren Alessi
Map Editors: Naomi Adler Dancis, Olivia Solís
Cartographers: Mike Morgenfeld, Landis Bennett, Kat Kalamaras
Indexer: Laura Welcome

Front cover photo: ©Lee Foster

Distributed by Publishers Group West

Printed in Hong Kong by Prolong Press, Ltd.

ABOUT THE AUTHORS

Mike Sigalas

© JOSEPH SIGALAS

Mike Sigalas's explorations of Southern Appalachia began in boyhood, when he played in the Smokies' streams, reenacted Civil War battles with his siblings in nearby pastures, and visited the homes of his childhood heroes, Davy Crockett and Andrew Johnson, in nearby towns. Later, as a college student on Spring Break, he awoke one morning in his freezing steel-walled utility van to find himself snowed in at the Smokemont Campground. On warmer days, Mike and his wife Kristin climbed mountain peaks, hiked to the waterfalls, rafted the Nantahala, and browsed the shops of Highlands.

Now a father, Mike's achieves new kinds of feats, such as weaving through a throng of toddlers to squeeze his sons onto Thomas the Tank Engine during Dillsboro's Day with Thomas Festival, and hiking to the top of Clingmans Dome pushing a hefty two-year-old in a stroller.

Mike's professional writing career began providentially in 1987, while he was working as a steamboat pilot and Jungle Cruise guide at Disneyland. An off-duty Frontierland popcorn vendor slammed into Mike's 1970 Nova coupe in the employees' parking lot. Mike pounded out the dent himself and used the insurance money to buy his first word processor, a $350 Amstrad. On this, he tapped out his first published articles, stories, and poems.

Mike is also the author of *Moon Handbooks: South Carolina* and *Moon Handbooks: Coastal Carolinas*. He lives with his wife and sons in South Carolina, a few hours from the entrance to Great Smoky Mountains National Park.

ABOUT THE AUTHORS
Jeff Bradley

© MARTA TURNBULL

Jeff Bradley wrote the Tennessee section of this book. Born in Kingsport, he remembers coming to the Smokies when he was too little to ride the chairlift in downtown Gatlinburg. At that time, he thought life would be perfect if he ever got that tall. He graduated from the University of Tennessee in Knoxville, and spent many happy days hiking in the Smokies. He became the East Tennessee stringer for *The New York Times* and wrote articles about the park for *The Times,* as well as for various magazines.

In 1979, the late Richard Marius, a fellow Tennessean, invited Jeff to teach writing at Harvard, which he did for eight years. Having a southern accent at Harvard took 50 points off Jeff's perceived I.Q., but he compensated for it by telling snake stories and various lies about the South to New Englanders, who have no snake stories of their own and will believe almost anything about Tennessee.

Jeff once stood in a Unitarian Church and told a small group of listeners about an alleged Tennessee folk remedy for getting rid of fleas on dogs—pour equal parts of whiskey and sand on the afflicted animal.

"How does that work?" asked an eager-eyed woman, who was holding a cup of herb tea.

With a straight face, he replied, "The fleas get drunk and stone each other to death."

This line, which would have provoked laughter in Tennessee, was greeted as if it were revealed truth.

In 1985, his *A Traveler's Guide to the Smoky Mountains Region* was published by the Harvard Common Press. His *Moon Handbooks: Tennessee,* the most thorough guide ever written about Tennessee, remains the best-selling guidebook to the state.

Jeff finally had enough of New England and in 1992—the 130th anniversary of the fall of Nashville in the Civil War—lit out for the territory of Boulder, Colorado. There he writes books, camps out year-round with Troop 171, and gets back to Tennessee as often as he can. Jeff can be reached at jeffbradley@earthlink.net.

*This book is dedicated
to all those who work
to preserve and restore
the wild and historic areas
of Southern Appalachia.*

Contents

SPECIAL TOPICS

CHATTANOOGA **168**

SPECIAL TOPICS

RESOURCES **193**

Map Contents

MAP SYMBOLS

═══ Divided Highway	⬭ U.S. Interstate	◉ State Capital
═══ Primary Road	⬡ U.S. Highway	○ City/Town
─── Secondary Road	◯ State Highway	★ Point of Interest
------- Unpaved Road	☐ County Road	• Accommodation
──-·-─ State Boundary	✗ Airport	▾ Restaurant/Bar
------- Trail	⬧ State Park	▪ Other Location
	ᴧ Campground	▲ Mountain

Keeping Current

It's unavoidable: between the time this book goes to print and the moment you read this, a handful of the businesses noted in these pages will undoubtedly change prices, move, or close their doors forever. Other worthy attractions will open for the first time. If you see anything that needs updating, clarification, or correction, or if you have a favorite gem you'd like to see included in the next edition, we'd appreciate it if you dropped us a line. Address comments to:

Moon Handbooks: Smoky Mountains
Avalon Travel Publishing
5855 Beaudry St.
Emeryville, CA 94608
USA
email: atpfeedback@avalonpub.com
(please put "Smoky Mountains" in
the subject line of your email)

Introduction

It's easy to see why more than 10 million people visit the Great Smoky Mountains National Park each year. Standing on the brittle granite ridge that divides Tennessee and North Carolina, you can gaze out over entire square miles where the only evidence of humans, if any, is an overhead jet trail. The tree-covered mountains seem to go on and on and on. For a moment, taking in the view, you share a deep breath back across time—with visitors from the 1930s, with dogged settlers who scraped for survival here in the 19th century, and with hundreds of generations of Cherokee, for whom these rolling mountains were not a place to escape the world, but were the world itself.

In a world where buildings go up in a month and come down in a day, where bulldozers can stop a river, dig a lake, or flatten a hillside in a single year, the Smokies are remarkably constant. As U.S. wilderness areas go, the Smokies stand out as home to more species of plants than any comparable area in the country. In fact, as you drive from outlying towns up the mountains, you'll see the vegetation change as much as you would if you were driving from Tennessee to Canada. The mountains are even more remarkable when considered regionally. By far, the Smokies compose the largest wilderness area in the eastern United States.

Not surprisingly, then, the Smokies are also the most heavily trafficked wilderness area in the United States. More than 10 million people visit Great Smoky Mountains National Park every year. Add to that the number of visitors who never make it to the park proper, drawn by Pigeon Forge's dinner shows and Cherokee's slot machines, and you have a titanic number of people vying for the Smokies' abundant but not unlimited resources.

That's where this book comes in. The Smokies' offerings *are* worth the time for a prolonged visit. In this book we'll show you what's out there, but more importantly we'll suggest which sights, attractions, lodgings, and restaurants you'll want to visit and which ones you'll want to leave to the masses.

HIGHLIGHTS OF THE SMOKIES REGION

THE QUIET SIDE OF THE SMOKIES
Cherohala Skyway
The Townsend Y
Fontana Lake and Village
John C. Campbell Folk School, Brasstown

THE TOURISM CORRIDOR
Arrowmont School of Arts and Crafts, Gatlinburg
Dixie Stampede, Pigeon Forge
Dollywood, Pigeon Forge
Smoky Mountain Knife Works, Sevierville

KNOXVILLE
Knoxville Museum of Art
Old City

EAST SIDE OF THE SMOKIES
Ramp Festival, Cosby
Rafting the Big Pigeon River

ASHEVILLE
The Biltmore Estate and Winery
Biltmore Village
Pack Place: Education, Arts and Science Center

CHEROKEE AND VICINITY
Great Smoky Mountains Railroad, Dillsboro
Highlands
Maggie Valley Opry House, Maggie Valley
Oconaluftee Indian Village, Cherokee
Rafting the Nantahala Gorge

THE LAND

Origins

According to many scientists, an ancient mountain range once stood where the Smokies stand today. Over the millennia it wore down, until eventually an ocean covered the old rocks. As oceans do, this one deposited thousands of feet of sediment over the mountain remnants, and the resulting pressure transformed the lower layers into metamorphic rock.

Then the African tectonic plate slammed up against its North American counterpart, and the old compressed rock layers popped up and over the more recent ocean deposits. Thus came the Smokies, which in those days presumably looked as jagged and bold as the Rockies of our time. Erosion has worn them into the gentle shapes that people enjoy today.

Climate

The weather in the Smokies is generally wetter and colder than in the surrounding parts of Tennessee and North Carolina. The first snow of the year in both Tennessee and North Carolina usually falls upon the Smokies' highest reaches; snowfall at Newfound Gap averages almost six feet

per year, and temperatures can drop to 20° below zero. Winters usually close Newfound Gap Road.

The Smokies are at their most whimsical in spring, when hikers might set off in balmy weather only to encounter snowstorms or freezing rain just a few hours down the trail. College students often encounter such changes on spring break backpacking trips.

Summertime brings heat and humidity, even up here. The Smokies get a lot of convectional rainfall, usually in the afternoons—or anytime someone sets off far from the campsite without raingear.

Fall is perhaps the best time to visit. The rains of summer have subsided, replaced by cool days and chilly evenings.

Flora

Designated a United Nations International Biosphere Reserve, Great Smoky Mountains National Park contains more than 1,500 species of flowering plants, including 143 species of trees—more tree species than in all of northern Europe combined. Part of this biodiversity is due to the variety of elevations, but the lush soil and annual 40 inches of rainfall don't hurt either.

Springtime brings the wildflowers. The park

offers special programs and walks led by botanists who identify the plants and describe their uses. Mushrooms and fungi grow abundantly in this moist environment, as do stinging nettle, poison ivy, and other carbon-based trials.

Most folks note that "woods" cover most of the park, but botanists don't see it this simply. They can point out five different types of forest within the park boundaries. One of the first ones visitors encounter is a **cove hardwood forest.** Deciduous trees such as sugar maples, yellow birches, and yellow poplars dominate, and their fall colors attract the multitudes. Three other forest groups, named for the trees that occur there, are **pine and oak, hemlock,** and **northern hardwood.**

The tops of the mountains contain **spruce-fir forests,** coniferous collections of red spruce and Fraser fir. More than 95 percent of the latter have been wiped out by the balsam woolly adelgid, which has left hundreds of acres of dead trees in its wake. **Blackberries** also grow at this altitude. Oddly enough, way up here, the plants bear few thorns.

Vegetation in the Smokies, as in much of the South, can grow so thick that a person can stand within four feet of a hiking trail and not be seen. Mountain laurel and rhododendron grow so thickly that mountain people referred to them as "hells."

Perhaps the most intriguing botanical phenomenon of the Smokies is the **balds**—treeless areas on mountaintops or ridges. These occur as grass balds or heath balds—those covered with shrubs. Either is a delight for hikers, for the balds open onto wide vistas with ample area for picnics or other frolics. No one knows for sure what caused these balds. Lightning fires, fires set by Indians, and overgrazing have all been suggested as reasons for Gregory Bald, Andrews Bald, Spence Field, Silers Bald, Little Bald, and Parson Bald. Mountain residents used to use grass balds as summertime pastures for cattle and sheep, since the land didn't have to be cleared of trees. Taking livestock up to the mountains also kept them from eating important crops such as corn.

Fauna

Black bears are the best-known animals in the Smokies. In the park, whenever a member of

Ursus americanus emerges from the woods along a road, traffic grinds to a halt, and the air fills with the sound of clicking camera shutters. It's a classic American vacation experience.

Unfortunately, despite endless warnings, some people persist in feeding bears. Doing so not only threatens the feeder's life but also threatens the bear's life: When bears lose their natural fear of humans, they're far more likely to cause problems and have to be moved or even killed. Feeding bears—or any wild animals in the park—can subject the feeder to a fine of $5,000 and six months in jail.

Despite the dangerous humans prowling the area, some 1,700 bears call the park home. They spend the winters in dens or high in trees, and during this time their young are born. Bears eat berries, acorns, other nuts, seeds, and insects.

You won't find any grizzlies in the Smokies, and black bears usually leave people alone. But not always: in May, 2000, a black bear and her cub fatally mauled a 50-year old Cosby schoolteacher hiking solo near the Elkmont campground—the first deadly bear attack on a human in park history. An examination of the victim's footprints showed that she had run when the bears moved close to her, which apparently caused them to view her as food.

You're far more likely to be struck by a lightening bolt than by a bear claw during your visit, but it's still wise to treat these animals with caution. Don't feed, taunt, or pester a bear in any way. If you want to take a close-up shot, use a zoom lens. While hiking, tie a cowbell or whistle a tune to warn bears of your approach and give them time to move on. Follow these guidelines and your chances of having a run-in with a bear are virtually nil.

Shortly before the fatal attack in 2000, a pair of hikers encountered an aggressive bruin, quite likely the same adult bear involved in the later incident. One hiker grew frightened and ran. The bear ran after her. The other hiker shouted to his partner and told her to freeze. She did, and the bear—which had drawn to within five yards—immediately quit the pursuit.

The lesson is clear. Avoid confrontations if at all possible, but if a bear approaches, don't run away—they can outrun even the most motivated human. Instead, most experts argue that you should stand your ground, and make yourself appear as large as possible by lifting your shirt or jacket over your head. Put children on your shoulders. Make as much noise as possible. Throw rocks and pinecones to discourage the bear from approaching further.

If worst comes to worst and a black bear attacks, fight back with everything you've got. Black bears are not overly aggressive by nature, and it's possible you may be able to convince your attacker that there are easier meals to be found in the forest.

Of course, bears are only one type of animal you'll find up here. More than one visitor, squinting at a herd of cattle grazing in Cades Cove, has said, "Hey! That's not a cow!" They've actually spotted a **white-tailed deer,** *Odocoileus virginianus.* These deer are never hunted in the park, so they sometimes seem as tame as cows. But if you approach too close, these fleet animals will bolt, leaping tall fences in a single bound.

The Smokies are plagued by nonnative species—animals that somehow invaded an area where they never occurred naturally. These critters tend to upset the ecological balance and make nuisances of themselves. The Smokies' chief nonnative is the **European wild hog,** *Sus scrofa,* a prolific pig that can top 200 pounds and stand three feet high. These fierce hogs come equipped with sharp tusks. If cornered, they don't hesitate to attack humans or eviscerate pursuing dogs. That's the bad news. The good news is that they are largely nocturnal and tend to avoid people.

They probably descended from hogs who escaped from a North Carolina game preserve in 1912. Since then, the animals have interbred with domestic swine and slowly moved into the park, where they root up wildflowers, foul streams, and compete with bears for berries, acorns, and other food. Currently, the Park Service is working to eliminate the pigs.

One animal that might not be so happy to see the free pork dinners herded off is the **red wolf,** *Canus rufus.* Long absent from the Smokies after being wiped out by farmers and a loss of habitat, the wolves were reintroduced in 1991 and again in

ELK REINTRODUCTION

Maybe wolf reintroduction didn't work so well in the park, but elk may have a chance. Twenty-five elk—13 males, 12 females—were released in the Cataloochee Valley in early spring 2001. Fitted with radio collars for monitoring their movements, the Kentucky-born elk have attracted visitors since they first arrived. If all goes well, by the end of 2003, the park will be home to 75 imported elk and some that have been born within the park. Signs looked good in late June 2001, when a female elk gave birth to the Cataloochee herd's version of Virginia Dare—the first elk born in the Smokies in 150 years.

Sometimes folks stare at a larger-than-normal deer with antlers and wonder if it might possibly be a elk, but if you see a real elk, you'll know the difference. They are SUVs with hooves: A full-sized male can weigh over 1,000 pounds. If you see one, follow your instincts and give it plenty of space.

1992, but when one group of wolves moved outside the park boundaries and members of the second group attacked local cattle, the animals—many of them underfed and diseased—were removed.

During the last 10 years, naturalists have reintroduced about 140 **river otters,** *Lutra canadensis,* to the Little River, Middle and West Prongs of the Little Pigeon River, Cosby Creek, and Abrams Creek.

Most people think of **turkeys,** *Meleagris gallopavo,* as the fat birds that appear on Thanksgiving tables. The ones that live in the park, however, are lean and incredibly fast—once aloft they can hit 50 miles per hour. The most likely place to see them is in the fields of Cades Cove.

Environmental Challenges
While the surge of visitors is a chief challenge facing the Smokies, the mountains also suffer from air pollution, including acid rain. The Smokies' topography invites pollutants to linger longer here than in flatland cities. Burning coal at power plants in Tennessee and as far away as Illinois

leads to haze that reduces visibility in summertime as much as 80 percent. Rainfall in the park has a pH of 4.4—five times the natural acidity.

Ground-level ozone results when sunlight breaks down pollutants from vehicles and power plants. Unlike the ozone layer high in the atmosphere, which shields the earth from ultraviolet rays, ground-level ozone damages plants and people. Monitoring stations in the Smokies give off the highest ground-level ozone readings in the East.

Another challenge facing the park is a tiny insect called the **balsam woolly adelgid,** which attacks Fraser fir trees. This nonnative pest has killed off most of these firs, which make up the bulk of the high-country forests in the Smokies. Park workers have saved some trees by spraying a soap and water mixture that wipes out the bugs, but the great bulk of trees, located far from roads, don't get sprayed.

More recently, the balsam woolly adelgid's dreaded cousin, the **hemlock wooly adelgid,** has made inroads into the Nantahala National Forest. In mid-2001, forestry officials were toying with the idea of introducing a rare beetle that feeds on the hemlock woolly adelgid, although some oppose introducing another exotic insect into the forest. Whether the beetles will be given the go-ahead—and whether they can significantly help the hemlocks—was unknown at the time of publication. Hemlocks make up only about 1 percent of the forests of the Smokies, but they provide needed shade in creeks and rivers, allowing local fish to live and reproduce in the cool waters.

A final challenge to Great Smokies Mountains National Park—and to all national parks—is their limited resources. With more revenues, the parks could hire more people to maintain the trails, walkways, and railings that keep folks from trampling wildlife. The park can't legally charge admission to increase these funds; early covenants from the park's founding stipulate that no admission charge could ever be levied. Voluntary donations are welcomed, of course, but they're not common enough. In early 2001, park officials were trying to find out if the no-admission law could somehow be bypassed.

© GREAT SMOKY MOUNTAINS NATIONAL PARK

Never feed a wild bear.

HISTORY

The Cherokee

The Cherokee claimed a huge part of the American Southeast as their own, ranging, by some estimates, west to northeast Mississippi, east to the upper coastal plain of South Carolina, north to the Kentucky/Ohio border, and south to central Georgia. The Cherokee called themselves Yun'wiya or Ani Yun'wiya, meaning "Principal People," and their control of the southern Appalachians earned them the nickname Mountaineers of the South.

The Cherokee lived in mud and grass houses, generally laid out around a central plaza. Tribal life was solidly patriarchal—men were the hunters and leaders. They were allowed multiple wives, but their wives were expected to remain monogamous. Women did most of the farming and container making. Older women were generally the tribal matchmakers.

Coexisting with Outsiders

The Cherokee's initial contacts with rapacious Spanish explorers were miserable but short lived. But, after all, the Spanish were adventurers in search of gold—not settlers. Relations with the English colonists of the 17th and 18th centuries seemed, at times, to hold more promise: The Cherokee were already an agricultural people when the British arrived, and in some ways both groups benefited from their initial interactions. The Carolina colonists had plenty to learn from the Cherokee about farming in the New World, and the Cherokee enjoyed English-made steel knives and firearms. They also benefited financially by trading furs with the new settlers and by capturing slaves from other tribes and selling them to British slave traders in Charleston. Many Cherokee admired and converted to Christianity, which further eased tensions.

The Cherokee and English were generally military allies. Cherokee warriors helped rout the Tuscarora tribe in 1711, and the Cherokee's intercession against their old rivals the Creek during the Yamasee War of 1719–23 saved the fledgling Carolina colony from being wiped out entirely. In 1730 Sir Alexander Cumming negotiated with the Cherokee and arranged for them to open up their lower land—much of the upper one-third of South Carolina—for English settlement. He took seven Cherokee leaders to London to meet George II. They gave the king a crown to show their tribe's submission to his authority. They promised that the Cherokee would forever remain faithful to the British crown.

In 1750 a smallpox epidemic killed roughly half of the Cherokee people. Shortly afterward, faithful to their words, the Cherokee broke with most other Native Americans and fought on the side of the British in the French and Indian War.

After South Carolina governor James Glenn brokered a treaty between the Cherokee and their Creek enemies in 1753, the Cherokee rewarded Glenn by granting South Carolina a few thousand more acres of land. There, the Carolinians built Fort Prince George on the Keowee River. It was built not only to protect British citizens and interests but also to protect the Cherokee from the Creek.

Further treaties continued to shrink the Cherokee domain. In January 1760, angered at British encroachments and broken promises, the Cherokee began massacring white settlers in the South Carolina Upcountry, an uprising referred to as the Cherokee War. Carolinians acted quickly, spreading their own brand of terror into Cherokee villages and burning out crops and winter stores. In 1761 a number of Cherokee chiefs led by Attakullakulla petitioned for peace. A year later, another contingent of Cherokee leaders went to London to reconfirm their loyalty to the crown. In 1763, attempting to protect the Cherokee and stifle further hostilities, the British government declared white settlement beyond the ridge of the Appalachian Mountains to be illegal. The tactic didn't work, of course: Settlers kept slipping over the line and establishing homesteads in the farthest reaches of the western Carolinas and Georgia.

While the Cherokee leadership generally got along with the British government, they did not much trust the Carolinian settlers, who seemed to be held back from Cherokee lands only by the long, red-coated arm of the British army. Perhaps it was inevitable that the Cherokee, like many eastern tribes, sided with the

THE ORIGINAL
CHEROKEE LANDS

PENNSYLVANIA

OHIO

INDIANA

ILLINOIS

WEST
VIRGINIA

KENTUCKY

VIRGINIA

TENNESSEE

NORTH
CAROLINA

SOUTH
CAROLINA

MISSISSIPPI

ALABAMA

GEORGIA

0   100 mi

0   100 km

ATLANTIC OCEAN

© AVALON TRAVEL PUBLISHING, INC.

British during the American Revolution. This was their downfall.

In conjunction with British regulars and Carolinian loyalists, the Cherokee first wrought havoc on colonial troops in the Carolinas and Georgia. British officers ordered the Cherokee to attack only organized bodies of colonial soldiers, but the Cherokee employed a more holistic fighting style, and soon stories of brutal murders and cabin burnings plagued the frontier. Their hands full with the British, the Americans were in no mood to negotiate another tenuous peace with the powerful Cherokee. They would hit the Cherokee swiftly and fiercely.

In August 1776, American general Griffith Rutherford took 2,400 men, crossed the Blue Ridge at Swannanoa Gap, and proceeded to burn down 36 Cherokee towns and murder many of the inhabitants, including the elderly, women, and children. At the same time, Tennesseans and South Carolinians launched their own devastating raids against the Cherokee. Overwhelmed and demoralized, the Cherokee sued for peace. In 1777 they ceded their remaining lower lands to the South Carolina government.

After this, the Cherokee made gigantic strides toward assimilation. In 1796 President Washington promoted an "educational experiment" involving the Cherokee—a study to see just how far these obviously intelligent Indians could "advance." From the Euro-American point of view, the Cherokee were the most "civilized" of the

"Five Civilized Tribes"—the Cherokee, Seminole, Creek, Choctaw, and Chickasaw.

Intermarriage with whites was common. As it happened, an important force in all this "civilizing" was the child of one such marriage. George Guess (1773–1843), half Cherokee and half English, favored his mother's Cherokee ties and went by the name Sequoyah. Convinced that the power of the whites came from their literacy, he single-handedly created a written alphabet that put all the sounds of the Cherokee language in 86 symbols. This work launched a literacy drive by Cherokee leaders and Baptist missionaries dedicated to seeing the tribe survive and flourish in the new world order. Cherokee teachers hurriedly taught the language to the tribe's children. In 1824 Baptist missionaries translated sections of the Bible into Cherokee.

In 1820 the tribe published its own constitution, establishing a democratic republic based on the U.S. system. In 1827 they formally declared themselves a sovereign nation under U.S. protection—not unlike, say, Puerto Rico today. In 1828 the *Cherokee Phoenix* appeared, a bilingual, English-Cherokee paper. If they wanted to assimilate into U.S. society without completely losing their tribal identity, the Cherokee were doing everything right. But given the political realities of the time—including that year's election of former Indian fighter Andrew Jackson as president—ultimately, it didn't help.

Trouble was brewing. Ever since Eli Whitney's invention of the cotton gin at the turn of the 19th century, Carolinians and Georgians had been farming the bolls out of their land until they stripped it of its nutrients. Farm families were anxiously moving westward from the "Old South" (the coastal South) to the "New South" in western Georgia, Alabama, Louisiana, Texas, and Arkansas. As if there weren't enough pressure to open up their lands to white settlers, in 1829 Cherokees found gold in the foothills of Georgia. Word got out, and a gold rush ensued as prospectors poured over the Cherokee's borders.

In 1830 the tribe took another major blow—the Jacksonian Congress passed the Indian Removal Bill, which ordered all Native Americans moved west of the Mississippi. The Cherokee protested, and the U.S. Supreme Court promptly declared the bill unconstitutional. Jackson saw the ruling as only a minor setback.

Though they'd assimilated and prospered so well that they were more likely to strike envy than fear into the hearts of their fellow Southerners, the Cherokee had still kept their identity as a separate people and a separate political entity, and this fact came to haunt them. To help clear the way for white settlement, the Georgia state government declared that within state boundaries, all Cherokee laws were void—including those that kept whites out of Cherokee lands.

The Cherokee again went through the proper channels and sued the Peach State in the landmark case *Cherokee Nation v. Georgia*. Since 1791 the Cherokee tribe in Georgia had been legally considered a foreign country, but the Supreme Court dismissed the case, arguing, in the words of Chief Justice John Marshall, that Indian tribes were "domestic dependent nations," acknowledging the Cherokee's separate status but allowing them no recourse to the Supreme Court. With the federal government taken out of the equation, the Georgia government promptly declared the Cherokee government within state lines as null and void.

This ruling pleased Jackson, who had long before decided that the only good Indian was a distant Indian. His solution to the "Indian problem" was to separate the two races by sending the East Coast's natives packing to unsettled—and until the discovery of oil many years later, largely undesirable—points west. In 1832 Marshall's Supreme Court gave the Cherokee a respite of sorts. In *Worcester v. Georgia*, Marshall argued that the Cherokee were dependent upon the federal government, not the state governments, and thus within the Cherokee nation "the laws of Georgia can have no force." Only the national government could have direct Indian affairs.

Jackson was not happy, since this ruling not only threatened to stall his plans for removal but also to put the federal government back into direct conflict with a state government—this in the shadow of the 1831–32 South Carolina Nullification Crisis, wherein the South became united around John C. Calhoun's new phrase, "states' rights."

Rather than risk another federal-state confrontation by sending in troops to protect the Cherokee's rights according to the 1791 treaty—which he had no interest in doing anyway—Jackson decided to do nothing. "Marshall has made his decision," he grumbled. "Now let him enforce it." Without the U.S. government standing in its way, the Georgia government instead enforced its own will on the Georgia Cherokee. The lands were opened to white settlement.

In 1838 the U.S. Army, sent by Andrew Jackson's protégé, President Martin Van Buren, entered the area, rounded up every Cherokee it could find—more than 15,000 people—and put them into specially constructed forts in Tennessee and North Carolina. From these holding areas, over the next two years, the Cherokee and their one thousand African American slaves were forced—sometimes under army escort—to walk and/or take boats to Oklahoma, some 800 miles away. The four different paths the Cherokee traveled to the new "Indian Territory" are now spoken of collectively as the Trail of Tears. Along the way, some four thousand Cherokee—mostly the elderly and children—died, as did many of their slaves and some of the Baptist missionaries who insisted on traveling with them.

For a decade, federal agents searched after the refugees for would-be Oklahomans, but in 1848 the government finally relented. With Mr. Manifest Destiny himself, North Carolina–born President James K. Polk, in office, and flush with victory in Texas and California (which made the country a lot roomier, all of a sudden), the U.S. Congress decided it could afford to recognize the North Carolina Cherokee's rights to this land.

Fortunately for the Cherokee, the southern Appalachian highlands were generally considered worthless for settlement at the time. Back when most Americans spent most of their days outdoors working the land, it was inconceivable that someday people would travel hundreds and thousands of miles simply to listen to a mountain brook, smell a pine tree, or walk through the woods. Certainly, no one in the 19th century could imagine that the Cherokee's barely accessible heights would someday border one of the most popular visitor attractions in all of America.

Only one hitch remained: For the U.S. government to recognize the tribe's rights, the state of North Carolina would need to first recognize the Cherokee as permanent state residents. This would take another 18 years. Finally, in 1866, the same Reconstruction-era state government that gave voting rights to African Americans also officially recognized the Cherokee as rightful state citizens. In 1889 the band received a state charter. In 1925, as Chief Justice John Marshall had argued a hundred years earlier, tribal lands within the Qualla Boundary were formally placed under federal protection—ensuring that the 56,688-acre reservation would remain in Cherokee possession for at least as long as there is a United States government.

Today's population within the boundary is over 6,300, and tribal enrollment is 12,500. The biggest news in recent years came in the 1990s when the tribe got permission to open up a huge new Harrah's Casino on its land outside the park. The 60,000-square-foot, 2,300-machine casino cost an amazing $80 million to build, but it draws 3.5 million guests and *clears* $120 million annually. Major expansions, including new gaming space, restaurants, and a 15-story, 252-room hotel, were nearing completion at the time of publication.

What do the Cherokee get out of all this? At present, each registered tribal member receives payments totaling around $5,000 a year, and this figure grows every year. But the benefits go well beyond individual payments. The tribe has built a dialysis center and plans a $12 million wellness center with its profits. The casino also provides jobs for some 1,900 people, a healthy boost to the local economy.

Settlers, Loggers, and Tourists

As more white people came to the area, they found the good land gone. They moved into "hollers" and onto hillsides that earlier arrivals had disdained. These folks lived hard lives, but they were very proud of their self-sufficiency and independence. Many of them traded and bartered for the things they needed and never dealt with cash.

INTRODUCTION

The biggest change on the land derived from a situation far beyond the mountains—the incessant demand for wood along the Eastern Seaboard. From the 1880s on, as immigration swelled the population of the United States, many of the trees up and down the East Coast were cut, so timber companies began eyeing far-flung lumber sources. Newly completed railroads made it all possible, and by the 1920s the sound of sawmills filled the valleys of the Smoky Mountains. Within 10 years, only the most remote areas of the Smokies remained un-logged.

Of course, those lumber trains ran both ways. On their return trips, chugging engines began to haul in tourists, and soon a few enterprising locals opened restaurants and motels. These early visitors to the Smokies were so impressed with what they saw that they joined Knoxvillians in suggesting a national park. Prominent among the group was Horace Kephart, who had moved to the Smokies to restore his health. He was so captivated that he devoted his life to founding the park.

Fortunately for the preservationists, the federal government was willing to listen. The large national parks in the West had proved very popular, but hardly anybody lived out there, so visitation was limited largely to the upper classes. The government wanted to replicate this success in the East, where parks would be more accessible to the average American family. It created the National Park Service in 1916 to establish and manage the growing number of federal parks.

Creating parks in the East was far more complicated than in the West, however. To begin with, the federal government already owned most of the land in the West; setting up a park on federal land was inexpensive. Since few people lived in or near western parks, there were few if any howls of protest. All this would change back east.

Birth of the Park

The federal government didn't want to spend any money acquiring land, so Tennessee and North Carolina contributed, each hoping to land the park within its borders. Private citizens and companies gave land and money, and eventually John D. Rockefeller Jr. donated $5 million, which put the fund drive over the top.

FRONTIER IN THE SKY

Just how isolated were the Smoky Mountains at the end of the 19th century? Consider this. Though the nation's first commercial line had been established only a few hundred miles away near Augusta in the 1820s, rail travel—that harbinger of 19th-century American modernization—arrived in Dillsboro only in 1884 and didn't reach the Elkmont region of the Smokies until 1902. The transcontinental railroad reached all the way to California by 1869. The Southern Pacific linked San Antonio with El Paso by pushing through the wild, outlaw-infested Pecos River region—home of Judge Roy Bean and considered the last and wildest of the Wild West—in the first half of the 1880s. But the Little River Railroad wouldn't reach into the modern-day park area until nearly 20 years later.

Not everyone was in favor of the park, however. Lumber companies led the opposition, but they could be and were bought out. More intense and more personal opposition came from the people whose small farms sat within the proposed boundaries of the park. By 1930, about 7,300 people lived on 1,200 farms in the area. These people, who had had little if any contact with the federal government all their lives, found it outrageous that strangers from far away were going to take their land. A few managed to negotiate for lifetime leases on their property; the Wonderland Hotel, several dozen vacation cabins, and Mount LeConte Lodge were grandfathered in. However, as the Cherokee before them, most mountain people were driven from their homes—in this case to make room for vacationing city folk.

On June 15, 1934, the Great Smoky Mountains National Park formally came into existence, but it was a while before the park was ready to receive visitors. The Civilian Conservation Corps built trails and roads, and on September 2, 1940, President Franklin D. Roosevelt bumped along in a caravan up the dirt road to Newfound Gap to attend the dedication, along with thousands of others arriving by car. Thus began Great Smoky Mountain National Park: Even in the beginning, there was traffic.

But road woes aside, you've really got to credit the park's founders with some foresight. The park in those days would shock current-day visitors. Whole sections had been clear-cut, large gullies ran down the hillsides, and streams were in some cases filled with silt and almost devoid of life. Left alone, however, nature quietly reclaimed the land. Now towering trees grow along former rail beds, and the vegetation is so lush that most people who blissfully drive by probably think they are seeing virgin forest.

Visitation levels have climbed with the treetops. The interstate highway system put the Smokies within a day's drive of an estimated one-third

Even in the beginning, there was traffic.

the U.S. population, and a great many of those people have made the trip, along with millions of visitors from the rest of the United States and the world. Yet while the number of visitors has doubled and doubled and doubled again, the roads in the park have largely stayed the same, causing intense congestion during summer and even worse traffic during the fall foliage season. The Park Service has doggedly resisted efforts to widen the roads and ignored other schemes over the years, among them a plan to run a chairlift from Gatlinburg to Clingmans Dome. In doing so, the Park Service has probably prevented thousands of good, gridlock-fearing people from experiencing the park. But then, too, it has helped preserve a wonderful wilderness area, one that continues to provide inspiration and joy to those who do come to see it.

The People

Most people come to Great Smoky Mountains National Park to experience the wilderness, not their fellow humans, but unless you leap out of your car and run straight into the woods (and it's been done), you'll come into contact with three groups of Southerners: fellow vacationers who hail from the South, locals, and, in places like Cades Cove, the ghosts of people who formerly inhabited the Smokies.

Fellow Travelers

Most of your Smokies-visiting compatriots will hail from the South: North Carolina sends Great Smoky Mountains National Park more visitors than any other state, followed by Tennessee and Georgia. These Southerners will generally be friendly. People standing in line with you will strike up a conversation; they'll ask where you're from, make some favorable comment about that place, and probably ask you if you know their wife's cousin's stepson, who used to live there before his rheumatism got bad and he moved to Panama City.

The student of dialect will notice subtle variations in regional speech among those hailing from different areas within the former Confederacy, from the lilt of the Carolina Low Country to the twangs of Texas. Travelers with New York accents are likely from Florida.

Smokies Natives

Of the mountain locals, most you meet will probably work in the service industry, in restaurants, hotels, and other travel-related jobs. While you may run across exceptions, you'll find that these folks are much more polite than they need to be. They can't help it—that's how they were brought up to behave, even to people who don't return the favor. No corporate trainer at Holiday Inn or McDonald's has ever had to teach Sevierville natives to say "sir" and "ma'am"; they've been saying it since they learned to speak.

Smokies Ghosts

The final group of folks you'll encounter up here, you'll meet less directly. Long dead, the men and women who farmed the Smokies lived out their lives in the mountain shadows on rocky farms passed down from generation to generation. The thoughtful visitor, upon ex-

BEAR HUNTING IN THE 1920S

"The Tennesseeans stalked their bears. The Carolinians used Plott hounds, a mixture of the hound, which chased, and the Mississippi bear dog, which fought. Sometimes it took several days to drive out the bears. Division of meat was made by 'selling out': to insure impartial distribution, one man behind a tree called the name of one of the party as a piece of meat was held up, out of his sight."

—*North Carolina: The WPA Guide to the Old North State, 1939*

amining the engineering of the Mingus turbine mill on the North Carolina side of the park or the innovative design of the cantilever barns in Cades Cove, comes to the realize that the people who lived in these mountains were not the stupid hillbillies trotted out in popular culture. The families who settled the Smokies were intelligent, resourceful people who scratched out a living in a hard country, created genuine art in quilts and music, and lived lives in many ways superior to the frantic ones the rest of us come here to escape.

COLORFUL SPEECH AND STORYTELLING

The vast majority of these mountain people read and believed the King James Version of the Bible. Myriad linguistic idiosyncrasies point to a strong biblical tradition in the South, particularly in the hills and mountains where churches were poorer and more egalitarian than in the coastal areas. In these mountain churches, the Reformation concept of the "priesthood of all believers" was taken very seriously, resulting in a high degree of biblical literacy among laypersons in a region not otherwise especially literate.

Elizabethan Archaisms

The powerful influence of the 1611 King James

Version—for many mountain Baptists, Methodists, and Presbyterians, the *only* inspired English translation—combined with the geographic isolation of the Smokies to preserve bits of the Elizabethan tongue among the mountain people. In the early 1900s, researchers and writers like John Fox and Horace Kephart catalogued hundreds of phrases and words that hadn't been heard in mainstream English since the days of Shakespeare. Even today, most mountain people don't "think"—they "reckon." They don't "plan"—they "aim."

Figurative Language

Another thing outsiders will notice is the Southern way with figurative language. To some degree, this too derives from the strong biblical tradition of the region. For centuries, Southern evangelical Christians have striven to illustrate the intangibles of life with easy-to-visualize parables, following the example of Jesus, who used illustrations drawn from situ-

© GREAT SMOKY MOUNTAINS NATIONAL PARK

This couple once lived in the area that is now the national park.

ations familiar to his unschooled 1st-century audiences (a shepherd's concern for his sheep, wheat planted among briars, a disobedient son returning home) to explain complex theological doctrines.

Hence, a mountain man deluged with work is not just busy, but "busier than a one-legged man at a tail-kicking." A known liar in the Smokies is not just someone people don't trust, but a person who "has to hire someone just to call his dog."

Storytelling

Which leads to another distinction about the Southern oral tradition: Southerners are natural storytellers. Anecdotes are woven into nearly every verbal exchange in the Smokies, whether you've just requested directions or idly asked a store clerk, "How are you?"

It's no accident that the National Storytelling Festival is held just 60 miles from the Smokies in Jonesborough, Tennessee. But you certainly don't have to attend the festival to hear tales in the mountains. Just engage a gas station attendant in conversation or sit in with several natives at a watering hole or lunch counter, and the stories will gradually emerge.

A SMOKY MOUNTAIN LINGISTER

Excerpted from *Smoky Mountain Voices, A Lexicon of Southern Appalachian Speech,* edited by Harold F. Farwell Jr. and J. Karl Nicholas.

Big Ike: superior; boldly. "He tried to act Big Ike and sass her."
foreigner: anybody from out of the immediate region
goozle: throat
jedgmatically: shrewdly evasive. "Jedgmatically, I don't know if Ray's a blockader."
lingister: an interpreter
Old Ned: fat pork. "Jake, hand me some Old Ned."
slantdicular: not perpendicular
toothbrush hunt: to meddle or pry after secrets

Stereotypes and Sensitivity

Many Southern highlanders are simultaneously proud of and embarrassed by the way they speak. "Southern accent equals stupid" is an equation played out daily in television, movies, and other forms of popular culture. Fed this sort of fodder, many people from the North and the West Coast seem to assume, whatever their own level of education or intelligence, that anyone with a pronounced Southern drawl is their intellectual inferior.

Consequently, while Southerners are quick to poke fun at themselves—witness the long-term regional popularity of *The Andy Griffith Show, Hee-Haw,* and comedians Jerry Clower and Jeff Foxworthy—the same jokes are not generally appreciated from outsiders. Perhaps the quickest way to make Southern hospitality vanish is to laugh at the way someone from around here speaks.

Because of the stereotypes attached to Southern speech, socially mobile natives of Tennessee and North Carolina often try, consciously or unconsciously, to sound more like the voices they hear in the media. One telling piece of evidence: Except on the smallest rural stations, few Southern disc jockeys and news anchors show any sign of a Southern accent.

THE BUCKLE OF THE BIBLE BELT

Southerners will seldom ask where a person went to college the way New Englanders do, but they may inquire where he or she goes to church. This question is not meant as a probing, personal inquisition, but as a means of seeking connection.

Evangelical Christianity has a powerful influence on this part of the world, often expressed through music. Many folks who wind up shouting the blues or fronting a rock band cut their musical teeth in church. Elvis warmed up for his all-night recording sessions by singing gospel harmony, and Tina Turner had a spot in her church choir. Sun Studio's Sam Philips was once recorded arguing theology with Jerry Lee Lewis between musical

MIXED BLESSINGS

Southern women have developed a wonderful technique for delivering an utterly cutting remark about another person without appearing mean-spirited. The trick comes from the phrase "Bless her/his heart." As long as the comment is prefaced with these three words, the speaker is freed from all charges of malice. An example: "Bless her heart, her rear is so big that she has to fly first class everywhere she goes."

takes, and even today no one blinks an eye when a country or bluegrass performer releases an album of gospel standards.

Blue Laws

The values of the local majority have been codified into law in these parts. You'll notice this in several ways. Many Appalachian towns, including Sevierville and Pigeon Forge, allow no liquor stores, although such establishments would no doubt make money. Bed-and-breakfast owners may matter-of-factly prohibit alcohol in their establishments. Many country and bluegrass venues are similarly alcohol-free. In some areas, blue laws keep stores closed until 1 P.M. on Sundays, when employees are finished attending church services.

Southern Preaching

Anyone worried that the United States has become a dreary, homogenous place where everyone speaks the same way and listens to the same things, should turn on a radio hereabouts to the AM band on Sunday morning. A twist or two on the knob will bring forth an out-of-breath preacher pouring it on, perhaps punctuating his sentences with a periodic and rhythmic "Hah!" The truly adventurous can see this sort of thing in the flesh by stopping off on Sunday morning at small churches—anything with "Holiness" or "Pentecostal" on the sign will do.

MUSIC

Kentucky-born Bill Monroe is generally credited as the founding father of bluegrass music,

though the music evolved over the centuries from Scotch-Irish and English ballads carried up into these mountains by early settlers and allowed to ferment in the damp mountain hollers for several generations. Monroe's original Bluegrass Boys—for which the genre received its name—first focused on fiddles rather than the banjo, nowadays one of the genre's three defining instruments, along with mandolin and guitar. The five-stringed interloper didn't come into play until rapid-picking Earl Scruggs, ever the innovator, joined Monroe's band in the mid-1940s. Up until then, the banjo had been known as an African American instrument, imported by slaves in the 17th century. It caught on with Euro-Americans only in the 1800s, when white musicians began playing it in minstrel shows. A four-stringed version of the instrument became popular in the early days of vaudeville, and finally Scruggs helped make it a standard with bluegrass and country musicians.

Banjos in tow, bluegrass bands enjoyed popularity in the late 1940s and early 1950s. Bands from the mountains and foothills, including the Bluegrass Boys (from Hickory, North Carolina), Reno and Smiley (from Spartanburg, South Carolina, and Asheville, North Carolina, respectively), the Dixon Brothers from Rockingham, North Carolina, and Virginia's Stanley Brothers enjoyed strong regional popularity. By the late 1950s, however, the music

SMOKY MOUNTAIN COFFEE

"Few mountaineers use sugar, and none cream. Grounds [are] never cleaned from pot until accumulation is so great that they must be. Coffee [is] bitter from long boiling, almost invariably very weak."

—*A description of early-20th-century Appalachian coffee making from the notebooks of Horace Kephardt, published in* Smoky Mountain Voices, A Lexicon of Southern Appalachian Speech, *edited by Harold F. Farwell Jr. and J. Karl Nicholas*

CLOGGING

Though derived in part from the Irish jig, clogging, like bluegrass music, is a relatively new phenomenon, a formalization of a long-gestating Appalachian art form. In 1938, at Asheville's Mountain Dance and Folk Festival, Sam Queen's Soco Gap Dance Team from the Maggie Valley area shocked the do-si-do out of the square dancers. The team employed unique, high-knee, foot-slapping steps—now acknowledged as the first example of bona-fide clogging on record. Sam's team went on to appear in Westerns, and the dancing caught on in a big way. Today, more than 600 clogging groups operate in the United States, with a handful in other nations. They meet in national competitions and vie for prizes and clogging glory.

As in square dancing, a leader—the "cuer"—stands in front of the cloggers and calls out the stomps, er. . . steps. Dancers stand in lines, facing the cuer. Traditionally, dancers each performed their own steps, but synchronized dancing has become the norm, especially in competitions. In *Folk Dance Scene* magazine, longtime dancer Marilyn Devin explains the nuts and bolt of the clog:

> With the counts, the notation of a basic clog (also called a "basic") looks like this:
>
> DTS Rk S (Double toe step, rock, step)

> L R L (Left, right, left)
> & a 1 & 2

> But the characteristic of clogging that you can't see from the written-out steps is its up and down movement. This relaxed, bouncing motion is the other essential of clog dancing: the knees must bend slightly on the downbeat and straighten on the upbeat. Both knees bend and straighten simultaneously: on the downbeat both knees are bent, on the upbeat both are straight. Naturally, the extent of this vertical movement varies with the style (and knee power) of the individual clogger . . . but even if it barely shows, this knee action must be part of the "feel" of the dance—otherwise it just won't be clogging.

To see some Smokies cloggers in action, head to most any bluegrass festival. Better yet, visit the Stompin' Grounds on Highway 19 in Maggie Valley, tel. 828/926-1288. It may look like a big old barn, but it's the Studio 54 of the clogging world. Doors are open nightly from May to October. Just stomp on in. For a peak at the larger world of clogging, visit www.clog.org.

---

was losing popularity in favor of honky-tonk and rockabilly, and many groups disbanded. Then, with the burgeoning interest in folk music in the late 1960s, many old-time musicians were asked to play various festivals around the country, earning a new audience for the music.

And then the floodgates really opened. Oddly, the film version of James Dickey's *Deliverance*—a movie depicting mountain men as inbred savages and most remembered for its horrifying rape scene—helped popularize the genre more than ever before. It even spawned a Top 40 bluegrass pop hit with Eric Weisberg and Steve Mandel's "Dueling Banjos"—based on an old Arthur "Guitar Boogie" Smith-Don Reno recording titled "Feuding Banjos" (as subsequent successful lawsuits confirmed).

Bluegrass in the Smokies

Today, bluegrass is an international music movement with a broad fan base that reaches across America's sociopolitical divide. When played by musicians who know their stuff, the life-charged music cuts through the air like sunlight.

Some of the best venues for bluegrass music

in the Smokies are festivals, including the Cosby **Ramp Festival** and Asheville's **Mountain Dance and Folk Festival.** Year-round venues include **The Front Porch** on Highway 321 halfway between Cosby and Newport, **Hillbilly's Music Barn** in Del Rio, Asheville's **Grey Eagle Music Hall,** the **Maggie Valley Opry House,** and Maggie's **The Stompin' Grounds,** which in addition to bluegrass music offers more clogging than a slab of deep-fried bacon. See the destination chapters for further information on these venues.

On the Road

Sights and Recreation

The Smoky Mountains region offers a greater variety of vegetative life than all of Europe. And the same is true for recreational choices. You'll find an incredibly broad variety of attractions, entertainments, and amusements—vegetative and not. The Smokies may not boast the world's highest peaks, hippest nightlife, or finest cuisine, but from primeval waterfalls to wax museums, from steam trains to river rafts, from homegrown bluegrass parlors and barbecue shacks to Vegas-style shows and an 80,000-square-foot Harrah's Casino, the region offers such an incredible combination of diverse, quality, and sometimes quirky attractions that as a vacation destination it's hard to beat.

PUBLIC LANDS

Federal Lands

The U.S. government manages much of the land in the Smokies, most famously the 520,000-acre, 800-square-mile **Great Smoky Mountains National Park,** but also its large, less-visited neighbors, the **Cherokee, Nantahala,** and **Pisgah National Forests.** If you're looking for Smokies-like forests without Smokies-like crowds, be sure to check into the national forests, which together offer 50 campgrounds and scores of trails.

On the Tennessee side in historic Greeneville, you'll discover the **Andrew Johnson National Historic Site,** a worthwhile memorial to Abraham Lincoln's fiery, stump-speaking successor. In Knoxville, the National Park Service also operates the **Gateway Regional Visitor's Center,** at 900 Volunteer Landing Lane, an excellent place for eastbound travelers to gather information on the Smokies.

At present, it won't cost you a dime to enter **Great Smoky Mountains National Park,** but this may change. Entrance to the national forests is similarly free. Most of the Andrew Johnson site is free, although a small fee is charged to tour the late president's homestead.

© GREAT SMOKY MOUNTAINS NATIONAL PARK

OUTSMARTING THE CROWDS IN THE SMOKIES

Visiting the most crowded park in the country will go more smoothly if you take a little time to plan your trip. Here are a few tips.

Go when school is in session. If you have no school-age kids (or you home school), visit the Smokies before June or after the last week in August.

During football season, avoid University of Tennessee home-game weekends. UT's stadium seats more than 104,000 people, and guess where a lot of them go after the game?

Get up with the chickens. Do your driving before most of the mob has eaten breakfast. Try to enter the park before 9 A.M. If you plan on hiking, you'll find plenty of parking places and have the trail to yourself.

Stay in Gatlinburg. It may cost a little more than outlying areas, but you're paying for time. You'll get to the park and back to your accommodations more quickly.

Use the Gatlinburg bypass. If you are coming from Pigeon Forge, drive around Gatlinburg, not through it.

Stay on the North Carolina side. If you crave the tourist amenities and shows of Pigeon Forge and Sevierville, remember that both Cherokee and Maggie Valley offer scaled-down versions with much smaller crowds. Cherokee boasts a full-sized casino to boot. And you can always make a day trip to the carnal pleasures of the Tourist Corridor from your North Carolina inn.

On crowded weekends, come in the back way. Don't approach the park by way of I-40 Exit 407. This route puts you in line with all the outlet shoppers and horrendous hordes of traffic in Sevierville and Pigeon Forge. Drive to Exit 443 and enter Gatlinburg and the park via Highway 321.

Bring food into the park. Don't drive back to town to eat lunch—carry food with you. If you're taking a hike, leave dinner in the car (in the trunk, out of the sight of bears). When you emerge from the woods, you can eat in leisure until the traffic thins out.

Drive the Newfound Gap Road early in the day. Almost everyone makes the drive from Gatlinburg to Clingmans Dome. Do it early and then take your hike.

See Cades Cove by bike. If you're physically up to the trek, bring or rent a bike for touring the mostly flat cove. You'll be able to pass up the motorized masses on the often RV-crammed, 11-mile, one-lane road. Even better, on Saturdays and Wednesdays from May to September, the road is open to bicyclists and pedestrians only until 10 A.M.

State Forest

North Carolina's **DuPont State Forest,** off Highway 64 between Brevard and Hendersonville, offers visitors 10,400 acres of forest featuring four major waterfalls on the Little River and several on Grassy Creek. Several of the falls were used as backdrops in *The Last of the Mohicans.* The area is crisscrossed with over 90 trails, most of them set on old gravel roads, including several that welcome mountain bikes. Fishing and horseback riding are also permitted here. Thus far, camping is not. Hunting is, so be sure to wear fluorescent colors in season.

HIKING

You'll find more than 800 miles of trails within national park boundaries. But there's no reason to hike only within the park—good trails with beautiful views, usually involving a waterfall, wind throughout the mountain region. For more information on the hikes below, see the appropriate destination chapters, but here's an overview of the sorts of hikes available.

Incidentally, if you want to camp along any trail in the park, you'll need to pick up a permit from a ranger station. See "Camping" under "Practicalities" for details.

THE APPALACHIAN TRAIL

If you think each trail in the Smokies is as a hiker's road, then the Appalachian National Scenic Trail is an interstate, cutting through the park for 68 miles on its 14-state, 2,167-mile cannonball run from Maine to Georgia.

Within the park, the trail runs along the mountain crest that divides Tennessee and North Carolina, offering some of the best views in the park. Here, Maine-to-Georgia hikers mingle with weekend hikers and day-pack wearers, who stroll along with packless tourists who just want to say they've been on the trail. (Since Newfound Gap, one of the park's most crowded areas, lies on the state line, even those who trudge a mere hundred yards can boast, "Sure, I've hiked the Appalachian Trail. Not the whole thing, you understand—just from North Carolina to Tennessee.")

© MIKE SIGALAS

You don't need a permit to day hike on the trail, but you'll need one to camp in one of the rustic shelters, which come along every 8 to 12 miles or so, or at a backcountry site.

The Appalachian Trail began as the vision of forester Benton MacKaye. Encouraged by friends, he first proposed the trail in the dark months after his suffragette wife committed suicide. MacKaye's plan appeared in the *Journal of the American Institute of Architects* in October 1921, detailing a trail along the ridges of the Appalachian Mountains. He felt that Americans living on the East Coast—by far the majority of Americans in 1921—needed to experience nature as an antidote to the increasing pressures of industrialized life.

The idea caught on. Two years to the month after MacKaye's article appeared, volunteers laid out the first stretch of the Appalachian Trail in a state park in New York. By 1934, through the efforts of only around 100 volunteers, 1,937 miles of the trail had been blazed. On August 14, 1937, with the opening of a two-mile section near Sugarloaf Mountain in Maine, the Appalachian Trail was completed.

For years, much of the trail lay on privately owned land that was subject to development. Then the trail was designated the first national scenic trail by the National Trails System Act of 1968. The federal government and the various states began buying up tracts of land along the trail. Today, only about 100 miles remain unprotected, and Congress has appropriated money for purchasing this land, as well. For more information contact the Appalachian National Scenic Trail, National Park Service Office, Harpers Ferry Center, Harpers Ferry, WV 25425, tel. 304/535-6278, website: www.nps.gov/appa.

Annually, more than 4,000 volunteers contribute over 175,000 hours of work on the trail. The **Appalachian Trail Conference,** a collective of volunteer organizations that helped establish the trail, provides excellent information for hikers, as well as opportunities to pitch in on the trail's upkeep. Contact the Appalachian Trail Conference, P.O. Box 807, Harpers Ferry, WV, 25425-0807, tel. 304/535-6331, website: www.appalachiantrail.org.

ON THE ROAD

Appalachian Trail

The most famous trail in America plunges southwesterly from Virginia into Tennessee and then lopes back and forth across the Tennessee/North Carolina border, in between the Cherokee and Pisgah National Forests. Then it enters the national park and pushes along the mountain ridge for 68 miles (a solid week of hiking in itself) before exiting due south to spend some quality time with North Carolina alone, passing through the Nantahala National Forest and toward its southern terminus in Georgia.

On most of the trail, you'll find whatever solitude you might hope for on a trail as famous as this one. But in the national park, Maine-to-Georgia hikers tramp alongside weekend hikers, who mingle with day-trippers. As a result, the in-park trail sections, especially near Newfound Gap, can be very crowded.

Other Park Hikes

A couple great hikes leave from the park's midway point at the Newfound Gap parking lot. From the lot, you can hike east for four miles to **Charlies Bunion,** a sheer drop of 1,000 feet. A spectacular view awaits. You can also hike to **Clingmans Dome** along a 7.5-mile section of the Appalachian Trail, the highest climb in the park. An easier, gravity-assisted way to cover the same trail, obviously, is to park at Clingmans Dome and hike downhill to Newfound Gap.

Leaving from Cades Cove, the five-mile round-trip **Abrams Falls** hike is a good one for people with kids, who love to play in the water at Abrams Creek, which drains Cades Cove. The **Rich Mountain** trail begins on a one-way road out of Cades Cove and offers a good view of the mountains and the cove itself.

Mount LeConte features not only magnificent views but also a rustic lodge at the top. Five trails lead to the summit; the **Boulevard Trail** and the **Alum Cave Trail** are two of the best. For optimal sight-seeing, take the former on the way up and the latter on the way down.

If you're staying in Gatlinburg and feeling guilty about that heavy breakfast buffet, you might consider taking the **Bullhead Trail,** a 7.25-mile (one-way) hike that gains 4,017 feet. It begins in the Cherokee Orchard parking lot near Gatlinburg. Right outside of Gatlinburg on the Newfound Gap Road, **Chimney Tops,** one of the more popular trails in the park, is only two miles one-way, with an elevation gain of 1,335 feet. By the steep end, most people are using hands and feet—but the view is worth it.

The 1.5-mile (one-way) **Grotto Falls** hike is cool on the hottest days. Hikers gain only 500 feet in elevation and can look for members of the park's 23 species of salamanders on the way. The trail ends at a waterfall.

So does the mild, four-mile **Hen Wallow Falls** hike, which gains just 600 feet through a forest of magnificent poplars and hemlocks. The namesake falls are two feet wide at the top and 20 feet wide at the bottom.

The **Ramsay Cascades** trail is one of the few dead-end trails in the Smokies, but the finale makes it well worthwhile. The 100-foot Ramsay Cascades waterfall, while not a straight drop, is the highest waterfall in the park.

Other Hikes

The waterfalls of the Nantahala National Forest offer an excellent end point for hikers who need motivation. Even falls with parking lots and overlooks can entice couch potatoes with the promise of a better view from a different angle.

An excellent guidebook for hikers is *Hiking Trails of the Smokies,* which offers a full-color map, detailed narratives, and trail profile charts for 165 trails. Printed on lightweight paper, the book is easy to carry, costs $16.95, and is available at visitor's center gift shops.

MORE RECREATION

Bicycling

Riding a bike in the most crowded park in the country is not easy. First of all, biking is prohibited on all of the park's trails. Second, with all the motor vehicle traffic, if you're going to bike the park's roads, you'd best get out there early.

The park's best biking area is Cades Cove. A concessionaire at the campground store rents bikes, or you can BYOB. The best times to ride are Saturday and Wednesday mornings (before 10

A.M.) in spring and summer, when Cades Cove Loop Road is closed to motor traffic. It also closes at sunset each evening, so if you've got a bike light or really good vision, you might try a moonlight ride.

A few unimproved roads make for good in-park mountain biking. Try the Cataloochee Valley on the eastern end of the park or the Parson Branch Road out of Cades Cove, but keep in mind that it's one-way out of the cove.

In North Carolina's Nantahala National Forest, the famed **Tsali** area offers more than 40 miles of single-track trails, as well as a campground at the trailhead. For more information contact the U.S. Forest Service, tel. 865/479-6431, or Nantahala Outdoor Center, tel. 865/488-6737. Some say they're getting a bit crowded, but most agree that the Tsali trails, located on a peninsula in Fontana Lake with the Smokies as a backdrop, provide the best all-around mountain biking on the North Carolina side. Then again, it's hard to beat all the scenery and choices at **DuPont State Park** between Hendersonville and Brevard—though at present you'll mostly be riding on roads there.

If you're visiting the Biltmore Estate in Asheville, you're welcome to bike the trails crisscrossing the extensive grounds, but only after you've paid your admission fee. For more information on trails in the region, see the Mountain Bike Western North Carolina site at www.mtbikewnc.com.

On the Tennessee side, the **Cherokee National Forest** has worked with mountain bikers to construct and maintain biking trails, including the **Tanasi trail complex,** which will eventually encompass more than 40 miles. Knoxville-area parks are bike-friendly and include **Lone Mountain State Forest** and **Haw Ridge Park.** For more information on the Tennessee side, visit the Chattanooga Bicycle Club's website at www.chattbike.com.

Fishing

Approximately 730 miles of trout streams thread through Great Smoky Mountains National Park, and bass-filled Fontana Lake lies on the park's southern border. You'll also find fishing through-

out the Nantahala and Pisgah National Forests and in the DuPont State Forest near Brevard. The Smokies are one of the last refuges of the brook trout, the only species native to these parts; anglers who catch one must release it. Efforts to restore brook trout populations have led to the closing of some streams; rangers can tell you which ones. Rainbow trout are fair game, however.

Trout season never stops in the Smokies; visitors can fish all year. A Tennessee or North Carolina fishing license enables you to fish all over the park. Trout stamps are not required. You can use one-hook artificial lures only—no bait allowed. You can pick up a fishing license at a bait store or online from the Tennessee Wildlife Resources Agency: www.state.tn.us/twra. Contact the North Carolina Wildlife Resources Commission at 1709 Mail Service Center, Raleigh, NC 27699-1709, tel. 919/662-4370, or online at www.state.nc.us/Wildlife. Licenses cost around $15 for the year or $5 for three days. The two states have a very limited reciprocal agreement, which means that only in very limited areas of Tennessee can you use a North Carolina license, and vice versa. But within the park, either state's license will do.

While your choice of bait is limited within the park, your choice of location is not. You can fish right beside the road or backpack into the most remote streams in the park. Or you can hire guides who will take you to the best places. Many of them are based in Gatlinburg. They include **Old Smoky Outfitters,** 511 Parkway in the Riverbend Mall, tel. 865/430-1936, website: www.oldsmoky.com; **Smoky Mountain Angler,** 376 E. Parkway, tel. 865/436-8746, and **Smoky Mountain Guide Service,** tel. 800/782-1061 or 865/436-2108. A good book for independent anglers is Don Kirk's *Smoky Mountains Trout Fishing Guide,* which costs $8.95.

Horseback Riding

If you own your own horse, you can bring it to the park and even ride it on overnight trips, but first you'll need permission from the Park Service, and you'll need to bring your own feed. Because of the damage that horses do to trails, rangers limit the numbers allowed. The park provides a complete set of guidelines for riders; call tel.

865/436-1200 or write to Superintendent, Great Smoky Mountains National Park, 107 Park Headquarters Rd., Gatlinburg, TN 37738.

Rental horses are available from several places in the park. All rides are guided, usually at a most sedate pace, and children under six have to ride with an adult. On the Tennessee side, you'll find horses for rent at the stables near park headquarters, tel. 865/436-5354; **Cades Cove Riding Stables,** tel. 865/448-6286; and east of Gatlinburg on Highway 321, tel. 865/436-5634.

Outside the park, **McCarter's Riding Stables,** tel. 865/436-5354, 1.5 miles south of Gatlinburg (close to the Sugarlands Visitor Center), offers less stringently regulated horseback adventures. Lead horses are available for children. McCarter's is open daily 8 A.M.–6 P.M. from early spring through late fall.

Smoky Mountain Stables, four miles east of Gatlinburg on Highway 321, tel. 865/436-5634, offers guided trail rides lasting one or two hours. It's open March through Thanksgiving.

On the North Carolina side, try **Smokemont,** tel. 865/497-2373, or **Deep Creek,** tel. 865/488-

8504. You'll also find horses for rent at **Cataloochee Ranch** above Maggie Valley.

White-water Rafting

Not all that far north of the National Wild and Scenic Chattooga River, the Smokies region offers rafting that's generally not quite as wild, though it's usually pretty scenic—if you can ignore the dozens of other colorful rafts bobbing down the river alongside you. South of the park, southwest of Bryson City, the Nantahala River flows parallel to Highway 19 from Topton to Wesser, about 10 miles from Robbinsville. The gorge walls vary in height from 500 to 1,500 feet, offering the area's top opportunities for white-water rafting, canoeing, and kayaking. Along the road you'll find several picnic areas and places with access to the rushing water. Guided white-water trips are offered by **Wildwater Ltd. Rafting,** 12 miles west of Bryson City on Highway 19, tel. 800/451-9972; **Nantahala Outdoor Center,** another mile along at 13077 Highway 19 West, tel. 800/232-7238 or 828/488-6900, website: www.noc.com; and **Nantahala Rafts,** Gorgarama Park, at 14260 Highway 19 West, tel.

rafting the Ocoee

© CHATTANOOGA AREA CONVENTION AND VISITORS BUREAU

RAFTING IN THE MOUNTAINS

Rafting and kayaking have become big business in the Smokies. Floating down a river—white-water or the calmer variety—is a lot of fun and a great way to experience this part of the world. With the exception of the Ocoee River near the Georgia border, boating on the Tennessee side of the Smokies is considerably milder than on the Nantahala River in North Carolina. In choosing a trip, consider the age and condition of the youngest or most fragile member of the group. Also pay careful attention to the put-in and take-out points and how long it will take to get there.

Some people get confused by the names of the rivers in Tennessee. The Little Pigeon River flows out of the Smokies through Gatlinburg, Pigeon Forge, and Sevierville. It is a small and gentle stream. The Pigeon River, used by various rafting companies, flows along I-40 close to the North Carolina state line. Its rapids range from a gentle Class I up to a thrilling Class IV.

Prices and packages change seasonally, so it's a good idea to comparison shop. Consumer tip: If you're from out of state, book your trip before leaving home by phone or on the Web and avoid local sales tax, which can add 8 percent or more to the cost.

Big Pigeon Rafting, tel. 800/438-9938, website: www.bigpigeon.com, offers trips on the Pigeon River from Hartford.

Blue Ridge Outing in North Carolina, tel. 800/572-3510, website: www.raftwithkids.com, specializes in rafting trips for children. It's located on the banks of the Tuckaseigee River on U.S. Highway 74/441 at the southeast end of Uncle Bill's Flea Market.

Carolina Outfitters Whitewater Rafting is located at 12121 Highway 19 West in Bryson City; tel. 800/468-7238, website: www.carolinaout fitters.com.

Endless River Adventures, tel. 800/224-RAFT, runs the Nantahala and Ocoee. It's located at 14157 Highway 19 West in Bryson City; tel. 800/224-7238 or 828/488-6199, website: www.endless riveradventures.com

The **Nantahala Outdoor Center,** tel. 800/232-RAFT, takes rafters on the Nolichucky, Nantahala, Ocoee, Pigeon, and French Broad Rivers. It's located at 13077 Highway 19 West in Bryson City; tel. 800/232-7238.www.noc.com.

Rafting in the Smokies, tel. 800/776-7238, operates on the Pigeon, Nantahala, and Ocoee Rivers. It's located between Gatlinburg and Cosby. Contact www.raftinginthesmokies.com.

828/488-2325. Of the three, Nantahala Outdoor Center is the largest. It offers a fairly mild, family-friendly run, but if you're looking for whiter water, the center also has trips of various lengths and skill levels on the Ocoee, Nolichucky, Pigeon, and Chattooga Rivers.

On the Tennessee side there's the Pigeon River, which parallels I-40 from the North Carolina border until it reaches Douglas Lake. The good news is that the river is very accessible; the bad news is that it flows alongside an interstate highway—not exactly a wilderness experience. It's more like a bizarre combination of Burt Reynolds films: *Deliverance* meets *Smokey and the Bandit.* At least two companies offer trips on the Pigeon, **USA Raft,** tel. 800/USA-RAFT, and **The White-**

water Company, tel. 800/723-8462.

Except in spring and after torrential downpours, the rivers and streams in the park are not big enough for canoeing, rafting, or kayaking. But those who want a milder experience can ride inner tubes down the Sinks area of the Little River.

Skiing

If you've come to the Smokies in pursuit of the world's best ski slopes, you'd best recheck your sources. However, **Cataloochee Ski Area** above Maggie Valley has nine slopes (seven with snow-making equipment), three ski lifts, and a rope tow. Night skiing is available, too. **Ober Gatlin-burg** is Gatlinburg's ski resort. You can either

ON THE ROAD

drive up the mountain or take the aerial tramway, which departs from downtown.

The park itself offers no downhill skiing, but during winter, cross-country skiers practice various forms of their sport on roads and trails. Clingmans Dome Road, the Cherokee Orchard Road, and the Roaring Fork Motor Nature Trail provide excellent skiing when the weather cooperates.

WINE-TASTING

Believe it or not, the Smokies region contains the most visited winery in America. The 96,500-square-foot **Biltmore Winery** is located on the grounds of the Biltmore Estate in Asheville. Stop by to sample the extensive list of wines, including nonalcoholic sparkling drinks. Over in Pigeon Forge, **Mountain Valley Vineyards,** 2174 Parkway, tel. 865/453-6334, produces 16 different kinds of wine—mostly sweet and medium sweet. Muscadine wine is the best seller, although berry wines run a close second. Visitors can watch wine being made in August and September. Mountain Valley is open for tastings all year, seven days a week.

BASEBALL

Minor-league fans will find several professional teams in the greater Smokies region. If you're approaching the Smokies from the southeast, you might be able to attend an **Asheville Tourists** game. See www.theashevilletourists.com for more information. Further out, the **Greenville Braves** (a.k.a. the "G-Braves"), the AA affiliate for the Atlanta Tribe, play in Greenville, South Carolina. See www.gbraves.com for information. On the Tennessee side, the Cincinnati Reds–affiliated **Chattanooga Lookouts** compete in the Southern League from their new stadium on Hawk Hill. Games usually start at 7 P.M. Catch them on the radio at WYYU 104.5, and check out www.lookouts.com for more information. North of Sevierville on SR 66, the affiliate for the Toronto Blue Jays, **Tennessee Smokies,** 3540 Line Drive, Kodak, tel. 865/286-2300, join the G-Braves and Lookouts in Southern League play. See them online at www.smokiesbaseball.com.

AMUSEMENT PARKS

Pigeon Forge's **Dollywood** combines live music—more than 40 performances daily—with more than 30 amusement park rides and a genuine Appalachian flavor. Craftspeople, a steam-powered train, and a museum devoted to Dolly Parton all add to the down-home ambience that puts this park a cut above your local Six Flags.

Also in Pigeon Forge is **Ogles Water Park,** not nearly as original or regionally conscious, but still a darn nice place to visit on a hot day. It features 10 water slides, a wave pool, and a "lazy river"-a creation that testifies to the South's desire to retain its native pace while welcoming new technologies.

Ober Gatlinburg, Gatlinburg's ski resort, is also its summertime amusement park. Visitors can either drive up to the park or take the aerial tramway, which departs from downtown and goes 2.5 miles up the mountain. Summertime attractions include bungee jumping, batting cages, go-carts, water slides, indoor ice-skating, and an alpine slide.

Located high above Maggie Valley, **Ghost Town in the Sky** is a small, aging amusement park—and a funky, homegrown bit of Americana. Think Roy Rogers, Howdy Doody, and wagon-wheel chandeliers. For young children and their parents, the park can be a real hoot. In the same spirit, just east of Cherokee on U.S. 19, **Santa's Land Park and Zoo** features the kiddie "Rudi Coaster" (with antlers), a miniature steam train, a petting zoo (including "reindeer," of course), and Santa's House, where kids can get cheek-to-rosy-cheek with Saint Nick himself. The park includes some nods to the mountain culture of the Smokies: a cabin from before the War Between the States, a gristmill, and a moonshine still.

Maybe "Amusement Parks" isn't the right category, but **Fields of the Wood,** on Highway 294 near Murphy, North Carolina, is a 200-acre Bible park where you can see the Ten Commandments laid out in huge stone letters across an entire mountainside, along with the All Nations Cross and replicas of Golgotha and Jesus' tomb.

WHAT TO DO WITH KIDS IN THE SMOKIES

Great Smoky Mountains National Park is a wonderful place for children. Here are a few suggestions for making their trip more enjoyable. **Keep time in the vehicle to a minimum.** Children who are not used to spending long hours in a car—particularly if they've ridden a long way to get to the Smokies—will not relish riding 22 more miles to Clingmans Dome. Get out of that vehicle as soon as possible.

Don't worry about the destination on hikes. Adults tend to be goal-oriented—"We're going to climb Mount LeConte!" Kids tend to enjoy the experience along the way. If a child is having a good time playing on a fallen log or climbing on a rock, don't repeatedly insist on moving on. You don't want the trip to the Smokies to resemble the Bataan Death March.

Take advantage of special programs for kids. The visitor's centers can provide information about storytelling, ranger walks, and other programs designed for kids. The Junior Ranger program is an especially good one.

Get in the water. Children love playing in streams. Take their shoes off and let them pick up the smooth stones and look for crawfish. Take a picnic lunch out of Gatlinburg to the Chimneys Picnic Area and play in the water. Don't let anyone drink it, however, no matter how clear it looks. Older kids may want to jump from boulder to boulder. Caution them not to jump from a dry rock to a wet rock. Have a towel, a change of clothes, and dry shoes on hand.

Use horse sense. Cades Cove offers hayrides, and stables around the park have horseback riding.

Spend time in town. No matter how much the heathen pleasures of Gatlinburg and Pigeon Forge may make adults grit their teeth, kids love these places. Don't be a stick in the environmental mud.

ON THE ROAD

ZOOS

The **Knoxville Zoo** shelters more than one thousand creatures representing 225 species, most of which live in re-creations of their natural surroundings. The zoo boasts an extensive large cat collection, and visitors can walk through habitats like Gorilla Valley, Cheetah Savannah, and Tortoise Territory. Kids particularly enjoy the petting zoo. The whole of **Soco Gardens Zoo** in Maggie Valley is mainly for kids, and it largely features exotics: a jaguar, alligators, llamas, monkeys, ostriches. **Santa's Village** in Cherokee also features a small petting zoo. So does Asheville's seven-acre **Western North Carolina Nature Center,** home to wild and domestic animals including a bear, cougar, golden eagle, deer, skunks, snakes, foxes, and more.

LEARNING IN THE SMOKIES

During the peak visiting season—roughly June through August—the Park Service provides daily walks, strolls, and talks involving various aspects of the Smokies. Some events are geared for children, while others can be enjoyed by all ages. Check at the visitor's centers for information on what's happening on specific dates.

Two groups provide educational experiences for teachers, children, families, and individuals who wish to immerse themselves in some aspect of the park. The **Smoky Mountain Field School,** tel. 800/284-8885, offers courses ranging from two days to one week involving topics such as geology, stream life, waterfalls, hiking, birds, insects, mammals, bears, and mushrooms. Classes are run in conjunction with the park and the University of Tennessee, and tuition is $36–295. Participants are responsible for arranging their own lodging and meals.

By contrast, the **Great Smoky Mountains Institute at Tremont,** 9275 Tremont Rd., Townsend, tel. 865/448-6709, offers a package deal—program, lodging, and food all for one price. The institute, on the Middle Prong of the Little River in Walker Valley, offers days filled with geology, wildflowers, forest ecology, and cultural history. Evenings include Appalachian music, guest speakers, night hikes, and other activities.

The institute has a dormitory with 125 beds, and participants sleep Shaker style—males on one side and females on the other. It serves hearty meals, family-style. Typical programs include a summer adult backpacking trip for $110; a naturalist-led LeConte trip for $230; and a women's backpacking trip for $110. Other programs include photography workshops, grandparent-grandchild weeks, and teacher escape weekends.

In Gatlinburg, the **Arrowmont School of Arts and Crafts** brings 1,500 students and 150 instructors together in summer to work on carving, weaving, pottery, and more than 15 other media at a 70-acre campus. The school originated in 1912 when Pi Beta Phi opened a settlement school in the economically depressed town of Gatlinburg. Noting the high value people put on local crafts, the school added crafts instruction along with the other subjects. When improved public schools eliminated the need for the settlement school, the emphasis was shifted entirely to crafts. For information write to the Arrowmont School of Arts and Crafts, P.O. Box 567, Gatlinburg, TN 37738.

Outside the park's western perimeter, just down Highway 29/19 from Murphy, Brasstown is home to the 380-acre **John C. Campbell Folk School,** 1 Folk School Rd., tel. 800/365-5724 or 828/837-8637. Founded in 1925 and modeled after Danish schools, the school tries to preserve the crafts, music, dances, and other traditions of the Appalachian people by teaching outlanders about them. You can visit the school's history center for free and browse the craft shop, a founding member of the Southern Highland Craft Guild, which features the work of more than 300 local and regional artists. You can also take the local trails and visit artist studios to watch work in progress. For a longer stay, the school offers 3- to 12-week classes in mountain music, dance, and crafts.

Practicalities

WHERE TO STAY

The Smokies have a long history of tourism, and with this comes **lodges, inns, cabins,** and even a **dude ranch.** Of the lodges, one of the best is the **Mount LeConte Lodge,** the only lodging inside the park. It is hard to get to (you have to hike 5.5 miles uphill from the nearest road) and harder to get into (it's normally reserved a year in advance), but if you can swing it, do so. Like Yellowstone's Old Faithful Inn, Yosemite's Ahwahnee, or the Grand Canyon's Phantom Ranch, the LeConte is a national park landmark.

While the LeConte has reasonable rates considering its enormous popularity, most of the other local lodges cost $150 a night and more, although they certainly provide a memorable experience for the money. Above Maggie Valley, **The Swag** is built of hand-hewn logs and sits on 250 acres bordering the national park, to which guests enjoy a private entrance. Another great mountain lodge, the sort of oversized place where one might shoot a remake of *The Shining,* is Asheville's 1913 **Grove Park Inn and Spa,** F. Scott Fitzgerald's regular haunt while here visiting Zelda.

Gracious old inns are common up here as well, many of them built between 1880 and 1910 (when the railroad finally reached this area) or in the 1930s (right after the opening of the park). On average, they tend to price out lower than the lodges, partly because they offer fewer amenities. In Gatlinburg, the grande dame is the **Buckhorn Inn,** open since 1938. The inn contains six rooms and has four cottages on 32 wooded acres, six miles from downtown Gatlinburg. Sitting a thousand feet above Gatlinburg, the **Tennessee Ridge Inn Bed and Breakfast** offers stunning views of the Great Smokies. For sheer tradition and pretense-free mountain hospitality, Dillsboro's **The Jarrett House** is hard to beat. It's been renting rooms and serving up its famous fried ham to visitors since 1884. Asheville's **Beaufort House Victorian Inn,** a historic 1894 home with big bay windows and pleasant views of the mountains, was recently ranked number one of all western North Carolina inns.

Bed-and-breakfasts have been popping up all over the residential blocks of the mountains' quainter neighborhoods. In this book, we've especially sought to include B&Bs that will give you a real taste of Appalachian life—lodgings whose relationship to the land and the people goes deeper than mere physical location. **Grandma's House Bed and Breakfast** in Kodak is one of these. It sits on a country lane that leads to the French Broad River and offers a big front porch with rockers and a swing. Inside you'll find genuine Appalachian decor, with such quilt patterns as Double Wedding Ring, Maple Leaf, and Snowball. Guests enjoy a big country breakfast. Another such spot, over in Waynesville, helps guests grasp the agrarian lifestyle that existed up here before the tourists came. The five-bedroom **Ketner Inn & Farm** was built in 1898 and rests on 27 acres of rolling farmland. You'll find country and Victorian antiques throughout, porches, and full country breakfasts. Children are welcome.

Cabins and cottages are a time-honored way to stay around here, especially if you're traveling with children or you just want privacy. Maggie

The National Park Service takes a rather stoic stance toward campers: Tent here and you're going to rough it, like it or not.

Valley's **Twinbrook Resort** is a 20-acre property featuring 16 cottages tucked beneath the hemlocks. Each cabin offers a fireplace, kitchen, cable TV, and phone. There are also mountain brooks to wade in, trails to hike, horseshoes, basketball, volleyball, barbecue grills, picnic tables, and a playground for the kids. Not far away are **Country Cabins,** the same sort of simple, hand-hewn cabins you'll see at Cades Cove in the park. Located beside a quiet creek, the cabins seem much more out of the way than they are, just off Maggie's main drag. Each of the log cabins offers a wood-burning fireplace, a kitchen, and a porch, and you can walk to a number of shops and restaurants.

Finally, another memorable stay awaits at **Cataloochee Ranch** above Maggie Valley, founded in 1933 and bordering the park at the top of Fie Top Mountain, elevation 5,000 feet. Activities in the 1,000-acre spread include horseback riding, hikes, and fishing. Amenities include a private entrance to the park.

CAMPING

The park itself offers 1,008 campsites at 10 developed campgrounds: 5 in Tennessee and 5 in North Carolina. They book up during the busy season, and none of them offer a whole lot of privacy, though some people prefer the Cataloochee campground due to its location off the beaten path. The larger campgrounds offer campfire programs in the evenings. Call 865/436-1200 for information.

Backcountry Camping

For even more privacy than you'll find in Cataloochee, the park offers close to a hundred backcountry sites for backpackers. Reservations are required for some sites, but there is no charge. Write to Backcountry Permits, Great Smoky Mountains National Park, Gatlinburg, TN 37738 or call 865/436-1231.

Park rangers are very strict about camping in unauthorized places. This means that campers

DOGS IN THE SMOKIES

Here are three good reasons to leave your dog(s) at home:

1) Consideration: The wildlife that typically wanders through campsites—raccoons, skunks, and bears—tends to make dogs bark like maniacs, especially in the wee hours of the morning when your fellow campers are trying to sleep.

2) Dogs and other pets are not allowed on the park's trails, since they scare off the very wildlife people hike miles to see.

3) Dogs bring back poison ivy. They cannot count, and hence the "leaves of three, let it be" law is lost on them.

cannot spend the night at parking areas, picnic areas, or roadsides, even if all the campgrounds are full. The same holds true for the backcountry. Allow enough time to get to your destination before nightfall.

SERVICES AND INFORMATION

Emergencies

In case of trouble, call **Park Headquarters,** tel. 865/436-1230; **Gatlinburg police,** tel. 865/436-5181; or **Cherokee, North Carolina, police,** tel. 865/497-4131.

The closest hospital to the Gatlinburg entrance is 15 miles away: Sevier County Hospital, Middle Creek Rd., Sevierville, TN, tel. 865/453-7111. The closest to the Cades Cove area is 25 miles away: Blount Memorial Hospital, Hwy. 321, Maryville, TN, tel. 865/983-7211. In North Carolina, Swain County Hospital in Bryson City, tel. 865/488-2155, is 16 miles from Smokemont.

Information

If your route to the Smokies brings you through Knoxville, you might want to visit the National Park Service's **Gateway Regional Visitor's Center** at 900 Volunteer Landing Lane, an excellent place for eastbound travelers to gather information on the Smokies. Within the park proper, the best place to get oriented and to get information is the **Sugarlands Visitor Center,** just outside Gatlinburg. It offers a small natural history museum, a slide show, free maps, and people who can answer questions. A bookstore offers helpful volumes and films. The **Oconaluftee Visitor Center** sits on the North Carolina side. Both centers are open daily 8 A.M.–7 P.M.

ENTERTAINMENT

The mountains feature a broad variety of shows and entertainment—much but not all of it centering around country music. You'll find ticket prices and other information on these shows in the destination chapters.

Country Music

Pigeon Forge's **Dollywood,** tel. 865/656-9620,

is the place for the biggest country music names. Stars such as Kathy Mattea, John Anderson, Patty Loveless, and the Statlers sing here in summer. Dolly herself usually makes one appearance per year—usually at the opening of the season. Weekend concerts begin in May and run through October; from the last week in June through the first week in August, every day is show time. The music plays at 2 and 7 P.M., and those who come to the later show do not have to pay to get into Dollywood.

To see big-name stars—country and not—on the North Carolina side of the park, head over to **Harrah's Cherokee Pavilion Theatre** at Harrah's Casino. The 1,500-seat theater has hosted Loretta Lynn, BB King, Charlie Daniels, Wynonna Judd, Bill Cosby, Brooks and Dunn, Kenny Rogers, and Mr. Wayne Newton.

Elvis in concert, 1957

© ELVIS PRESLEY ENTERPRISES

Mountain Music

For something more homegrown, the **Maggie Valley Opry House,** 3605 Soco Rd., tel. 828/926-9336, features Maggie Valley's unqualified bluegrass star, Raymond Fairchild, one of the best living banjo pickers. If at all possible, get over to the Opry House at 8 P.M. on any night April–October and catch this man in action. And speaking of mountain music, the nearby Stompin' Grounds, tel. 828/926-1288, may look like a big old barn on Highway 19, but it might just be ground zero for—or the Studio 54 of—clogging. The Stompin' Grounds throws open its doors nightly from May to October.

The family-oriented **Diamond K Dance Ranch** (1 Playhouse Dr., Maggie Valley, tel. 828-926-7735) offers classic and contemporary country music (live and not), teen nights, Friday night fish fries ($5.95), and award-winning chili. No alcohol is allowed on the premises.

In the same alcohol-free vein, Cherokee's **Smoky Mountain Jamboree,** located on Acquoni Road opposite the Best Western, tel. 828/497-5521, boasts a "country music extravaganza." It's open daily June through October and on weekends only during April, May, and November.

Variety

In Sevierville, the **Southern Nights Theater,** tel. 800/988-7804 or 865/908-0600, puts together a show with elements of country, rock, oldies, bluegrass, and comedy. Another part of the Dollywood empire, **Music Mansion,** tel. 865/428-7469, presents an exuberant group of 25 men and women amid scene and costume changes that pay homage to big bands, patriotic music, country, gospel, and oldies.

Maggie Valley's 300-seat **Carolina Nights,** on Highway 19 across from Microtel, tel. 828/926-8822, offers a prime rib dinner and a show that stakes a claim somewhere between Nashville and Vegas, which, if you check your atlases, is awfully close to Branson.

Gatlinburg's 200-seat **Sweet Fanny Adams Theatre,** 461 Parkway, tel. 865/436-4038, is smaller and homier than those listed above. The entertainment consists of musical comedy, a sing-along, and a vaudeville-type review six nights a week.

The King

You'll find scads of mock-King up here. Specializing in the art is **Memories Theatre,** tel. 865/428-7852, home to first-class Elvis impersonators.

Outdoor Drama

Over at the Qualla Reservation you'll find the stirring **Unto These Hills,** tel. 828/497-2111. With a cast of 130, this show depicts the history of the Cherokee people from the point of first contact with Europeans to their 1838 deportation along the Trail of Tears.

Repertory Theatre

Beside the Shelton House in Waynesville stands the 250-seat **Performing Arts Center,** 250 Pigeon St., where the Haywood Arts Repertory Theatre (HART) produces two main stage musicals, five main stage plays, and up to six Studio Theater shows every season. The main stage plays and musicals tend toward mainstream classics. Call 828/456-6322 for show information and reservations.

Comedy

All of the variety shows feature a good bit of comedy (as well as some good comedy bits), but **Comedy Barn** on the north side of the Parkway in Pigeon Forge sticks its neck out and claims to specialize in the stuff. It's a corn-fed sort of comedy, perfected during years of work on cruise ships. A one-man band, live country music, and juggling round out the act. The Barn door is open late April through December. Call 800/29-LAUGH or 865/428-5222 for information.

More Entertainment

At Dolly Parton's **Dixie Stampede,** at the intersection of Mill Creek Road and the Parkway, tel. 800/356-1676 or 865/453-4400, a thousand patrons sit side by side on five tiers of seats (eating rotisserie chicken and ribs) as a kindler, gentler version of the Civil War takes place before their eyes. Visit www.dixiestampede.com for more information.

ON THE ROAD

FESTIVALS

Spring

The **Townsend in the Smokies Spring Festival** takes place in April. In May, Waynesville's **Ramp Festival** celebrates the tarnation out of Appalachia's favorite leek, something of a cross between the onion and the garlic clove. As with most celebrations in this neck of the mountains, the festival includes live bluegrass music, clogging in the streets, and lots of food for the sampling—including, in this case, various manifestations of the ramp. For information on this festival, founded in 1931, call 828/456-8691.

Knoxville's **Dogwood Arts Festival** gets its name from the many dogwood trees that grace the town. Held in April, the festival offers all manner of performing arts, big-name concerts, athletic activities, and various events all over the city. For information call 865/637-4561 or visit www.dogwoodarts.org.

Cosby holds its own **Ramp Festival** the first Sunday in May. This one-day affair consists of music, crafts, the selection of the Maid of Ramps, and plenty of handpicked bluegrass music. Call 423/487-3492 or 423/623-5410 for information.

The Greeneville **Iris Arts and Crafts Festival** takes place in May. Traditional and contemporary crafts are available, plus food. Some craftspeople give demonstrations. For further information call the Greene County Partnership at 423/638-4111.

Summer

Cosby's **Dulcimer and Harp Festival,** run by Musicrafts, begins the second Friday in June. Other, smaller gatherings are held Memorial Day, the Fourth of July, and Labor Day weekends. Each event takes place on Saturday and features traditional mountain music, covered-dish meals, old-time dancing, and other events. For information call 865/487-5543.

Probably Asheville's top annual event, and by some accounts the largest street festival in the Southeast, **Bele Chere** contains road races, mountain music and dancing, cooking, craft demonstrations, games, and lots of other shenani-

gans, all on the (closed) streets of downtown Asheville in late July.

For 10 days in July, Waynesville hosts the **North Carolina International Folk Festival.** Call 828/452-2997 for information.

Held in July and October in the Gatlinburg Convention Center, the very popular **Craftsmen's Fairs** bring in about 150 craftspeople from all over the United States. The dates fluctuate every year—usually one week in July and one in October—so call 865/436-7479 for information.

August brings the **Mountain Dance and Folk Festival,** tel. 828/258-6107, to Asheville, Held annually since the 1920s, the event features old-time and bluegrass music and mountain dancing. For a complete listing of events, contact the Asheville Chamber of Commerce at 828/258-3858.

In late August, Cherokee's Ceremonial Grounds beside the tribal office on U.S. 441 host the **Intertribal Traditional Dances.** Various tribes from around the United States come for dance competitions and demonstrations. For information call 800/438-1601.

Townsend's **Autumn Leaves Arts and Crafts Fair** is held for a week in September. Contact the **Townsend Visitors Center,** 7906 E. Lamar Alexander Pkwy., tel. 865/448-6134 or 800/525-6834, for more information.

If you somehow miss the Fourth of July, then Knoxville's **Boomsday,** held the night of Labor Day, will catch you up very quickly. Said to be the largest fireworks display in the Southeast, it's held on the waterfront. Call 865/693-1020 for details.

Autumn

The biggest fair in the area is the **Tennessee Valley Fair,** held every year beginning the first Friday after Labor Day. The usual agricultural contests and exhibitions take place, along with live entertainment, usually of the country music persuasion. To get to the fairgrounds, take the Cherry Street Exit off I-40 east of downtown Knoxville, go south, then turn left onto Magnolia. Or just follow the crowd. Admission is $7 for adults; $3 for children 6–11. For further information call 865/215-1470 or visit www.tnvalleyfair.org.

Fall also brings the **On Cosby Drama and Festival,** with local musicians, fireworks, an outdoor theatrical performance, antique tractors, and crafts. The music includes bluegrass, gospel, and country. The drama, performed on Friday and Saturday nights, centers on a topic seldom addressed in these parts: the forced removal of locals from the land that now makes up the national park. For details call 423/487-5700.

In early October, the **Cherokee Indian Fall Festival** takes place at the Cherokee Ceremonial Grounds. The festival includes ceremonial dancing, blowgun demonstrations, archery, stickball games, and beauty pageants. For information call 800/438-1601.

Santa's Land Park and Zoo, east of Cherokee, hosts a **Fall Harvest Festival** on weekends in October. Visitors will enjoy mountain craft exhibits, fresh apple cider, apple butter, and more. Call 828/497-9191 for information.

The **Battle of Blue Springs,** a Civil War reenactment, takes place west of Greeneville, Tennessee, in Mosheim on the third weekend in October. Those who attend will see authentic military and civilian campsites, the firing of full-scale cannons, cavalry maneuvers, a battle with about 200 participants in period dress, a battlefield hospital, and a period church service. For further information call Earl Fletcher at the Mosheim Town Hall, tel. 423/422-4051, or visit www.members.tripod.com/bluesprings2.

Winter

Sevierville, Pigeon Forge, and Gatlinburg all get together to promote **WinterFest,** a November to February celebration of the season that gives shops and other businesses a great opportunity to don thousands of lights. The festival events differ from year to year but generally consist of concerts, storytelling, wine-tastings, and so on. For details, contact each town's chamber of commerce or tourist bureau. In Sevierville, the number is 865/453-6411 or 800/255-6411. Or hit the Web at www .seviervilletn.org/tourism/accomod/htm.

The first two Fridays and Saturdays in December, Dillsboro's shops stay open late and lit for their picturesque **Christmas Lights and Luminaries** festival. Thousands of Christmas lights and candles brighten the evening, and brass ensembles and carolers fill the cold night air with music. It's a memorable atmosphere for some Christmas shopping. Call 828/586-2155 for information.

Christmas brings Asheville a host of events including **A Dickens Christmas in the Village,** tel. 828/274-8788, and alcohol-free **First Night Asheville,** tel. 828/259-5800.

ON THE ROAD

Great Smoky Mountains National Park

Introduction

Forget the Grand Canyon, Yellowstone, and Yosemite: Great Smoky Mountains National Park attracts more visitors than any other national park in the country—more than 10 million guests visit every year.

Since this 520,000-acre, 800-square-mile park appeals to so many people, if you're looking for some quality time with Mother Nature, you'll need to get off the beaten path. Fortunately, doing this is easy for the most part: Simply get out of the car. Roughly 95 percent of all visitors to the Smokies never venture more than 100 yards from their vehicles. Simply hike 101 yards down the nearest trail, and you can escaped near-ly 9.5 million of those 10 million visitors. And the remaining half million, fortunately, don't all come at once.

Why do so many people visit here? Accessibility is one important factor. Even with the prevailing southwestern migration patterns, one-third of Americans still live within a day's drive of the park. For easterners, other than the very-out-of-the-way Everglades National Park at the tail end of Florida, the Smokies are the largest natural area available. To westerners and international visitors touring the country in a car or RV, the Smokies make a reasonable mid-point destination. And the park is closer to a major airport (in Knoxville) than most other national parks.

And then, for better or worse, there's the

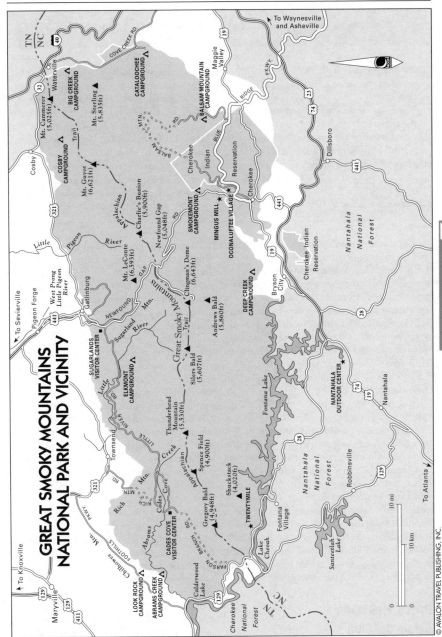

GREAT SMOKY MOUNTAINS NATIONAL PARK AND VICINITY

To Waynesville and Asheville

GREAT SMOKIES

Mt. Cammerer (5,025ft)
BIG CREEK CAMPGROUND
Mt. Sterling (5,835ft)
CATALOOCHEE CAMPGROUND
BALSAM MOUNTAIN CAMPGROUND
Maggie Valley
COSBY CAMPGROUND
Mt. Guyot (6,621ft)
Charlie's Bunion (5,900ft)
Newfound Gap (5,048ft)
Cherokee
Indian Reservation
SMOKEMONT CAMPGROUND
MINGUS MILL
OCONALUFTEE VILLAGE
Cherokee Indian Reservation
Nantahala National Forest
Mt. LeConte (6,593ft)
Clingman's Dome (6,643ft)
Andrews Bald (5,860ft)
DEEP CREEK CAMPGROUND
Bryson City
SUGARLANDS VISITOR CENTER
Gatlinburg
ELKMONT CAMPGROUND
Thunderhead Mountain (5,530ft)
Silers Bald (5,607ft)
Spence Field (4,900ft)
Shuckstack (4,020ft)
Gregory Bald (4,948ft)
TWENTYMILE
Fontana Lake
NANTAHALA OUTDOOR CENTER
Nantahala
Pigeon Forge
West Prong Little Pigeon River
Townsend
Fontana Village
Nantahala National Forest
Robbinsville
CADES COVE VISITOR CENTER
Abrams
LOOK ROCK CAMPGROUND
ABRAMS CREEK CAMPGROUND
Calderwood Lake
Lake Cheoah
Santeetlah Lake
Maryville
Cosby
Waterville
Little Pigeon River
Little River
Sugarland River
Little River
Great Smoky Mountains
Appalachian Trail
Appalachian Trail
Cades Cove Creek
Rich Mtn.
Chilhowee
To Knoxville
To Sevierville
To Atlanta
Dillsboro

10 mi
10 km

© AVALON TRAVEL PUBLISHING, INC.

GREAT SMOKY MOUNTAINS NATIONAL PARK HIGHLIGHTS

The Appalachian Trail: The 2,160-mile, Georgia-to-Maine pathway experiences some of its heaviest traffic between the park's boundaries. Those who just want to say they've walked a part of this famous trail will find a number of day hikes.

Cades Cove: The best-preserved collection of Appalachian buildings inside the park.

Clingmans Dome: The highest spot in the park. About as rugged as a trip to Macy's, but the view is beautiful.

Cataloochee Valley: If you're overwhelmed by the crowds, this out-of-the-way former settlement may be the Smokies you were looking for. Keep an eye out for elk, recently reintroduced here.

LeConte Lodge: An amazing thing to find at the top of a mountain trail. Stay if possible.

Mount LeConte: A seminal hike with several compelling trails to choose from.

Newfound Gap: The center of the park and a nice piece of WPA craftsmanship. Standing here astraddle two states captures the imagination of kids and not a few adults. The Appalachian Trail crosses here.

park's proximity to all the buffets, motel rooms, and miniature golf courses in Pigeon Forge and Gatlinburg. These human-made attractions and amenities make the park a good destination for tepid nature enthusiasts—those who want to see waterfalls and smell the pines but also want HBO and a Jacuzzi tub at night. And the region's schizophrenic personality also makes it just right for families mixed in their interests. How many other vacation spots offer both a Ripley's Believe It or Not! *and* the Appalachian Trail as local attractions?

And then there's the park itself. Unlike most other parks, Great Smoky Mountains National Park preserves a considerable amount of historical structures along with its natural splendor. At preserved settlement sites like Cades Cove and Cataloochee, 21st-century visitors can view a 19th-century lifestyle caught in amber. Meanwhile, the park's natural beauty continues to charm the masses. The Smokies feature more different flowering plants than any other national park in the United States—or Canada for that matter. The total stood around 1,500 at publication time, but botanists seem to discover new species in the park every year.

PARK HISTORY

Before the Park

The sanctuary that is Great Smoky Mountains National Park was, like most sanctuaries, born from necessity. The devastation that led to the birth of the park came at the sharp end of an ax—by way of the railroads. Once railroads gave eastern lumber interests access to long undisturbed areas of timber, the trees began falling at a disturbing rate.

Influential Knoxville businessman Willis P. Davis and his wife returned from a trip to the western national parks in 1923 and suggested that the Park Service make a park in the Smokies—before it was too late. Fortunately, as lumbermen decimated the area's forests in the 1920s, the same trains that hauled out lumber began to haul in tourists, an important (if inadvertent) step in raising public support for a park.

The early visitors to the Smokies were so impressed with what they saw—and so mortified by the encroaching devastation from logging—that they joined the Davises and their Knoxville friends in asking Washington to step in and declare the area a national park.

The Coolidge administration was willing to talk. The large national parks in the West had proved popular, but for the vast majority of Americans, these parks were a thousand or more miles away. In practice, these "parks for the people" served mainly moneyed folks like the Davises who had the leisure time and funds to travel to, say, Yellowstone or Yosemite. The Department of the Interior was looking to create new, more accessible parks in the East.

However, the government had run into problems. Creating parks in the trans-Mississippi region had mostly involved setting aside lands already owned by the federal government. But the East had been settled earlier and more thoroughly than the West. Most areas of natural beauty in the East had long histories as summer or winter playgrounds for the upper classes, who held expensive deeds on their vacation properties and sway with those in power. Thus, it would not do to turn, say, the Poconos, Cape Cod, or Miami Beach into a national park. What was needed instead was an eastern area of scenic beauty, sparsely populated with people of negligible political power—people who could be bought out cheaply and forced out quietly.

Making Room

In the Smokies, the National Park Service found its prize. Some subsistence Appalachian farmers would undoubtedly be happy to sell for what seemed like a good price, and those who weren't would not be well connected enough to stand up against the pro-park forces. Though many wealthy Knoxvillians owned vacation homes in the area, many were willing to allow and even support the creation of a national park as a way of protecting the scenic beauty around their weekend cabins and lodges. Once all the proper donations had been made and strings had been pulled, the National Park Service allowed these people to lease for as long as they, and in some cases their children, were alive.

Even still, the farmers and lumber companies who owned land in the Smokies did have to be paid *something*. Congress balked at paying the bill. However, the states of North Carolina and Tennessee, which had been working to build their economies through increased tourism and improved roads, willingly contributed. Both state governments hoped to rope the park within their borders. Eventually, the present-day border-straddling location of the park would serve as a nice compromise.

In 1926, President Calvin Coolidge—himself a flinty son of the Appalachians of southern Vermont—signed the bill that authorized and protected the area as a federal park, but it could not be created until the NPS had acquired 150,000 acres in the area.

Private citizens and companies gave land and money, but it would take nearly $12 million to acquire all the desired parcels. North Carolina finally gave up its quest to have the park completely within its borders and agreed to donate $2,162,283 toward a park straddling the Tennessee line—but only if Tennessee coughed up $2 million of its own. Tennessee's legislature raced into session and came out with $2,345,330, and Congress eventually came through with $2,293,265 from Washington. Then a couple of major park supporters buttonholed John D. Rockefeller Jr. and persuaded him to cut a check for $5 million. Suddenly, the fund-raising portion of the venture was over.

But having the money and owning the land were two separate things. Over 6,000 parcels had to be purchased, including some 1,200 small farms owned by mountain families, many of whom had lived on the land for generations. Eventually, the 150,000 acres—and more—would come: All the money suddenly floating around the mountains mollified most of the park's opponents quickly enough. The lumber companies, which had initially led the opposition to the park on economic grounds, could be and were bought out. Entire lumber company towns such as Smokemont were evacuated and dissembled. The companies were compensated for their losses.

More sustained opposition came from some of the area's 7,300 farmers. Roughly half gladly took the money and moved into cities or down to more fertile farming lands, but the other half wanted to stay. They became the biggest obstacle to the park's founding. In the days before Social Security cards, most mountain people had experienced little if any contact with the federal government. They found it outrageous that flatlanders in business suits were suddenly going to take their land—to make, of all things, a park for flatlanders. Some gave up, bewildered, but others stood up courageously to the strange, powerful forces that had come for their land. Courage, however, doesn't buy good attorneys, and nearly all of these opponents ended up expelled from the park's boundaries within the next several years. By 1939, the *WPA Guide to North Carolina* would describe the park as "largely deserted by its inhabitants."

In a humane gesture, the government allowed a few elderly and sick mountain people lifetime leases to their own land. But they couldn't hunt and fish, cut firewood, or farm using the old ways. Many who had permission to stay ended up leaving anyway, out of frustration. Others, over the next decades, saw their ex-neighbors making a good living providing tourist amenities in the gateway towns and moved outside the park to share in the bonanza.

One last group of park opponents consisted of local conservationists who favored national forest rather than national park status for the Smokies. They believed that a national park would attract huge crowds of visitors, compromising the mountains' peaceful atmosphere and threatening its distinct vegetation and wildlife. They lost the battle, of course, but you can't fault this group for a lack of foresight.

> *Botanists have identified more than 143 different tree species within the park—more than in all of Europe.*

A Park Is Born

By 1934 the governments of Tennessee and North Carolina had purchased more than double the required acreage—more than 300,000 of the park's present-day 520,000 acres—and signed it over to the Department of the Interior. On June 15, 1934, the U.S. Congress formally bequeathed national park status to the Smokies, freeing up the Park Service to develop the area for visitors. The Depression was on, but the Civilian Conservation Corps (CCC) was at full throttle. The corps went on to build the park a strong infrastructure—roads, bridges, trails, and campgrounds—and other sturdy, often inspired, amenities.

Although as late as 1939 not a single campground had yet opened for business, on September 2, 1940, President Franklin D. Roosevelt bumped along in a caravan up the dirt road to Newfound Gap for a dedication ceremony. Thousands of others arrived in hundreds of cars to attend. Thus, from the beginning, traffic and crowds have been part of the park scene.

Humans and Nature

Great Smoky Mountains National Park, as it appeared in those days, would shock us today. Under private ownership, whole sections had been clear-cut; large gullies ran down the hillsides, and many streams were filled with silt and nearly devoid of life. Bear, deer, and other game had been hunted to the edge of extinction and were only slowly beginning to reassert themselves in the area. Left alone, however, nature quietly reclaimed the land. Now towering trees grow along roads that were once rail beds, and the vegetation is so lush that most folks drive blissfully by what they assume to be virgin forest.

Visitation has steadily increased in the Smokies over time. The interstate highway system soon put the park within a day's drive of an estimated one-third of the U.S. population, and a great portion of that one-third made the trip. While the number of visitors has doubled and doubled and doubled again, the roads in the park have largely stayed the same, causing congestion during summer and even worse traffic during the fall foliage season. The Park Service has resisted efforts to widen the roads and ignored other schemes meant to increase accessibility at the expense of ecology, among them a suggestion to run a chairlift from Gatlinburg to Clingmans Dome. In doing so, the Park Service has preserved a wonderful wilderness area, one that continues to provide inspiration and joy to those who come to see it.

Recent Developments

In October 2000, Mike Tollefson became the park's new superintendent. A Seattle native, the new chief came straight from the head position at Sequoia and Kings Canyon National Parks in central California. Even though these parks see as many visitors annually as Great Smoky Mountains National Park attracts in October alone, Tollefson may just be the man for the job. At Sequoia and Kings Canyon, he oversaw the removal of nearly 300 park buildings as part of an effort to protect ancient sequoias, so it seems

THE NATION'S SIX MOST VISITED NATIONAL PARKS

1. Great Smoky Mountains National Park, 10.1 million visits annually, 521,621 acres (19.4 visits per acre)
2. Grand Canyon National Park, 4.4 million visits annually, 1,217,403 acres (3.6 visits per acre)
3. Yosemite National Park, 3.4 million visits annually, 761,266 acres (4.5 visits per acre)
4. Olympic National Park, 3.3 million visits annually, 922,650 acres (3.6 visits per acre)
5. Rocky Mountain National Park, 3.1 million visits annually, 265,722 acres (11.7 visits per acre)
6. Yellowstone National Park, 2.8 million visits annually, 2,219,790 acres (1.3 visits per acre)

likely that he'll prioritize the park's natural attractions over its human-made amenities. His announced priorities include improving air quality and (not unrelated) reducing traffic in the Cades Cove area. One possible solution, Tollefson suggests, might be a tram system similar to one that has helped reduce congestion on the crowded floor of Yosemite Valley.

ORIENTATION
Getting In

For now at least, nearly everyone who visits the park arrives by car, usually via one of three roads. Over one-third enter via the **Gatlinburg entrance,** on the Tennessee side, making this the park's de facto main entrance—a reality that has its good side and its bad side. On the good side, the Park Service has sensibly loaded up most of its best visitor amenities near this entrance, including the Sugarlands Visitor Center and Park Headquarters. From here, you can either head up the Newfound Gap Road over the mountains or turn right and head for the Cades Cove area along Little River Road.

The downsides of the "main" entrance are the crowds and the tourism gauntlet you'll have to

run in Pigeon Forge and Gatlinburg just to get into the park. If you've come to the Smokies to get away from it all, accessing the park via Sevierville, Pigeon Forge, and Gatlinburg may bring to mind the old Steve Miller line about having to go through hell before you get to heaven.

At the reservation outside of North Carolina's **Cherokee entrance,** the trend seems, thankfully, to be away from the concrete tepees and Sioux headdresses of the past and toward lower-key, Cherokee-respecting attractions—and modern-day, Cherokee-enriching casinos. Once inside the park, you'll find the interesting Oconaluftee Visitor Center and Pioneer Farmstead and the photogenic Mingus Mill—but then you've got to continue on up Newfound Gap Road (U.S. 441) for about 10 curvy miles before you hit the next roadside pull-over—Newfound Gap.

Townsend is the least-used of the three main entrances to the park. It leads to an intersection of the Little River Road, which heads toward the Sugarlands Visitor Center and Gatlinburg, and Laurel Creek Road, which goes to Cades Cove.

Major Roads

Newfound Gap Road, a.k.a. **U.S. 441,** crosses the park and the park's namesake mountains at Newfound Gap. This is the road you'll travel if you enter the park by either the Gatlinburg or Cherokee entrances.

During the push to establish Great Smoky Mountains National Park in the 1920s and 1930s, supporters cultivated public interest in the project by including an over-mountain road in the plan. A direct route between east Tennessee and North Carolina, the supporters argued, would stimulate trade and help both areas' economies.

The route they chose largely followed the existing dirt path over Newfound Gap, first blazed as early as the 1850s. Until its discovery, travelers over the main range of the Smokies had to use the higher Indian Gap. This "new-found gap" was lower and hence more passable later into the winter and earlier in the spring. It soon replaced Indian Gap as the primary crossing point in this region.

Newfound Gap Road was paved, and the

GREAT SMOKIES

supporters were right about the economic development—probably more right than they knew. Today, Newfound Gap Road crosses the park from one tourist town to another, climbing from 1,465 to 5,048 feet at its highest point. Motorists sense that they're seeing most of the park, since they're crossing from one side to the other and even changing states along the way. Unfortunately, on most warm-weather days, what you'll mostly see traveling Newfound Gap Road is traffic, sometimes of the bumper-to-bumper variety.

For many, the highlight of the drive lies at the gap itself, where you'll find breathtaking views, the state line sign (a popular picture spot), a crossing point for the Appalachian Trail, and a monument where Franklin D. Roosevelt formally dedicated the park in 1940.

Clingmans Dome Road

Named after its endpoint, the highest mountain in the park, this road spurs off the Newfound Gap Road at Newfound Gap. Clingmans Dome was named for the man who first measured it accurately—a little-known, part-Cherokee, Confederate brigadier general, Thomas Lanier Clingman. Before that, the Cherokee knew the dome as Ku wa' hi—"Mulberry Place." They believed that bears had great "townhouses" under this and three nearby mountains. The Great White Bear, chief and doctor to the rest, lived at Mulberry Place. The bears would come here to chat it up and dance before heading downstairs to hibernate for the winter.

The dead-end, six-mile road (a.k.a. Skyland Drive), which leads to an observation tower, is the highest paved road east of the Mississippi. It hits 6,300 feet in elevation.

Roaring Fork Motor Nature Trail

This road is a one-way, five-mile loop just outside of Gatlinburg. It'll take you into the park and uphill to the **Grotto Falls** parking area, then downhill back to town along a rushing stream. The water cavorts over rocks, cooling the air and providing moisture for luxurious ferns and mosses. A great place for photographers, the road is off limits to RVs and it's closed in winter.

Little River Road

One of two main roads in the park, Little River Road leaves from the Sugarlands Visitor Center over Sugarlands Mountain, descends to the Little River, and follows it toward the Cades Cove area. Some of this 18-mile road was constructed on the remains of the Little River Railroad, which was used to bring logs out of the mountains in the early 20th century.

A turnoff to the left leads to the **Elkmont** community, a group of cabins long occupied by families who owned them when the park came into existence. Back on the road, a turnoff to the right leads to **Metcalf Bottoms,** where you'll see a log schoolhouse and several old cabins.

The Little River grows in volume the further it goes. It plunges over a small waterfall at **The Sinks,** a popular if bone-chilling swimming hole. Further downstream, you'll see people tubing on the river. The National Park Service takes a dim view of this sport, since it's hazardous, especially when the water is high. But it's allowed and people do it. Little River Road ends at an intersection with Laurel Creek Road, which leads to Cades Cove and the road out of the park to Townsend. **Laurel Creek Road** is a pleasant drive, but you won't see much but trees.

Cherokee Orchard Road

Here's a true back road, lying just outside Gatlinburg. Follow the Historic Nature Trail Road to Gatlinburg to Cherokee Orchard Road. It runs three and a half miles through an old orchard and past the site of several log cabins. In season, it's a great drive for wildflower viewing.

Cades Cove Roads

You can read about the Cades Cove Loop Road below, but here are a couple of good roads that lead *out* of the area. Cades Cove residents used to take **Rich Mountain Road** to do their shopping, trading, and hollering down in Maryville. Today this seven-mile road starts out one-way as it winds out of the cove, offering several views of farmland, and crosses Rich Mountain at the park boundary. Outside the park it becomes a two-way road and descends to U.S. 321 near Townsend. The one-way, eight-mile

Parson Branch Road is even prettier; it leaves the cove just beyond the Cable Mill parking area and wanders down to U.S. 129 between Fontana and Chilhowee. Beautiful, lush mountain laurel and fern surround the road, and it fords a creek several times. If Cades Cove is crowded—and it often is in summer—this is an excellent escape from the crowds. Both Rich Mountain Road and Parson Branch Road are closed in winter.

Sights and Recreation

HISTORIC SITES

Cades Cove

Consider this: Of the 10.1 million people who visit Great Smoky Mountains National Park each year, some 2.5 million of them visit the cove, a large, relatively flat area first settled in 1821. If Cades Cove were a national park all by itself, it would be one of the top 10 most visited national parks in the country.

Thousands of small-scale farmers once worked 1,200 farms within the boundaries of today's Great Smoky Mountains National Park. Although most of the farm buildings have fallen, the few that remain can help you get an idea of life before the park. The biggest collection of ante-park structures lies in Cades Cove. At its peak, the 5,000-acre valley supported 685 residents, who kept several churches and mills in operation. Today the park permits cattle grazing to keep the pastures from returning to forest, and it also maintains the farm buildings, churches, and a mill. A narrow, 11-mile, one-way road circles the cove, with 19 interpretational stops that explain the old ways of life here.

The restored and preserved buildings and farms of Cades Cove are well worth seeing. Bring or rent a bike, and you'll be able to pass up the motorized masses on the often RV-crammed one-lane road. Even better, on Saturdays and Wednesdays from May to September, the road is open to bicyclists and pedestrians only until 10 A.M.

Along the road you'll see **Tipton Place,** which features a cantilevered barn. This sort of structure is an example of mountain ingenuity: The build-

GREAT SMOKIES

© JEFF BRADLEY

looking into Cades Cove

ing spreads out at its second story to provide shelter for various outdoor chores and for animals.

The best part of the cove, however, centers on **Cable Mill,** a working mill alongside a frame house and several farm buildings. During visiting season, crafts and farming demonstrations take place. One weekend in October, re-enactors at the mill make sorghum molasses the old-fashioned way.

The Cherokee called this area Tsiyahi, meaning "Otter's Place," but the settlers renamed it, presumably after a human—though nobody is quite sure whom. To many students of the subject, the name most likely refers to a Cherokee chief named Cade, or Kade, who once held land in the cove. Another story says that the cove is named for Kate, the settlers' name for the wife of Cherokee Chief Abram. Others argue that the cove was named after an early settler family named Cade, and yet another story says that the name was originally Cage Cove, referring to the "cage" created by the mountains surrounding the cove.

One popular hike out of the area leads to 20-foot-high Abrams Falls, a worthwhile trek. And the Cades Cove campground, though often crowded, offers the only camp store in the park.

Elkmont

Pennsylvanians Colonel W. B. Townsend, J. W. Wrigley, and F. H. McCormick acquired over 75,000 acres of Smokies timberland in 1902 and formed the Little River Lumber Company, headquartered outside current park boundaries in the little community of Tuckaleechee (renamed Townsend). The company built the Little River Railroad to span the 18 miles between Townsend and Elkmont, from where Shays—geared locomotives designed for steeper grades—climbed even higher into the mountains to pick up the prized lumber. Before long, sportsmen were riding up from Knoxville to Townsend on the Southern Railroad Line and then switching over to the Little River Railroad to be carried deeper in the mountains than they'd ever ventured before. Making a base camp in Elkmont, they then headed up further to hunt and fish. Shrewdly, Colonel Townsend,

the LRLC's president, quickly added passenger and observation cars to the train and raised the passenger fare.

By 1907, many of Townsend's regular customers, men who came up on weekends from Knoxville, Maryville, and Chattanooga to hunt, fish, and rub dirty elbows with the loggers, had founded the Appalachian Club. To show its appreciation for their business, in 1910 the Little River Lumber Company deeded the club a 50-acre tract for a clubhouse. The company also agreed to lease hunting and fishing privileges on some 40,000 acres above Elkmont exclusively to the Appalachian Club for 10 years. In exchange, the club was expected to manage the fish and game and to patrol the area for poachers.

Of course, once the large, comfortable clubhouse went up, the tough logging camp went the way of Crane's Yellow Sky. A less sports-minded breed of flatlander soon wanted to join the club. Men began bringing their wives for the weekend. The whiskey and games of dice and five-card stud were replaced by teas and dances and bridge tournaments. Soon the town had a post office, boardinghouse, theater, and church. Men of leisure began building cottages and bringing their families not just for the weekend but for the entire summer. With ruggedness and stamina no longer requirements for admission in the Appalachian Club, wealth and connections became key factors. And the club denied access to its facilities and functions to all non-members.

Elkmont continued to grow. Though it no longer felt like a lumber town, timber was still the town's chief industry, and the trees continued to fall. As the trees were clear-cut, the lumber company had no more interest in the land and sold it for good prices. In 1912, three brothers bought 65 acres and built the two-story, white clapboard Wonderland Park Hotel. A couple of years later, a group of men from Knoxville who hadn't made the cut at the Appalachian Club bought the Wonderland and formed their own club. They reserved some rooms for club members, but left others open to the public.

The Little River Railroad shut down in 1926. The railroad bed became the base for today's

Elkmont Road, and as the cars rolled into town, a greater boom seemed on the horizon. But then the government came calling. Despite the best legal efforts of some Appalachian Club members, the land became a national park. However, though the members' lost their land, their lawyer was able to get them long-term leases to their cabins. The leases were renewed in 1972, but most of them expired in 1992—the same year the Wonderland finally closed its doors.

Nowadays, Elkmont is home to the park's largest campground and to a very rare phenomenon—**synchronized fireflies** (lightning bugs). For some reason, at only this elevation (2,200 feet) the fireflies light up and black out in sync with one another, creating a memorable sight. Look for them in May, June, and July (and sometimes early August) in the late evening—9–10 P.M.—on the nature trail past the campground and across the stone bridge.

NORTH CAROLINA

Cataloochee

If you want to see historic structures but find Cades Cove too congested, the hard-to-get-to Cataloochee Valley may offer you the Smokies experience you were hoping for. The Cat-

aloochee Historic District sits about 11 winding miles from I-40 and 16 twisting miles south of Big Creek. The upper Smokies were one of the last areas in the Southeast to be settled, and Cataloochee Valley was one of the last areas in the Smokies to be settled—just before the Civil War.

In the early 20th century, the Cataloochee Valley was home to two prosperous villages—Big Cataloochee and Little Cataloochee, with more than 200 buildings and more than 1,200 residents between them. It was the largest settlement in all of the Smokies—roughly twice as populous as Cades Cove.

Today, a thin, carefully preserved human residue lingers over the Cataloochee region. An old school, churches, and quite a few houses and barns still stand. While Cataloochee's restored structures can't compare to Cades Cove's, neither do its traffic and crowds. In fact, you can't even *get* to Little Cataloochee by car—that requires a two-mile hike. For some folks, the sheer quiet of the 29-square-mile area makes the entire experience superior to that found at Cades Cove. And the spot is so remote that when bears run into trouble with visitors elsewhere in the park, they're hauled up here and released so that they won't be able to find their way back.

GREAT SMOKIES

© MIKE SIGALAS

Split Log Cabin, Oconaluftee Homestead

Mingus Mill

The name Cataloochee, incidentally, comes from the Cherokee term for "waves of mountains," an accurate description of the view, even now. There's camping up here, including a very popular camp for equestrians.

Back on the beaten path—Newfound Gap Road—you'll find **Oconaluftee Mountain Farm Museum** right beside the visitor's center near the Cherokee entrance. It offers periodic demonstrations of old-time farming methods.

Nearby **Mingus Mill** is also worth a stop—especially if you're tired of the same old grind. That is to say, don't expect the vertical waterwheel usually found in the region's other mills. The Mingus Mill—a "tub" or "turbine" mill—features a wheel that lies on its side. And the old spattering wooden flume that scoops water out of the creek to feed the mill is worth a couple of snapshots all by itself.

The mill grinds corn and wheat. In fact, you'll find cornmeal and flour on sale inside the mill, packaged in miniature sacks. Unfortunately, these products aren't actually ground there at the mill—they're ground in a modern facility in Tennessee. Blame the newfangled health codes.

HIKING

Whether it's a stroll in the woods or a multi-day trek in the backcountry, hiking ranks high on the list of things to do in the Smokies, where more than 800 miles of trails await the walker. Below is a selection of good **day hikes** in the park. Most are on well-marked trails, but it's never a bad idea to carry a good map. An excellent guidebook for hiking is *Hiking Trails of the Smokies*. Printed on lightweight paper, it's easy for hikers to carry. It costs $16.95 and is available at visitor's center gift shops.

Anyone wanting to hike for longer than a day and to camp along any trail in the park needs a permit, available from ranger stations. See "Camping" under "Practicalities" for details.

Appalachian Trail Hikes

The most famous trail in America runs along the 68-mile mountain crest that makes up the Tennessee-North Carolina border. Here, Maine-to-Georgia hikers tramp alongside weekend hikers, who mingle with day-trippers who want to experience the famous trail. As a result, the section of

SMOKY MOUNTAIN BALDS

None of the Smoky Mountains—indeed, none of the Appalachians south of New Hampshire—extend above tree line. Heavy forests cover the highest peaks in the park. How then does one explain the balds—ridge-top areas where there are no trees? Some of these 10-plus-acre balds are covered with grass, while others are covered with heath (the family containing mountain laurels, rhododendrons, and azaleas). Theories as to the origin of the balds involved lightning fires, plant disease, or some sort of action by Indian residents.

Whatever created the grass balds, early European settlers put them to use as summer pastures for cattle and sheep. Since settlers usually had to carve every pasture or garden out of virgin hardwood forest, having a ready-made pasture was a godsend. In the spring of each year, men and boys would drive cattle to the mountain heights, always wary of marauding bears and mountain lions. All summer the animals would graze on the grass under the watchful eye of boys or an old man.

Meanwhile, down on the farms, families could raise gardens and fields of corn, free of trampling livestock that might knock down fences to get at the grain. In fall, when the weather began to turn cold and all the crops were in, the animals, fattened by summer grass, were driven home.

The balds make delightful hiking destinations. Coming out of the woods and onto a wildflower bedecked grass bald and a stunning mountain vista is enough to make persons of a certain age burst out singing "The Sound of Music."

The park contains eight named balds. Andrew's Bald, near Clingmans Dome, is the closest to a road, about a mile and half each way. To get there, go to the Clingmans Dome parking lot and look for the signs. Spence Field and Gregory's Bald can be reached from Cades Cove.

When people stopped grazing cattle on the balds, the surrounding forests slowly began to reclaim them, and the Park Service was faced with a quandary: Should officials let nature take its course and eventually cover the balds, or should the forest be restrained? Luckily for hikers, the park chose the latter course. The balds remain.

the trail near Newfound Gap can be very crowded.

Leave the Newfound Gap parking lot and head east four miles to **Charlies Bunion,** a sheer drop of 1,000 feet. A spectacular view awaits. The trail climbs 980 feet in the first three miles.

Newfound Gap to Clingmans Dome, a 7.5-mile, one-way trek along a section of the Appalachian Trail, is the highest trail in the park and the highest stretch along all of the Appalachian Trail's 2,100-mile length. The trail offers superb views as the elevation rises 1,600 feet. Of course, if you're adverse to fighting gravity, the easier way to walk this trail is to begin at Clingmans Dome and hike downhill to Newfound Gap.

Cades Cove Hikes

The five-mile round-trip **Abrams Falls** hike is a good one for kids; they love to play in the water at Abrams Creek, which drains Cades Cove.

Begin along the Cades Cove Loop Road and hike down to the falls, or go to the Abrams Creek Ranger Station off the Foothills Parkway on the west side of the park and hike upstream to the falls. The latter is the prettier route, even if it's a bit out of the way.

Two trails lead to **Gregory Bald,** a former summer pasture. The Gregory Ridge Trail, 11 miles round-trip, begins at the turnaround at the start of Parson Branch Road and climbs 2,600 feet up Gregory Ridge. The Gregory Bald Trail, nine miles round-trip, begins farther down the Parson Branch Road and climbs 2,100 feet. Keep in mind that Parson Branch Road is a one-way road leading out of the park. Hikers camping in Cades Cove are in for a long drive to get back to their sleeping bags.

The **Rich Mountain** trail begins on another of those one-way roads out of Cades Cove. Once motorists get to the boundary of the park—Rich Mountain Gap—traffic runs in both directions.

GREAT SMOKIES

Walk east from here along a fire road until the trail takes off to the left. Follow it to the top of the mountain and the intersection with the Indian Grave Gap Road. A good view of the mountains and Cades Cove awaits.

Hikers can reach the beautiful mountain bald of **Spence Field** by two trails. The first is the **Bote Mountain Trail,** a jeep road that begins on Laurel Creek Road, which leads into Cades Cove. Spence Field lies 13 miles ahead, a climb of 2,900 feet. The shortest trail is also the steepest. Begin at the Cades Cove Picnic Area and follow the **Anthony Creek Trail** to its intersection with the Bote Mountain Trail. Prepare to walk nine miles and gain 3,200 feet in elevation.

Mount LeConte Hikes

Mount LeConte is the third highest mountain in the eastern United States if you measure from sea level to each mountain's peak. But if you measure from the valley floor below each mountain to that mountain's uppermost point, LeConte ranks as the tallest mountain east of the Mississippi. Consequently, it offers some of the park's most striking views.

These views, and the lodge they inspired, have made Mount LeConte very popular with park visitors. In fact, in the late 1920s and 1930s, when the Great Smoky Mountains Conservation Association was trying to win support for a park, it used to bring influential people to a special camp on the top of the mountain to let the views work their magic.

The old Masonic argument that "all roads lead to the mountaintop" may or may not be true, but at least five trails lead to the top of Mount LeConte. If you're making the climb, you might want to spice things up by hiking up one trail and down another, though depending on which trails you choose, you may need two vehicles to pull it off.

One popular trail for the ascent is the **Boulevard Trail.** It begins at Newfound Gap, thus eliminating a good deal of the climb. To get to the trail, park at Newfound Gap and head east on the Appalachian Trail. The Boulevard Trail will turn off to the left. The total distance is eight miles one way, with an elevation gain of 1,545 feet. Since the trail follows a ridge top,

with lots of ups and downs, you'll feel like you're climbing much more.

The **Alum Cave Trail** is a steep, 2,800-foot, 5.5-mile climb that offers a lot to see. If your knees are sturdy, it's a good choice for the downward trek. Along the way, as you might guess, you'll pass Alum Cave, which incidentally was named all wrong. The spot is not a true cave, but really a large overhang. The "alum"—a mineral found in the overhang—is not truly an alum, but actually a "pseudo-alum."

Miners came up here starting in the 1830s to remove the pseudo-cave's deposits of pseudo-alum, used for dyeing fabric and stopping external bleeding. They also mined other non-pseudo-minerals up here, including Epsom salts and saltpeter (used in gunpowder). During the Civil War, with medicine and munitions in short supply, the Confederacy mined here extensively.

In addition to the un-cave, the trail also offers a rock arch and other great scenery. The trail be-

hikers on Alum Cave Trail

© JEFF BRADLEY

gins at the Alum Cave Bluffs parking lot off Newfound Gap Road.

The next three Mount LeConte trails leave from the Gatlinburg area. They'll come in handy if the park is jammed with cars that make it difficult to get to the other trails.

So named because the mountain it crosses resembles the head of a bull, **Bullhead Trail** begins in the Cherokee Orchard parking lot near Gatlinburg. The elevation gain is 4,017 feet, and the hike is 7.25 miles one way.

Rainbow Falls Trail, another trail setting off from the Cherokee Orchard parking lot, is a 6.75-mile, one-way hike that passes an 80-foot waterfall and gains 4,017 feet. Some hikers avoid this trail because it's rocky and steep with lots of gullies.

Hikers from the Gatlinburg area can save 700 feet of elevation gain by taking the **Trillium Gap** trail, which begins along the Roaring Fork Motor Nature Trail at the Grotto Falls parking lot. The elevation gain is 3,473 feet over seven miles one way.

More Trails on the Tennessee Side

Right outside of Gatlinburg on the Newfound Gap Road and one of the more popular trails in the park, **Chimney Tops** is only two miles one-way, with an elevation gain of 1,335 feet. By the end most people are using hands and feet, but the view is worth it.

The 1.5-mile, one-way **Grotto Falls** hike is cool on even the hottest days. Leave the Roaring Fork Motor Nature Trail at the Grotto Falls parking area and walk upstream to this waterfall. Hikers gain only 500 feet in elevation and can look for salamanders on the way. The park shelters 23 species of them.

The **Hen Wallow Falls** hike leaves from a less crowded area. Drive to the Cosby Picnic Area on the northeast end of the park for a two-mile, one-way hike. The elevation gain is 600 feet through a forest with magnificent poplars and hemlocks. The falls are two feet wide at the top and 20 feet wide at the bottom.

The **Ramsay Cascades** trail is one of the few dead-end trails in the Smokies, but what a finale! The 100-foot Ramsay Cascades, while not

SMOKIES HIKING REMINDERS

You've heard these rules before, and you'll see them on signs throughout the park, but here are a few points to keep in mind as you hike through the Smokies:

1. Stash a windbreaker or sweater in your pack. The higher you go, the colder it gets, so a shirt that feels cool and comfortable at the bottom of a mountain trail may prove inadequate for the cold weather at the mountaintop. Getting chilled is rarely any fun, and in bad weather it can prove life threatening.

2. Never drink from streams or creeks. Yes, you're getting "back to nature," but there's no reason to bring some of that nature home in your digestive tract. Carry your own drinking water or take a filtering device with you.

3. Keep kids close. Because of the park's dense foliage, kids can bolt ahead and get lost faster than you can say "Hansel and Gretel." Consider equipping young folk with a whistle, provided they use it only if necessary.

4. Bring bug repellent. Unless, of course, you want to walk along doing a Leonard Bernstein-at-the-podium impersonation.

5. Carry a poncho. The Smoky Mountains get an average of 40 inches of rain per year.

a straight drop, is the highest waterfall in the park. The trail begins in Greenbrier Cove, about six miles due east of Gatlinburg on Highway 321. Four miles one way, the trail gains 1,600 feet in elevation. Hikers should be careful at the falls; several people have fallen to their deaths.

More Hikes on the North Carolina Side

At Cataloochee you'll find the remote but popular, 7.4-mile **Boogerman Loop Trail,** which climbs around 800 feet (to a peak elevation of around 3,600 feet). As Allen R. Coggins recounts the story in his delightful book *Place Names of the Smokies,* the trail is named for Robert "Boogerman" Palmer, whose abandoned cabin you'll pass on the trail. Asked in school what he wanted to be when he grew up, the bashful Palmer supposedly put his head down, laughed, and answered, "the Boogerman." His friends laughed along and began using the name. The older Palmer got, the more his neighbors realized that he hadn't been kidding about his chosen vocation. He withdrew more and more from his mountain neighbors. He grew his beard long and enjoyed frightening children with his appearance. They rewarded him by creating tall tales about their encounters with "the Boogerman." When the lumber companies came around and bought up his neighbors' land, Palmer refused to sell—which is why his namesake trail threads in part through all-too-rare virgin Appalachian forest.

In addition to old-growth forest, the Boogerman Loop Trail also offers some wonderful color in autumn, remnants from settlers' cabins, and pretty views of *cataloochee*—"waves of mountains." To get there, take Cove Creek Road to the Caldwell Fork Trail and follow the signs.

MORE RECREATION
Bicycling
Mountain bikes are prohibited on all Smokies

trails—as are all vehicles—but a few unimproved roads make good riding. You might try the Cataloochee Valley on the eastern end of the park. Or try the Parson Branch Road out of Cades Cove—but keep in mind that even for bicycles, this is a one-way road.

In the more populated areas of the park, the roads can get quite busy with distracted drivers. So if you're going to bike the park, get out there early. The best place to ride is Cades Cove. A concessionaire at the campground store there rents bikes. When the Cove is jammed with cars, you'll be glad to be on your bike.

Fishing
Approximately 730 miles of streams thread through the park, and Fontana Lake lies on the southern border. Except for Fontana, which harbors smallmouth and rock bass, trout is the name of the game here. The park is one of the last refuges of the brook trout, the only species native to these parts; anglers who catch one must release it. Efforts to restore brook trout populations have led to the closing of some streams, and rangers can tell you which ones. Rainbow trout are the interlopers whose exploding populations have made the brook trout so rare, so they are fair game.

fishing for trout in Abrams Creek

© JEFF BRADLEY

Trout season never stops in the Smokies. A Tennessee or North Carolina fishing license enables you to fish all over the park year-round, and you'll find licenses for sale in the gateway towns. Trout stamps are not required, but you're only allowed to use one-hook artificial lures—no bait of any sort is allowed.

You can fish right beside the road or, if you're serious about it, backpack deep into the most remote streams in the park. (See "Camping" under "Practicalities," below.) You can even hire a guide to take you to the best places. A good book for anglers is Don Kirk's *Smoky Mountains Trout Fishing Guide,* which costs $11.95.

Horseback Riding

Horse owners can ride in the park and even take overnight equestrian camping trips with Park Service permission. The park limits the number of horse camps, and you'll need to bring your own horse feed. For a complete set of guidelines for horseback riding, call 865/436-1200 or write to Superintendent, Great Smoky Mountains National Park, 107 Park Headquarters Rd., Gatlinburg, TN 37738.

Horses are available to rent from several places in the park, generally for about $15 for a short ride. All rides are guided, usually at a sedate pace, and children under six have to ride with an adult. On the Tennessee side, visitors can rent horses near Park Headquarters, tel. 865/436-5354; at Cades Cove Riding Stables, tel. 865/448-6286; and east of Gatlinburg on Highway 321, tel. 865/436-5634. On the North Carolina side, try Smokemont, tel. 828/497-2373; or Deep Creek, tel. 828/488-8504.

Hayrides

May through October you can tour Cades Cove in a truck-drawn hay wagon in the evening. The rides costs $6 a person or $8 for a ranger-led trips. No reservations are required. The wagons depart from the Cades Cove Stables. If you've got a group of 15 or more, you can may reserve your own wagon for day trips.For group reservations, call 865/448-6286.

Water Sports

Except in spring and after torrential downpours, you'll have a bear of a time trying to canoe, raft, or even kayak the park's rivers and streams. You may spot some intrepid, experienced kayakers (or some foolish, inexperienced ones) within the park, but for true white water you'll probably need to go outside, preferably to the French Broad or Nantahala River.

If you're seeking a milder experience and don't mind taking a cool dip, you can ride **inner tubes** at the Sinks area of Little River Road. Use caution, though. Rocks—both underwater and not—can make this activity hazardous. Lots of people tube this area every year, and you'll probably be fine if you keep your head about you—specifically if you keep it away from the rocks.

Skiing

The park offers no downhill skiing, but during winter cross-country skiers practice various forms of their sport on roads and trails. Clingmans Dome Road, the Cherokee Orchard Road, and the Roaring Fork Motor Nature Trail provide excellent skiing when the weather cooperates.

GREAT SMOKIES

Practicalities

WHERE TO STAY

When it comes to a place to stay in the most visited national park in the country, **Mount LeConte Lodge** is the only game around—and it's 5.5 miles from the nearest road. Jack Huff built LeConte Lodge in the 1920s, and when the park came into existence the lodge was allowed to remain. Various environmental hardliners have argued for the demise of the venerable lodge, but public sentiment has overwhelmed them every time.

LeConte Lodge holds about 50 guests, either in cabins or private rooms within cabins. Rooms run $79 a night *per person,* and accommodations are extremely rustic: no electricity, hot water, or telephones. The flush toilets stop working in cold weather, so you may have to use a pit toilet. Most of dinner and breakfast comes out of cans carried up the mountain by pack llamas—used because they damage the trails less than horses. The staff serves hearty meals family-style—a great chance to mingle and swap stories with other travelers. The sunset over Clingmans Dome is the evening's sole planned entertainment, and guests retire to their toolshed-sized cabins with wool blankets and kerosene heaters to beat back the cold.

And most guests wouldn't have it any other way.

LeConte Lodge enjoys more demand for its rooms than any other hostelry in the region. Open from late March through November, the lodge accepts reservations for the following year beginning on October 1 (or the following business day if October 1 falls on a weekend). Call 865/429-5704 or write Wilderness Lodging, 250 Apple Valley Rd., Sevierville, TN 37862. Reservations for the entire year are usually snatched up completely within two weeks. But folks have been known to cancel—it won't hurt to call at the last minute to see if a bunk's opened up.

An alternate way to get a bunk at the lodge is to sign up for a Smoky Mountain Field School hike. The lodge reserves three Saturdays a year for these hikes—one each in the spring, summer, and fall. Call 800/284-8885 for dates.

CAMPING

The National Park Service takes a rather stoic stance toward campers: Tent here and you're going to rough it, like it or not. You'll find no sissy pay showers here, and only when the numbers overwhelm pit toilets do the flush toilets open up. Neither will RVers find electrical or water umbilical cords.

Sites run $12–17. You can reserve one up to five months in advance at the park's three most popular campgrounds, Cades Cove, Smokemont, and Elkmont, from May 15 through October 31. Just call 800/365-2267 and type in the park code, GREA, at the prompt. All sites at the park's other campgrounds, and any unreserved campsites at the campgrounds listed above, are available on a first-come, first-served basis. No more than

looking out a cabin at Mount LeConte Lodge

six people can occupy one site, either in two tents or one RV and one tent. During summer and fall campers can stay only seven days; the rest of the year they can stay 14 days. Pets are permitted in campgrounds but you'll have to restrain them.

Overall, the park offers 1,008 campsites at 10 developed campgrounds: 5 in Tennessee and 5 in North Carolina. The larger campgrounds offer campfire programs in the evenings. Call 865/436-1200 for information.

Tennessee Campgrounds

Cades Cove, with 161 sites, lies in a part of the Smokies rich in things to do. Besides the cabins and the Cable Mill, trails lead to a bald and a waterfall. This is the only campground with a store, and the Cades Cove Loop Road is the best place in the park to ride a bike. The campground can handle 35-foot RVs, is wheelchair accessible, and is open year-round.

Cosby, with 175 sites, features smaller crowds. It's also more convenient if you're planning to see the Greenbrier area and hike to Ramsay Cascade. Tubing Cosby Creek is a favorite activity here. Cosby can handle 25-foot RVs and is open late March through October.

Elkmont, with 220 sites, is the biggest campground in the entire park. It's close to the Metcalf Bottoms Historic Area and the delightful Little River. In late May, June, and early July, you can see the amazing synchronized fireflies along the

> *In the Parker Brothers National Parks version of Monopoly, Great Smoky Mountains National Park received the second most prestigious "address"— making it the "Park Place" of national parks.*

nature trail past the campground. Laurel Falls is nearby, and Elkmont is also the campground closest to the worldly pleasures of Gatlinburg. It can handle all size RVs, is wheelchair accessible, and is open year-round.

Look Rock offers 92 sites on the extreme western edge of the park. Since it's out of the way, it's a good place to look for a spot when other campgrounds are full. Look Rock offers access to Abrams Creek. It can handle 25-foot RVs and is open late March through October.

Abrams Creek, with 16 sites, is the smallest park campground in Tennessee. This gem lies in a forest of huge conifers that lend it a cathedral effect. It is the trailhead for a hike up to Abrams Falls and is also wheelchair accessible. It can handle 16-foot RVs and is open late March through October.

North Carolina Campgrounds

Balsam Mountain, with 46 sites, is a good base for exploring the Cherokee Reservation; Mingo Falls is a good day trip from here. The campground can handle 30-foot RVs and is open mid-May through October 18.

Deep Creek, with 108 sites, lies three miles north of Bryson City and within two miles of three waterfalls: Juneywhank Falls, Indian Creek Falls, and Toms Branch Falls. The campground can handle 25-foot RVs and is open mid-April through October.

Smokemont, with 140 sites, is the largest campground on the North Carolina side and a good place to take in the Mountain Farm Museum at Oconoluftee and Mingus Mill. It's also the park campground closest to Cherokee, North Carolina. Open year-round and wheelchair accessible, it can take all RV sizes.

Big Creek, with nine sites, is the smallest campground in the park. It lies on the far eastern end of the Smokies. It's open May 1 to November 2 and can take 26-foot RVs.

Cataloochee, with 27 sites, also on the eastern end of the park, lies at the end of a rough,

BLOCKADER'S GLORY

For many years, mountain people called Sugarlands "Blockader's Glory," which, roughly translated, meant "Moonshiner's Heaven." "Blockade liquor" was another name for moonshine, and the then-isolated valley—now the site of park headquarters and the visitor's center—was a haven for moonshiners.

GREAT SMOKIES

MOUNTAIN ARCHITECTURE: CANTILEVER BARNS

While log cabins in the Great Smokies were not all that different from log houses built anywhere else in a hardwood forest, the overhanging barns erected in East Tennessee were found in few other parts of the country. Writing in the *Tennessee Encyclopedia*, Marian Moffett reported that she and another researcher found "only six cantilever barns in Virginia and another three in North Carolina. By contrast, 316 cantilever barns were found in Tennessee, with 183 in Sevier County, 106 in Blount County, and the remaining 27 scattered from Johnson to Bradley counties." Professor Moffet coauthored *East Tennessee Cantilever Barns,* published by the University of Tennessee Press in 1993.

Cantilever barns imaginatively create shelter with a minimal use of material. As best seen at the Tipton Farm in Cades Cove, a cantilever barn begins with two boxlike log structures measuring 12 by 16 or 18 feet and placed about 15 feet apart. The logs at the top of these boxes extend out to support a second floor, which not only bridges the gap between the two structures but also stretches eight or ten feet out in each direction to create shelter underneath. In an area where annual rainfall can be 63 inches or more, sheltering animals and farm equipment was very important.

Most cantilever barns were built during a 50-year period beginning in 1870, yet innovative architects still use the form. The main building of Richmont Inn, a luxurious resort in Townsend (www.richmontinn.com), takes the shape of a four-story cantilever barn. And Maya Lin, the award-winning designer of the Vietnam Veterans Memorial, restored and re-created a cantilever barn as an ultramodern sky-lit reading room for the Langston Hughes Library at the Children's Defense Fund's conference and training center in Norris, Tennessee.

unpaved road that will guarantee campers freedom from crowds. The Cataloochee area contains several old buildings left behind by a community of 1,200 settlers. The campground is open late March through October.

Trail Shelters

Shelters, most of them on the Appalachian Trail, offer accommodations for hikers who do not want to carry tents or sleep under the stars. Each shelter has three walls and a chain-link fence across the front. Inside you'll find 8 to 14 beds made of wire mesh strung between logs. Outside you'll find a pit toilet. The good news is that shelters are dry and bear-proof, with beds up off the ground. The bad news for some folks is that you may find yourself in close quarters with up to 13 total strangers, any of whom may be champion snorers or Amway enthusiasts.

You don't have to pay to stay in one of the shelters, but you do need to reserve one in advance. Call Park Headquarters at 865/436-1231 up to one month before your visit.

Backcountry Camping

Despite all the talk of crowding in the park, it offers close to 100 backcountry sites where, some contend, the ultimate camping experience takes place. Park workers have established backcountry sites all over the park; they shift the locations from time to time to minimize the wear and tear on the land. A site can accommodate from 8 to 20 campers, who can stay up to three days before moving on. Reservations are required for some sites, but there is no charge. Write to Backcountry Permits, Great Smoky Mountains National Park, Gatlinburg, TN, 37738 or call 865/436-1231. If you're already in the park, stop by one of the visitor's centers—at Sugarlands, Cades Cove, or Oconaluftee—or one of the ranger stations.

To keep things as pristine as possible, the park requires backpackers to pack out all garbage. Don't bury it or throw it in a pit toilet. In general, practice zero-impact camping: Tents should not be trenched, and hand-dug toilets must lie well away from the campsite and any water sources. Campers can build fires in established fire rings, but park officials prefer that you use a portable stove to lessen the impact on the land.

A final note: Park rangers are very strict about camping in unauthorized places. You can't spend the night in a parking area or picnic area or on the side of the road, even if all the campgrounds are full. The same holds true for the backcountry. Be sure to reserve ahead and allow enough time to get to your destination.

SERVICES AND INFORMATION
Park Admission
The original park charter forever forbid the charging of an admission fee. So even today, you won't pay a dime to enter the park.

Emergencies
In case of trouble, call **Park Headquarters,** tel. 865/436-1230; **Gatlinburg police,** tel. 865/436-5181; or **Cherokee police,** tel. 704/497-4131. Sevier County Hospital on Middle Creek Road in Sevierville, tel. 865/453-7111, is 15 miles from Gatlinburg. Blount Memorial Hospital on Highway 321 in Maryville, tel. 865/983-7211, is 25 miles from Cades Cove, and Swain County Hospital in Bryson City, North Carolina, tel. 704/488-2155, is 16 miles from Smokemont.

Information
The best place to get oriented to the park and to find out what's happening is the **Sugarlands Visitor Center,** just outside Gatlinburg. It includes a small natural history museum, a slide show, free maps, and people who can answer questions. A bookstore offers helpful volumes and films. The **Oconaluftee Visitor Center** sits on the North Carolina side of the park. Both centers are open daily 8 A.M.–7 P.M. Rangers at stations scattered throughout the park can also answer questions and deal with problems.

GREAT SMOKIES

The Quiet Side of the Smokies and Fontana Lake

Townsend

Townsend bills itself as "the peaceful side of the Smokies," and, compared to Gatlinburg and Pigeon Forge, that's certainly the truth. Townsend lies in a cove—a flat area in mountain parlance—called Tuckaleechee Cove. Tourists have been coming to this area since 1904, when the railroad came through, but recent excavations show that this area has been popular with people for over 2,500 years.

When road crews began widening Highway 321 in 1999, they uncovered evidence of extensive Indian habitation, so work was halted while archeologists studied the newly exposed ground. Scientists found what was left of a big Cherokee town, as well as evidence of habitation dating back to 200 A.D. Human remains were found as well, and the Eastern Band of the Cherokee and Seminoles from Oklahoma, the presumed descendants of those who lived here, helped make

Millennium Manor in Alcoa

the decision to leave the 70 graves intact. Each was covered with a layer of concrete before the road was paved over.

Millions of people across the country have seen Townsend without realizing it. It is the site of CBS's (later the Family Channel's) *Christy*, the saga of a young teacher who comes to a remote mountain area to teach school. The story comes from the novel of the same name by Catherine Marshall.

People who want to see the greatest concentration of wildflowers in this region—400-plus species—should beat a path to **Hedgewood Gardens** on Bethel Church Road off Highway 321, tel. 865/984-2052. A woman named Hedy Wood designed the six acres of gardens to look as natural as possible, nurturing them for 23 years. She died in 1993 and her daughter, Hope Woodard, has opened the gardens to the public by appointment only.

You can view Townsend's history at the **Little River Railroad & Lumber Company Museum** on Highway 321, tel. 865/448-2211. Most people who look at the verdant forests hereabouts can't imagine that all of it was at one time cut down. This free museum gives a sense of what those times were like with a restored Shay locomotive, depot, and steam-powered sawmill. It is open every day in summer and October, and weekends only in May and September.

RECREATION

The Townsend Y has nothing to do with the YMCA, but it is perhaps the best swimming hole in these parts. In a region full of chlorinated water parks, this is the real thing and a wonderful way to escape the heat. Just inside the park on the left—look for hordes of parked vehicles—two streams come together to provide a variety of fun. Families will enjoy drifting down the stream in inner tubes, with just enough white water to make it fun. On the far side of the stream and conveniently over a deep pool, cliffs provide an opportunity for brave (and exceedingly warm-blooded) souls to take the plunge. There are no lifeguards here, which is the bad news and the good news.

Farther downstream is **River Romp Tubes,**

8203 Hwy. 73, tel. 865/448-1522. Located in the Bodywear outlet store at the junction of Highways 321 and 73, this place rents high-quality inner tubes and life jackets for the float down the Little River.

Tuckaleechee Caverns, 825 Caverns Dr., tel. 865/448-2274, also cools off visitors, but only to 58°. With the usual colorfully named features, this cave is a great rainy day excursion. Home to a huge room approximately 400 by 150 feet, it is open March 15 through November 15. Admission is $8 for adults, $4 for children 5 to 11, and free for children under 5.

On Horseback
Cades Cove Riding Stables, in the Walland area between Townsend and Maryville at 4035 E. Lamar Alexander Parkway, tel. 865/448-6286,

offers horseback rides, carriage rides, and hayrides through Cades Cove. It's open April through October.

Davy Crockett Riding Stables, 232 Stables Dr., tel. 865/448-6411, does not require customers to wear coonskin hats on its guided rides. It's open every day except Christmas.

Double M Ranch, 4033 Miser Station Rd., tel. 865/995-9421, has horseback rides, hiking, and a paved road for bicycling.

On Foot

Little River Outfitters, 7807 E. Lamar Alexander Pkwy., tel. 865/448-9459, is a guide service, fly shop, backpacking store, and clothing shop.

ENTERTAINMENT AND EVENTS

The **Townsend in the Smokies Spring Festival** takes place one week in April, and the **Autumn Leaves Arts & Crafts Fair** is held for a week in September. Contact the **Townsend Visitors Center,** 7906 E. Lamar Alexander Pkwy., tel. 865/448-6134 or 800/525-6834, for more information.

WHERE TO STAY

Bed-and-Breakfasts and Inns

Blackberry Farm, 1471 W. Millers Cove Rd., tel. 865/984-8166, website: www.blackberry-farm.com, harks back to the grand hotels of old, when guests went to one place, paid one price, and spent all their time there. This elegant inn sits on 1,100 acres and has 44 guest rooms, all furnished with English and American antiques and priced at $395–895 per night. The price includes three gourmet meals per day and fully stocked pantries. Once guests stagger from the table, they can work off the calories at a fitness center, four tennis courts, a swimming pool, a trout pond, a three-acre bass and bream lake, and two off-site golf courses. Mountain bikes, fly-fishing gear, golf carts, binoculars, and tennis rackets are available. Special programs include cooking schools and fly-fishing expeditions.

The **Richmont Inn,** 220 Winterberry Ln., tel. 866/267-7086 or 865/448-6751, was built to resemble the cantilevered Appalachian barns

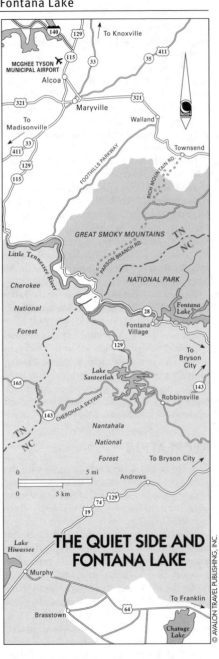

THE QUIET SIDE AND FONTANA LAKE

© AVALON TRAVEL PUBLISHING, INC.

© JEFF BRADLEY

making a splash at the Townsend Y

found in East Tennessee and western North Carolina. Inside, however, the traveler finds 18th-century English antiques, French paintings, and Swiss cooking. The 10 rooms are named for prominent Appalachian folks and contain whirlpool baths, king-sized beds, fireplaces, and balconies. Rates range $115–225 per night. Pets are not welcome, but children over age 12 are. The rooms are among the best to be found in these parts, but the food is icing on the cake—literally. Room rates include a candlelit dessert prepared by a chef who once won the grand prize in *Gourmet* magazine's dessert recipe contest. Breakfast might include French baked eggs or French toast à l'orange. Look for the inn online at www.richmontinn.com.

Terrapin Point Retreat, 426 Cameron Rd., tel. 865/448-6010, has a suite with mountain views, a private bath, and a whirlpool. Rates are $110 per night. See it online at www.geocities.com/heartland/ridge/8744.

At the **Twin Valley Bed and Breakfast Horse Ranch,** 2848 Old Chilhowee Rd. Walland, tel.

865/984-0980, energetic guests can pitch in with taking care of the horses, while the rest can just relax. This is not one of those B&Bs filled with antique English furniture. It is a comfortable place, housed in a hand-hewn log building decorated in country style, where guests don't have to worry about knocking into an expensive antique. The two rooms share a bath, and cabins are also available, as are backwoods wilderness shelters. The ranch serves a full country breakfast. Rates range $75–95. See them online at www.bbonline.com/ten/twinvalley.

Cabins, Condos, and Chalets

Perhaps the most delightful place to stay hereabouts is in a cabin overlooking the Little River. Falling asleep with the window open on a cool evening, listening to the sound of flowing water, is about as good as it gets.

A word to the wise: Some property owners have had problems with guests hosting loud parties and have resorted to draconian rules, such as no visitors without written permission. If an unauthorized guest is detected (or a smuggled-in pet is found where animals aren't permitted), the rental agency has the right to throw everyone out with no refund of the rental fee.

The following is a short list of what is available, on the water and elsewhere, in Townsend. For a more complete list, call 800/525-6834 or visit www.townsendcabin.com.

"Bear"ly Rustic Cabin Rentals, website: www.townsendcabin.com, offers more than 40 completely furnished cabins and cottages. Rates begin at $99 per couple per night for two bedrooms.

Dogwood Cabins and Realty, 7016 E. Lamar Alexander Pkwy., tel. 888/448-9054 or 865/448-1720, website: www.dogwoodcabins.com, offers waterside as well as mountain cabins for nightly and long-term rentals.

Carnes' Log Cabins, tel. 865/448-1021, website: www.carneslogcabins.com, is located approximately one mile from the park entrance.

Old Smoky Mountain Cabins, tel. 800/739-4820 or 865/448-2388, website: www.oldsmokymountaincabins.com, has cabins with one to eight bedrooms.

QUIET SIDE

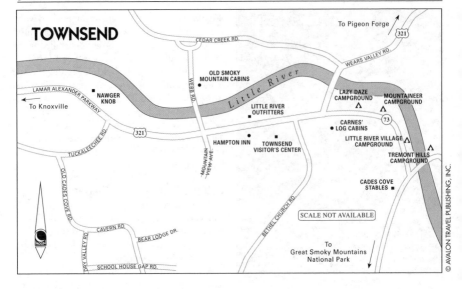

Wild Mountain Rose Log Cabin Rentals, tel. 800/736-1938 or 865/448-6895, website: www.wildrosetn.com, has cabins with fireplaces, mountain views, and large porches with rockers.

Motels

Among your motel options are the **Best Western Valley View Lodge** on Highway 321, tel. 865/448-2237 or 800/292-4844; **Big Valley Motel,** 7052 E. Lamar Alexander Pkwy., tel. 865/448-6639; **Hampton Inn,** 7824 E. Lamar Alexander Pkwy., tel. 865/448-9000 or 800/HAMPTON; **Highland Manor Motel,** also on Highway 321, tel. 800/213-9462; and **Talley-Ho Inn,** 8314 Hwy. 73, tel. 865/448-2465 or 800/448-2465.

Camping

Most of the campgrounds in the Townsend area lie between Wears Valley Road and the entrance to the park along the Little River.

The 75 sites at **Lazy Daze Campground,** 8429 Hwy. 73, tel. 865/448-6061, some of them along the Little River and all with cable TV, await campers here. The campground is open year-round.

Little River Village Campground, tel.

865/448-2241, also lies along the Little River, with 136 sites and all the amenities you'll need. The campground is open March to November.

Also on the Little River, **Mountaineer Campground,** tel. 865/448-6421, offers 49 sites and is open year-round.

The 144 sites at **Tremont Hill's Campground,** tel. 865/448-6363, are open from March 1 to the Sunday after Thanksgiving.

Ye-Olde-Mill Anderson's Campground, tel. 865/448-6681, offers 26 sites and fewer amenities than the larger places. It's open April to November.

MORE PRACTICALITIES
Food

The **Carriage House,** 8310 Hwy. 73, tel. 865/448-2263, serves three daily meals of country cooking from April to November 15.

The **Creekside Inn,** 7016 E. Lamar Alexander Pkwy., tel. 865/448-1215, offers steaks, seafood, pasta, and other dishes, including teriyaki chicken.

Laurel Valley Country Club, tel. 865/448-9534, serves dinner on Friday and Saturday, brunch on Sunday, and lunch Monday through Friday. Meals include shrimp marinara, wild boar

THE CULT OF *CHRISTY*

Christy began as a 1967 novel by the late Catherine Marshall, widow of Peter Marshall, chaplain to the U.S. Senate. The novel was loosely based on the experiences of Catherine's mother, Leonora Whitaker Wood, who as a young woman taught in a Presbyterian mission school near Del Rio, Tennessee, from 1910 to 1912. This school was one of 34 settlement schools in the state—mostly located in the mountainous east—where outsiders came in to help the impoverished locals.

The book tells the story of a devoutly Christian 19-year-old woman who comes to teach in a mission school in a remote corner of Tennessee—Cutters Gap in the book—and her inspiring adventures with the inhabitants of that mountain community. The plot in many ways prefigures the Luke Skywalker-Princess Leia-Han Solo love triangle in the *Star Wars* trilogy. Christy is caught between her affection for an earnest young minister and her attraction to a brooding, scampish local doctor—an agnostic—and meanwhile faces pedagogical challenges as she adjusts to the ways of the mountain people. The young woman's strong faith in the Force—er, God—however, sees her through her troubles. She decides that her love for the minister is more brotherly than romantic, and when the brooding doctor converts, the final obstacle is out of the way, and she ends up with him.

The novel became a best-seller, and the author hoped that it would be made into a film, as was her biography of her husband, *A Man Called Peter*. Marshall died in 1983, and it wasn't until Easter Sunday 1994 that *Christy* aired as a CBS made-for-television movie. It then became a weekly show in the same time slot as *The Waltons,* an earlier wholesome series. Some 20 episodes were filmed, four as two-hour specials. These were later shown on the Family Channel.

The filming was done in Townsend, a small town on the western end of Great Smoky Mountains National Park. After the show went off the air, an outdoor musical version of *Christy* was performed for several summers in Townsend.

Christy fans clamored for more episodes, however, and in 2001 a new miniseries, *Christy, Choices of the Heart,* aired on Pax TV. Christy finally marries!

The story of Christy has sparked a new series of books aimed at Christian teens. Now up to 12 volumes, they are published by the Tommy Nelson imprint of Thomas Nelson Publishers, website: www.tommynelson.com.

Christy fans who come to the Smokies region have two choices. The real Cutters Gap is in the mountains near Del Rio (see Chapter 7). Visitors to Townsend can drive past the church used in the filming of the series. People at the Townsend Visitors Center can give you directions.

The best time to come to Townsend is during **Christyfest,** held annually since 1997. Typical gatherings include a chance to meet cast members, watch a play, and meet fellow devotees. For more information, call the Townsend Visitors Center at 865/448-6134 or 800/525-6834 or go to http://come.to/ChristyFest.

tenderloin, and grilled chicken. To get to the club, take Old Tuckaleechee Road off Highway 321, drive two miles, and follow the signs.

Mill House Restaurant, 4737 Old Walland Hwy., tel. 865/982-5726, occupies the former home of a Little River mill owner. The mill is no more, but the house has been transformed into perhaps the best place to eat this side of the Smokies. The Mill House is a prix fixe restaurant—all meals cost the same, in this case around $20. Seven courses make up the meal, with entrées of steak, seafood, chicken, and pork. The ambience is very relaxed; diners linger for a long time over the delicious food. Reservations are a very good idea. To get there, leave Townsend and drive toward Maryville. Watch for the sign 1.5 miles past the Walland turnoff. The restaurant is open weekends only.

T.J.'s Smoky Mountain Bar-B-Q, 7305 E. Lamar Alexander Pkwy., tel. 865/448-9420, offers beef, pork, ribs, and chicken—takeout or eat in.

QUIET SIDE

Shopping

Townsend is home to the **Earthtide School of Folk Art,** 7645 E. Lamar Alexander Pkwy., tel. 865/448-1106, located in a yellow house next to the Townsend post office. The school offers classes that last an afternoon, three or four days, or sometimes longer. Subjects include basketry, drawing, pottery, spinning, weaving, wild foods, and medicinal plants. A gallery on the premises features the work of the school's instructors as well as other local craftspeople. Passersby are welcome to watch various artists at work.

Lee Roberson's Studio/Gallery, 758 Wears Valley Rd., tel. 865/448-2365, presents idealized scenes of the Smokies past and present. The artist's prints and other work are available at this gallery, located two miles outside of Townsend.

Nancy's Art & Frame Shop, 7249 E. Lamar Alexander Pkwy., tel. 865/448-6377, sells prints of local scenes by a variety of artists.

Nawger Knob Craft Settlement is a collection of two shops well worth a stop. If you've ever thought about taking up woodcarving, **Smoky Mountain Woodcarvers Supply,** tel. 800/541-5994, website: www.woodcarvers.com, has a great collection of tools, advice, and pieces of wood on which to begin. Just next door is **Wood-N-Strings,** website: www.clemmerdulcimer.com, a dulcimer shop featuring beautifully crafted versions of the old mountain instrument.

Information

Beside the Hampton Inn, you'll find the **Townsend Visitors Center,** 7906 E. Lamar Alexander Pkwy., tel. 865/448-6134 or 800/525-

door of Earthtide School of Folk Art, Townsend

© JEFF BRADLEY

6834. It's open daily 9 A.M.–6 P.M., except in January and February, when it is open only Friday to Sunday. Visit the website at www.blountweb.com/townsend/visitorsctr.htm. You'll find more Smokies information online at www.smokymountains.org.

QUIET SIDE

Maryville and Vicinity

The seat of Blount County, Maryville was named for the wife of Governor William Blount. This part of Tennessee saw a lot of conflict between Indians and settlers as the latter moved closer to the strongholds of the former. When the edge of the frontier was pushed west and south, Maryville lay on the route back east, and it prospered from travelers and trade.

Sam Houston, so instrumental in founding Texas, moved to this area from Virginia when he was 14 years old. When he was 19 he taught school for one term in a log schoolhouse that still stands here. In 1819 a Presbyterian minister founded a seminary that eventually became Maryville College. The college broke ground in many ways: It was the first seminary in the South, one of the first colleges to offer coeducation, and one of the few colleges open to black and Indian students.

Maryville is also the birthplace of Lamar Alexander, Republican governor of Tennessee from 1979 to 1987 and the first governor to be elected to consecutive four-year terms. He campaigned by wearing a plaid shirt and jeans and walking across the state. This technique, however, has not proven effective in the several times that Alexander has run for president.

SIGHTS

The **Sam Houston Schoolhouse,** tel. 865/ 983-1550, website: www.geocities.com/sam houstonschoolhouse, where the future president of the Republic of Texas served as a 19-year-old teacher, is a small structure built of poplar logs. It includes a visitor's center with a museum containing artifacts and pedagogical implements used by Houston and other teachers of that time. To get to the schoolhouse, drive three miles north out of Maryville on Route 33 to the intersection of Sam Houston Schoolhouse Road. Go right for two miles. The schoolhouse is open daily 10 A.M.–5 P.M. and Sunday 1–5 P.M. Admission is $.50 for adults; children get in free.

PRACTICALITIES

Where to Stay

Due to its proximity to Knoxville's McGee Tyson Airport, Maryville has an assortment of franchise motels. For something less generic try the **High Court Inn,** 212 High St., tel. 865/981-2966, which occupies a 1911 house down the street from the Blount County Courthouse. The house, which has been completely restored, has three guest rooms, all with private baths, four-poster beds, and claw-foot bathtubs. Rates range $59–69.

Also try the **Executive Lodge,** 215 Hall Rd., tel. 865/984-9958, or the **Princess Motel,** 2614 Hwy. 411/129, tel. 865/982-2490.

Food

Buddy's Bar-be-que, 518 Foothills Plaza, tel. 865/984-4475, is a Knoxville-based chain with good food. It's open daily for lunch and dinner.

Order in the Court Cafe, 212 High St., tel. 865/984-3861, presides Monday through Friday over lunches of soups, sandwiches, and salads. Brunch is served Sunday, 10 A.M.–1 P.M.

The Southern Skillet, 1311 E. Lamar Alexander Pkwy., tel. 865/984-9680, offers country cooking and homemade desserts. It serves all three meals seven days a week.

Shopping

Halls Furniture and Auction, 3501 E. Lamar Alexander Pkwy., tel. 865/983-1598, offers a down-home sort of entertainment every Friday evening with an auction of both junk and valuable treasures. The trick is knowing which is which. The bidding gets rolling at 7 P.M. and can continue past midnight.

Lee's World of Crafts, 370 Gill St., Alcoa, tel. 865/984-7674, sells prints, quilts, baskets, furniture, and other items.

Information

Visit the **Blount County Chamber of Commerce,** 309 S. Washington St., Maryville, tel.

QUIET SIDE

A HOUSE FOR THE AGES

© JEFF BRADLEY

Across the South, a variety of visionary folks have been led by their religious beliefs to create unusual works of art, gardens, and buildings. Millennium Manor in Alcoa is one of the more unusual specimens.

In 1937, William and Fair Nicholson moved to Alcoa. They were a very religious couple who took very seriously this verse from Revelations 20:6:

Blessed and holy is he that hath part in the first resurrection. On such the second death hath no power, but they shall be priests of God and Christ, and shall reign with him a thousand years.

According to the Nicholsons, to reign for 1,000 years they would need a house that would survive Armageddon. They decided to build a house based on Roman designs, since Roman buildings have proven they can last as long as two millennia.

And so, at age 61 and while holding down a full-time job, William and his wife began building their house. The old couple used tons of stone and more than 4,000 bags of cement. Millennium Manor contains 14 rooms and a two-car garage, totaling about 3,000 square feet. The thinnest inside wall is 19 inches thick. The thinnest exterior wall is 25 inches thick. The roof is three feet thick, and the floor is more than four feet thick. To ensure a water supply, the couple dug a 60-foot well that is five feet in diameter. Their work was completed by 1946.

And then they waited for the Rapture. Fair Nicholson died in 1950, and William lived for 15 more years, dying at the age of 88 in 1965. The couple had 10 children, none of whom wanted to take up residence in the stone house. Dean Fontaine bought the house in 1995 and is restoring it. He lives in the house and holds an open house each Memorial Day.

This house is just off U.S. 129. From U.S. 129, take the ramp toward U.S. 441/321 toward Townsend. Take Lincoln Street to the left, cross some railroad tracks, and go left on Wright Road to Millennium Manor at 500 Wright Road.

Most of the information in this article came from material assembled by Fontaine. He maintains a website about the Manor, www .millenniummanor.com.

865/983-2241; it's open Monday through Friday 8 A.M.–5 P.M. You'll find more information at www.smokymountains.org.

ALCOA

Several Tennessee towns were founded or controlled by industries that have extracted the natural resources of the state. Alcoa was perhaps the only company town whose raw materials did not come from Tennessee. As well as the name of the town, Alcoa is an acronym for the Aluminum Company of America. In 1910 it began buying land along the Little Tennessee River to create a series of lakes for waterpower to produce cheap electricity—a big part of the cost of making aluminum.

The company located its factory outside Maryville in 1913 and incorporated Alcoa to house workers. The town, which segregated blacks and whites, included parks, commercial areas, schools, and other facilities. Although labor strife plagued Alcoa in the 1930s, the town and its industry boomed during World War II, when the workforce hit 12,000 people. Alcoans had a high standard of living compared to the rest of the state, and that prosperity influenced Maryville and Blount County as well.

The company no longer owns the town, which is virtually indistinguishable from Maryville, but it still gets electricity from four dams on the Little Tennessee River. And the company continues to prosper, with a workforce of 2,000 that makes aluminum for beverage cans.

FOOTHILLS PARKWAY

To outlanders, this road makes no sense. It stops and it starts, one section dumps motorists into Wears Valley for no apparent reason, then it lurches back to life near Cosby for a short time before terminating onto I-40.

As is often with such matters, therein lies a tale. The Blue Ridge Parkway was proposed in the 1920s to link Shenandoah National Park and the Great Smokies. The proposal set off a political tug-of-war between politicians from North Carolina and Tennessee, each of whom hoped to bring the dollars and jobs to their state. North Carolina won, and today the Blue Ridge Parkway hosts around 27,000 people per day. They motor along the ridge tops, descending into valleys to fill up their gas tanks and empty their wallets.

Foothills Parkway represents an effort to replicate that golden goose, this time on the Tennessee side of the park. In 1944, Congress passed a bill creating the parkway but was slow in coming up with the money. The first mile was paved in 1960, and over the years the road has grown in fits and starts. Later, attitudes changed, and a good many people came to think that building a ridge-top road was not the best way to treat a wilderness area.

Pressure grew, however, for anything that would relieve the congestion of Highway 441 through the park. In 1999 money was approved for the first of 10 bridges that would complete the 1.6-mile missing link of the 16.1-mile Walland to Wears Valley segment of the parkway. The missing link consists of very rough terrain, and bridging just this 1.6-mile gap is likely to cost more than $60 million. Even after this segment is finished, the Foothills Parkway will be only half of its proposed length.

Even those who oppose completing the road have to admit that by buying the ridge-top property, the government has prevented philistines from building monstrous houses that would spoil the view for miles.

To outlanders, the Foothills Parkway makes no sense. It stops and starts, one section dumps motorists into Wears Valley for no apparent reason, then lurches back to life near Cosby for a short stretch before terminating onto I-40.

FONTANA

Below the North Carolina line and east on Highway 28, Fontana Lake is a child of the Depression-era Tennessee Valley Authority. The TVA built Fontana Dam to generate power for a Tennessee aluminum plant, just in time for the demands of World War II. Fontana Village arose to house the construction crews.

When the war was over, existentialist Jean-Paul Sartre, on a tour of the United States, visited Fontana Village. Writing in *Le Figaro,* he waxed rhapsodic about what he saw: "The striking thing is the lightness, the fragility of these buildings. The village has no weight, it seems barely to rest upon the soil; it has not managed to leave a human imprint on the reddish earth and the dark forest; it is a temporary thing."

He was wrong about the temporary part. When the 480-foot dam—for a long time the highest in the eastern United States—was completed, it may just have been the last hard day's work anyone's ever put in around Fontana; the town has been a resort since then. Unlike Norris, Tennessee—a village built under similar circumstances and eventually sold house-by-house—Fontana Village was leased in one piece from the government and turned into a resort when the construction workers left. Due to its out-of-the-way location, it's less crowded and less expensive than most of the other amenity areas circling the national park.

The **Fontana Village** resort consists of 250 cabins and a modern hotel. Rooms at the hotel run $49–149; cabins cost $69–209; camp cabins run $49–59. A campground costs around $20 a night. A 16-bunk hostel offers even cheaper, if less private, digs. Outdoor activities are the name of the game here, including tennis, golf, hiking, horseback riding, fishing, and boating. For information, call 800/849-2258 or go to www.fontanavillage.com on the web.

The **Log Cabin Museum,** set in an 1875 cabin, documents the history of the village. Also on Highway 28–inside the Fontana Motel, of all places—is the **Graham County Museum of Prehistoric Relics,** tel. 828/479-3677. Therein you'll find thousands of prehistoric Amerind stone weapons, tools, and other artifacts.

> *When the 480-foot Fontana Dam—for a long time the highest in the eastern United States—was completed, it may just have been the last hard day's work anyone's ever put in around Fontana; the town has been a resort since then.*

Robbinsville

South on Route 1147, Robbinsville is the seat of Graham County, about 60 percent of which resides within the Nantahala National Forest.

Before the current town was founded, the Snowbird Indians—Cherokee who lived in the Snowbird Mountains—dwelled here. Cherokee chief Junaluska, who commanded his warriors in an alliance with General Andrew Jackson against the Creek Indians in the 1814 Battle of Horseshoe Bend, was one inhabitant. According to tradition, Chief Junaluska saved Jackson's life when Old Hickory was attacked by a Creek warrior. The good chief received American citizenship and a good bit of Graham County as a reward. He's buried off Highway 143 Business; you can view the grave for free.

Today, Robbinsville serves as the southern starting point for the **Cherohala Skyway,** one of only 20-some national scenic byways in the nation, first opened in 1996. Robbinsville is also home to **Tapoco Lodge Resort,** 14981 Tapoco Rd., tel. 800/822-5083 or 828/498-2435, website: www.tapocolodge.com. It offers an American meal plan, which provides three full Southern meals a day. Rates start at $69 a person, but you can rent just a room (no meals) starting at $79, double occupancy. Other local lodgings include the **Phillips Motel,** 290 Main St., tel. 828/479-3370, which offers efficiency rooms.

MURPHY

This little town on Highway 19 is the seat of Cherokee County and one of the oldest settlements in far western North Carolina. Set where the Hiwassee and Valley Rivers meet, Murphy was founded in 1830 as an Indian trading post, but the Cherokee were here long before that. A mile and a half north of town, in Tomotla, settlers found an old mine shaft containing a cannon barrel, picks, and other mining tools apparently used by De Soto and his gold-hungry Spaniards when they passed through here in 1540. In 1567 Juan Pardo followed in De Soto's tracks, leading an expedition up from St. Augustine, via the South Carolina Low Country.

In 1715 British Major George Chicken of South Carolina led an expedition against the local Cherokee here. In 1817 Baptist missionaries to the Cherokee founded a school about three miles northeast of the town site. The town itself was originally named Huntersville, for the colonel who founded it, but it was renamed for Archibald Murphey, a politician and much-admired advocate of free popular education. As fate would have it, the town leaders misspelled Murphey's name. Fort Butler was built nearby in 1837, by General Winfield Scott's men as one of the staging grounds for the Cherokee removal to Oklahoma.

In spring of 1865, at the tail end of the War Between the States, a band of local men deserted the Confederate army for a federal unit. Charges of treason were filed against them in the Cherokee County courthouse. In those days before shredders, the scalawags destroyed the case documents the old-fashioned way—they burned down the courthouse. Confederates led by Major Stephen Whitaker caught up with the deserters at Hanging Dog Creek, about four miles northwest of town, on May 6, 1865. Today the town, with fewer than 2,000 citizens, still centers around the old courthouse square, which features a "new" (1926) courthouse of local blue marble and a Confederate monument.

Attractions

Murphy is home to a pair of interesting sites. The **Cherokee Historical Museum,** 87 Peachtree St., tel. 828/837-6792, contains artifacts from the Cherokee era and the early white settlements in this area. In the eclectic spirit of small town museums, it also contains an extensive doll collection. There is no charge for admission.

Fields of the Wood on Highway 294, tel. 828/494-7855, is a 200-acre Bible park where you can see the Ten Commandments laid out in huge stone letters across an entire mountainside, powerful visual testimony to the Bible's vital place in Appalachian culture, as well as an ethical reminder to birds and airplane passengers. For fun, you can have your picture taken beside your favorite commandment (or perhaps the one you most enjoy breaking). Also here are the All Nations Cross and replicas of Golgotha, the hill where Jesus was executed, and Jesus' tomb. There is no charge for admission. The park is open dawn to dusk daily. Go there at www .cogop.org/fow on the Web.

Lodging

The **Hilltop House,** 94 Campbell St., tel. 828/837-8661, is a bed-and-breakfast that offers three rooms and a meal plan. **Huntington Hall Bed and Breakfast,** 500 Valley River Ave., is another B&B option. **Park Place Bed and Breakfast,** 54 Hill St., tel. 828/837-8842, offers three rooms, meal plans, private golfing, and tennis privileges.

BRASSTOWN

Brasstown is just down Highway 29/19 from Murphy, and it's mainly known as the home of the 380-acre **John C. Campbell Folk School,** 1 Folk School Rd., tel. 800/365-5724 or 828/837-8637. Modeled after Danish schools, the school was founded in 1925 to preserve the crafts, music, dances, and other traditions of the Appalachian people. It makes a wonderful day trip from the park. You can visit the school's history center for free and browse the craft shop, a founding member of the Southern Highland Craft Guild, which features the work of over 300 local and regional artists. You can also take the local trails and visit artists' studios to watch work in progress. For a longer stay, the school offers 3- to 12-week classes in mountain music, dance, and crafts. Call for information or go on the Web to www.folkschool.com.

The Tourism Corridor

On September 2, 1940, President Franklin D. Roosevelt and thousands of other people rode in a caravan up the dirt road to Newfound Gap in the new Great Smoky Mountains National Park. The people in the villages they passed through—Sevierville, Pigeon Forge, and Gatlinburg—had no way of knowing the impact that the park would have on the places they lived.

Today the park is the most visited of all national parks, and those three towns thrive on industrial-strength tourism. Millions of cars from all over the country converge here, disgorging people looking for a good time and carrying money in their pockets to pay for it.

They find a myriad of ways to spend here.

Outlet shopping, country music shows, amusement parks, T-shirt shops, helicopter flights, and you-name-it await the charge card.

Amid the hokum, however, visitors will find high-quality crafts, wonderful inns and bed-and-breakfasts, and places where Appalachian music rings out clearly. And kids who are weary of traveling will utterly love the gateway area. Parents intent on getting into the sanctity of the Smokies should stop and take in a few indulgences; they'll make the wilderness all that much sweeter. Both Pigeon Forge and Gatlinburg have buses resembling trolleys that take visitors from place to place. They are exceptionally useful for dispatching older children to their favorite destinations.

© GREAT SMOKY MOUNTAINS NATIONAL PARK

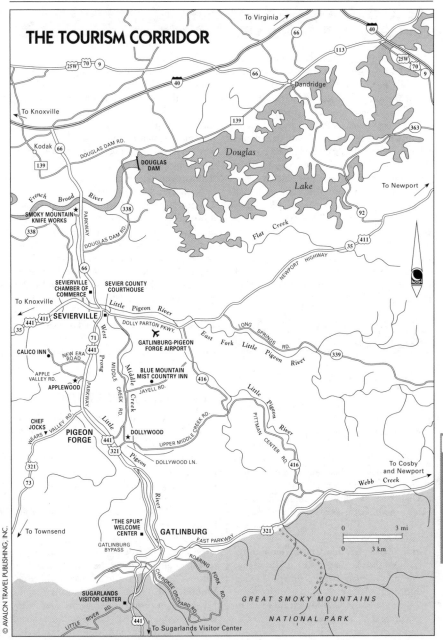

THE TOURISM CORRIDOR

To Virginia

To Knoxville

Dandridge

Kodak

DOUGLAS DAM RD.

DOUGLAS DAM

Douglas

Lake

To Newport

French Broad River

PARKWAY

SMOKY MOUNTAIN KNIFE WORKS

DOUGLAS DAM RD.

Flat Creek

NEWPORT HIGHWAY

SEVIERVILLE CHAMBER OF COMMERCE

SEVIER COUNTY COURTHOUSE

To Knoxville

SEVIERVILLE

Little Pigeon River

DOLLY PARTON PKWY.

LONG SPRINGS RD.

East Fork Little Pigeon River

WEST PRONG

GATLINBURG–PIGEON FORGE AIRPORT

CALICO INN

NEW ERA ROAD

BLUE MOUNTAIN MIST COUNTRY INN

JAYELL RD.

APPLE VALLEY RD.

APPLEWOOD

MIDDLE CREEK

Little Pigeon River

PITTMAN CENTER RD.

CHEF JOCKS

WEARS VALLEY RD.

PIGEON FORGE

Little Pigeon River

DOLLYWOOD

UPPER MIDDLE CREEK RD.

DOLLYWOOD LN.

To Cosby and Newport

Webb Creek

To Townsend

"THE SPUR" WELCOME CENTER

GATLINBURG

EAST PARKWAY

GATLINBURG BYPASS

ROARING FORK RD.

CHEROKEE ORCHARD RD.

0   3 mi
0   3 km

SUGARLANDS VISITOR CENTER

GREAT SMOKY MOUNTAINS

NATIONAL PARK

LITTLE RIVER RD.

To Sugarlands Visitor Center

© AVALON TRAVEL PUBLISHING, INC.

N TOURISM CORRIDOR

Sevierville

The town and the county were named for John Sevier, Tennessee's first governor, who negotiated with the Cherokee to secure this area for settlers. Like many towns in those early days, Sevierville had no courthouse, so judicial proceedings were held in a local stable. According to one account, this structure was so infested with fleas that the itching attorneys finally burned it to the ground. While it stood, however, the accused received perhaps the speediest trials in Tennessee.

Sevier County has produced some great music makers. Dolly Parton grew up here, as did two great Dobro players, both associated with Roy Acuff. Clell Summey, a.k.a. Cousin Jody, joined Acuff in 1933 and became the first person to play Dobro at the Grand Ole Opry. He was replaced by Pete Kirby, a.k.a. Bashful Brother Oswald, who became the foremost Dobro player in country music.

TOURISM CORRIDOR HIGHLIGHTS

Smoky Mountain Knife Works, Sevierville: For those who carry a knife except when wearing pajamas or bathing suits, this place is heaven on earth.

Dixie Stampede, Pigeon Forge: Tourism runs amok as more than a thousand people eat whole chickens, ribs, and soup without silverware while horse-drawn chuck wagons and costumed equestrians careen around an earthen arena. Think Civil War Ben Hur as dinner theater.

Dollywood: People come expecting an amusement park, but this place is true to its Appalachian roots.

Great Smoky Arts and Crafts Community: Far from the madding crowd of Gatlinburg, here one can enjoy meeting artists and seeing their work.

Arrowmont Shop, Gatlinburg: An island of serenity and high-end crafts amid a sea of T-shirt shops.

Close to 30 percent of Sevier County lies within the boundaries of the Great Smoky Mountains National Park, and tourists lured by the park are the town's focus nowadays. Not so long ago, motorists whizzed through Sevierville on their way to Pigeon Forge, Gatlinburg, and, if they made it that far, the park. About the only way Sevierville could get them to stop was to give them speeding tickets, which the local constabulary did with enthusiasm.

Nowadays Sevierville has come into its own and provides several reasons for visitors to slow down and spend a little time. The first is its downtown, an eddy in the stream of tourism that flows close by. The **Sevier County Courthouse** is a Victorian structure built in 1895–96, and its four-sided Seth Thomas clock still keeps time. Beside the courthouse is the **Dolly Parton Statue,** a bronze depiction of a young Dolly by Tennessee artist Jim Gray. The small-town atmosphere is perfectly captured by **Virgil's '50s Restaurant.** Down the street you'll find the **Sevier Country Heritage Museum** and several antiques shops.

SIGHTS AND RECREATION

The **Sevier Country Heritage Museum,** located at 167 E. Bruce Street in a former post office, contains the usual Indian artifacts as well as weapons from various wars. A portable camp-meeting organ is interesting, but the most unusual items are a robe and mask from the Sevier County Whitecaps, a vigilante organization that terrorized the area in the 1890s. The museum's hours change, so call 865/453-4058 to make sure it is open.

Between the Little Pigeon River and the intersection of the Forks of the River Parkway and Church Street lies the **McMahon Indian Mound,** all that is left of some Indians from the Mississippian period—long before the Cherokee. Excavations here revealed a village of about 75 people who lived in structures made of wood, thatch, and clay.

SHOWTIME IN THE TOURISM CORRIDOR

Taking a cue from Branson, Missouri, a small town that has enjoyed great success with nightly shows featuring over-the-hill but still popular entertainers, investors have tried the same thing here, with varying success. Country singer Lee Greenwood performed for years, and folks such as Anita Bryant and Jim Ed Brown have tried their hand as well. None have lasted. The most successful shows seem to be those that feature talented and enthusiastic unknowns who can be replaced without a major change in the marquee.

Shows emphasize family entertainment. Alcoholic beverages are not served in theaters, and patrons will never see any Dwight Yoakam look-alike making pelvic thrusts behind a guitar. Many shows include gospel music. All this is mildly ironic, for country music's staples through the years have been drinking, honky-tonking, and broken hearts. But the roadside tradition of "fightin' and dancin' clubs" gets no homage here.

Theaters generally open in April for weekends only and then expand to six or seven nights a week when summer arrives. They cut back on the number of shows as the fall winds down. Since most of these places seat hundreds of people and require vast parking lots, you will see none of them in Gatlinburg. "There's No Business Like Show Business," as the song goes, and that's very true here. Acts change, theaters open, theaters close, and a new Elvis periodically comes to town.

The talent lineup changes with the season, and sometimes so do the names of the theaters. To get the most accurate information about who's playing where, check the Web at www.seviervillechamber.org or www.mypigeonforge.com or stop in at a welcome center. Tickets cost from $20 one up, with generous discounts for kids—in many places children under 11 get in free.

Here are a couple of perennials:

The **Comedy Barn** is for those who could never get enough of *Hee Haw.* You'll find it in Pigeon Forge at 2775 Parkway, tel. 800/295-2844 or 865/428-5222, website: www.comedybarn.com.

Dixie Stampede Dinner and Show, at the intersection of Mill Creek Road and the Parkway, tel. 865/453-4400 or 877/782-6733, has to be the most unusual dinner show in the entire state. More than a thousand patrons sit side by side on five tiers of seats facing a U-shaped, dirt arena. The meal consists of whole rotisserie chickens, ribs, soup, and accompanying dishes, all enjoyed without silverware. The show involves 30 horses; people riding ostriches; people singing, trick riding, and roping; and performers dressed as Union and Confederate soldiers. The price for all this is approximately $33 for adults and $19 for kids 4 to 11. Children 3 and under get in free if they sit on an adult's lap and eat off that person's plate. Owned by Dollywood, Dixie Stampede runs March through December. Call for tickets or visit www.dixiestampede.com.

Outside of town, the **Harrisburg Covered Bridge** crosses the east fork of the Little Pigeon River. Built in 1875, this bridge is still in use. Go east of Sevierville on Highway 411, turn right onto Highway 339, and follow the signs. Highway 441 East leads as well to **Forbidden Caverns,** tel. 865/453-5972, a commercial cave whose name comes from an Indian legend involving the burial of a princess in a place that was forbidden. Later the cave was used for making moonshine. The caverns contain a large wall of cave onyx, a beautiful mineral, as well as un-

usual formations, all illuminated with special lighting and augmented with a sound system. The site is open seven days a week from April 1 through November 1. Call about December hours. Admission is $8 for visitors 13 and older, $4 for ages 5 to 12, and free for kids under 5.

The **Tennessee Museum of Aviation,** located at the Sevierville Airport, contains a collection of flyable "warbirds" from World War II and subsequent conflicts. The collection changes when airplanes are bought and sold, but visitors can count on seeing a MIG 17, a P-47, a Thunderbolt, a P-33, and an AT6. Kids will appreciate a flight simulator and various Learn to Fly exhibits. The facility also includes the Tennessee Aviation Hall of Fame. To get there from downtown Sevierville, take Highway 411 east a couple of miles to the airport, which will be on the right. For more information call 865/268-8738 or visit www.tnairmuseum.com.

Halfway between Sevierville and Pigeon Forge motorists will pass **Applewood,** a complex that began with a family-owned apple orchard but now offers a cider mill, cider bar, bakery, candy factory, smokehouse, winery, gift shop, and two restaurants. The winery produces eight apple wines—some of them mixed with other fruit. Cider production begins in late August and runs through February, depending on the supply of apples. The complex is open every day, with longer hours in the tourist season. For information about the restaurants, see below.

On Horseback

The **Cedar Ridge Riding Stables** on Highway 441, tel. 865/428-5802, are open daily year-round.

Douglas Lake View Horse Riding, 1650 Providence Ave., tel. 865/428-3587, offers short rides or the overnight variety.

ENTERTAINMENT AND EVENTS

Festivals

Sevierville, Pigeon Forge, and Gatlinburg all get together to promote **WinterFest,** a November to February celebration of the season that gives shops and other businesses a great opportunity to don thousands of lights. The events that make up WinterFest differ from year to year but generally consist of concerts, storytelling, wine-tastings, and so on. For details, contact each town's chamber of commerce or tourist bureau. In Sevierville, the number is 865/453-6411 or 800/255-6411. Or hit the Web at www.seviervillechamber.org.

WHERE TO STAY

Sevierville, Pigeon Forge, and Gatlinburg contain one of the greatest inland concentrations of places to stay in the South. Inns and bed-and-breakfasts

are available, but many other lodgings are of the franchise variety. "Chalet" is a term often used in these parts. Originally used to describe an A-frame or another building along that line, the word now usually refers to any detached structure. Often, a "cabin" and a "chalet" are virtually indistinguishable. Condominiums have become a big part of the lodging scene in the Smokies, and having a kitchen can help you keep costs down.

When inquiring about views of the mountains, visitors should ask if they'll be able to see Mount LeConte or Clingmans Dome. Almost every hill around here is called a mountain, and the promised "mountain view" may not be what you had in mind.

Potential visitors can call the Sevierville Chamber of Commerce, tel. 865/453-8574 or 800/255-6411, for a list of lodging places that are members.

Bed-and-Breakfasts and Inns

Blue Mountain Mist Country Inn, 1811 Pullen Rd., Sevierville, tel. 865/428-2335, consists of 12 guest rooms in a Victorian-style house and five guest cottages, all set on a 60-acre farm with views of the mountains. Each room in the inn has a private bath, and cabins come with whirlpool baths, fireplaces, porch swings, kitchenettes, television sets, and VCRs. Outside await a picnic table and grill. The Sugarlands Bridal Room—the top of the line—contains a whirlpool bath with views out of a turreted window. A large country breakfast appears every morning. Rates range $90–130 in the inn and $140 for the cottages. Visit the inn online at www.bbonline.com/tn/blue mtnmist.

The **Calico Inn,** 757 Ranch Way, tel. 865/428-3833 or 800/235-1054, is a log house sitting amid 25 acres. The three rooms have private baths and are decorated with folk art and antiques. Guests get a full breakfast, complete with bread or muffins. Rates are $89–99.

The **Little Greenbriar Lodge,** 3685 Lyon Springs Rd., tel. 865/429-2500 or 800/277-8100, overlooks Wears Valley and was built in the 1930s as a hunting lodge. It has survived various incarnations since and is now a pleasant inn with

10 double rooms and one single, all decorated with Victorian antiques. Three of the rooms share two baths, but the rest have their own. The lodge serves a full country breakfast. Rates are $75–110. Take a look on the Web at www.little-greenbrierlodge.com.

The **Von-Bryan Inn,** 2402 Hatcher Mountain Rd., Sevierville, tel. 865/453-9832 or 800/633-1459, has one of the best views you can get—360 degrees of mountain scenery from atop Hatcher Mountain. The inn contains seven guest rooms as well as a chalet. Each room has a private bath—some have a whirlpool or steam shower—and every guest can enjoy a large gathering room with a cathedral ceiling and large fireplace. Rates run $100–145 for two people in the guest rooms and $220 for four people in the chalets. Guests feast on a breakfast buffet. You can smoke in the chalet but not the inn. Extra guests can stay for $20. Take a look on the Web at www .bnblist.com/tn/vonbryan.

Cabins, Chalets, and Condos

The offices that rent cabins, condos, and chalets are usually not on-site; call these agents for complete listings.

Wildflower Mountain Rentals, tel. 800/726-0989 or 865/453-2000; **Echota Cabins,** tel. 800/766-5437 or 865/428-5151; **Great Smoky Mountain Real Estate and Rentals,** tel. 800/642-5021 or 865/429-3231; **Hidden Mountain Resorts,** tel. 800/541-6837 or 865/453-9850; and **Cornerstone Chalets,** tel. 800/205-6867 or 865/453-4331865/.

Hotels and Motels

Prices for lodging hereabouts depend mightily on when you go, and in October they can change dramatically from weekday to weekend. Most of the motels are of the franchise variety.

A few good choices among moderately priced places include the **Comfort Inn Interstate** on Dumplin Valley Road at Highway 66, tel. 800/441-0311 or 865/865/933-1719, and the **Mize Motel,** 804 Parkway, tel. 800/239-9117 or 865/453-4684.

More expensive are the **Best Western Dumplin Valley Inn,** 3426 Winfield Dunn Pkwy., tel. 865/933-3467; the **Comfort Inn Mountain Suites,** 806 Winfield Dunn Pkwy., tel. 800/441-0311 or 865/428-5519; and the **Hampton Inn,** 681 Winfield Dunn Pkwy., tel. 800/426-7866 or 865/429-2005.

Camping

It's heads or tails at the bare bones campgrounds at **Douglas Dam Headwater** or **Douglas Dam Tailwater,** above and below the TVA's Douglas Dam. A total of 113 sites—20 with hookups—are open from early April through October.

Knoxville East KOA, 241 KOA Dr., tel. 865/933-6393, with 200 sites, has all the amenities and is open all year. Take Exit 407 off I-40 and go north. You can't miss it.

River Plantation RV Park, 1004 Pkwy., tel. 800/758-5267 or 865/429-5267, features 166 large sites—40 by 60 feet. It offers rental cars, full hookups, an outdoor pool, satellite TV, and camping cabins, and is open all year.

Riverside Campground on the French Broad River, tel. 865/453-7299, has 165 sites, most of them with full hookups, along with planned group activities, a swimming pool, a pavilion, a playground, and more. Take the Highway 66 Exit off I-40 and go south four miles, then right a quarter mile on Boyds Creek Road. The campground is open all year.

Smoky Mountain Campground, tel. 865/933-8312 or 800/684-2267, weighs in with 246 sites and is open all year. With all the amenities, it lies off I-40 at Exit 407. Go south on Highway 66 for about 100 yards, then go a half mile east on Foretravel Drive.

FOOD

Sevierville is a dry town; there are no liquor stores. Visitors who want wine have to buy it at the winery or bring it themselves. Restaurants do not serve alcoholic beverages, although some will allow diners to carry in their own. To be sure, call ahead.

The Applewood complex, on Apple Valley Road off the Parkway between Sevierville and Pigeon Forge, tel. 865/428-1222, includes two restaurants. The **Applewood Farmhouse Restaurant** and the **Farmhouse Grill** offer dishes such as chicken à la orchard and other varieties of country cooking. Both places really shine when it comes to desserts: apple cider pie, apple fritters, apple butter—you name it. Both are open for all three meals every day.

Josev's, in downtown Sevierville at 130 West Bruce Street, tel. 865/428-0737, serves lunch Tuesday through Sunday and dinner Tuesday through Saturday. It specializes in American food and homemade desserts.

Virgil's '50s Restaurant, just off the town square at 109 Bruce Street, tel. 865/453-2782, is a fun place to go. The black-and-white tiled floor, pink neon, and colorful booths seem just right for the fifties music that's always on tap here. The cuisine includes burgers, sandwiches, and country cooking.

SHOPPING AND INFORMATION

Shopping

The **Robert A. Tino Gallery,** 812 Old Douglas Dam Rd., tel. 865/453-6315, website: www.roberttinogallery.com, offers original paintings and limited-edition prints of mountain and country scenes by this native Tennessee artist. The shop is located in an old house, now on the National Historic Register.

Information

The **Sevierville Chamber of Commerce,** 806 Winfield Dunn Pkwy., tel. 865/453-6411 or 800/255-6411, is open Monday through Saturday 8 A.M.–5 P.M. and Sunday 1–5 P.M. Find it on the Web at www.seviervillechamber.com.

Pigeon Forge

Pigeon Forge has been visited by millions for a long time. The first notable influx involved enormous flocks of passenger pigeons attracted by beech trees that lined the river. "Pigeon" became the name of the river, and in time it powered an ironworks built by Isaac Love and operated until the 1930s—thus the "Forge." In the years that followed, Great Smoky Mountains National Park came into being, and an ever-growing number of tourists started coming through town.

For years Pigeon Forge struggled along as a Gatlinburg wannabe—a place that would do anything to grab passing tourists. In the last 15 years, however, Pigeon Forge has begun to shed its tacky image. Part of this change has to do with geography—Pigeon Forge has room to expand (Gatlinburg, all but surrounded by Great Smoky Mountains National Park, doesn't). An important element fell into place when local girl Dolly Parton bought Silver Dollar City and trans-

THE BACK DOOR TO DOLLYWOOD AND PIGEON FORGE

Highway 441 through Pigeon Forge and Gatlinburg is often just called the Parkway. When traffic clogs this artery on weekends and during leaf season, the name is apt: It feels like all the cars are parked. Here are some alternative routes to Dollywood and Pigeon Forge.

From I-40, take Exit 432-A west of Newport. Get on Highway 411 east toward Sevierville. When you pass the Sevierville/Gatlinburg Airport on your left, begin looking for Middle Creek Road, also on your left. Turn there and follow the directions below.

From Highway 66 heading south, turn left onto Highway 411 at Sevierville. Less than two miles east of Sevierville, turn right on Middle Creek Road, which runs parallel to the infamous Parkway. Go 4.7 miles, passing the hospital on the way, and turn left on McCarter Hollow Road. This is the back entrance to the Dollywood parking lot. Jump on a tram and try to keep from smiling as you listen to everyone else complain about the traffic.

To get to Pigeon Forge, stay on Middle Creek Road, which comes out near the Old Mill on the Parkway.

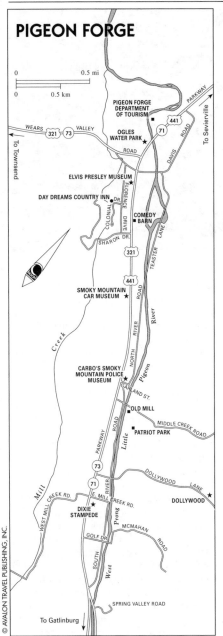

PIGEON FORGE

0   0.5 mi

0   0.5 km

PIGEON FORGE
DEPARTMENT
OF TOURISM

To Sevierville

WEARS   VALLEY

321 73

OGLES
WATER PARK ★

To Townsend

ROAD

DAVIS ROAD

441

PARKWAY

71

ELVIS PRESLEY MUSEUM ★

FLORENCE DR.

DAY DREAMS COUNTRY INN ■

COLONIAL DRIVE

COMEDY
BARN ★

SHARON DR.

TEASTER LANE

321

441

SMOKY MOUNTAIN
CAR MUSEUM ★

NORTH   RIVER   ROAD

Pigeon   River

Creek

CARBO'S SMOKY
MOUNTAIN POLICE
MUSEUM ★

GARLAND ST.

OLD MILL ■

MIDDLE CREEK ROAD

■ PATRIOT PARK

PARKWAY

Little   River   ROAD

73

DOLLYWOOD   LANE

71

E. MILL CREEK RD.

WEST MILL CREEK RD.

DOLLYWOOD ★

DIXIE
STAMPEDE ★

Mill   Creek

MCMAHAN   ROAD

GOLF DR.

SOUTH   West   Prong

SPRING VALLEY ROAD

To Gatlinburg

© AVALON TRAVEL PUBLISHING, INC.

formed it into Dollywood. Then the town took a look at the success of Branson, Missouri, and went into the music business. -While these music halls have not always made the cash registers sing, they provide the closest thing to nightlife that that visitors will find hereabouts. Finally, outlet shopping came to town to an extent that some surveys show that more people come here to shop than to visit the national park. Whatever the reasons for coming, millions of people do so, and most of them cruise down the Parkway. When it's 90°, traffic is bumper to bumper, and radiators and tempers are boiling over, driving through here can be anything but fun.

SIGHTS AND RECREATION

Dollywood

Let's take it from the top. Dollywood, tel. 865/428-9488, combines live music—more than 40 performances daily—with more than 30 amusement park rides. Dollywood puts an Appalachian spin on all this activity, with 20 artists working on traditional crafts such as weaving, pottery, and woodcarving. The Dollywood Express, a steam-powered train, rides along a five-mile track, and Dolly Parton's Museum tells the extraordinary entertainer's life story. The Eagle Mountain Sanctuary displays bald eagles that for one reason or another cannot be released into the wild. Dollywood Boulevard focuses on the movies, offering a ride simulator and a restaurant with a Hollywood theme.

Dollywood opens in late April and closes at the end of December, with long hours during summer. All-day admission for one adult is $28.99, for children 4–11 $18, and for seniors (60 and older) $22; children 3 and under get in free. The best deal is to enter the park after 3 P.M.; you can come back the next day free of charge. Preview the park online at www.dollywood.com.

The Dollywood Story

What is now the biggest attraction in Tennessee began over 30 years ago when Dolly Parton was just a teenager.

Dollywood began life as Rebel Railroad, a steam train that made a loop around an 1860s

N **TOURISM CORRIDOR**

© DOLLYWOOD PUBLICITY

Dolly at Dollywood's Gristmill

town complete with general store, blacksmith shop, etc. Before boarding the train, passengers were warned that a holdup that might occur. Children were encouraged to bring toy weapons—which just happened to be for sale at the souvenir shop—to repel the invaders.

Sure enough, along the way, marauders dressed as Union troops would attempt to rob the train.

New owners, among whose assets were the Cleveland Browns football team, bought Rebel Railroad in 1970 and transformed it into Goldrush Junction. Perhaps because they were Yankees, they kept the train but ditched the Civil War theme. Goldrush Junction was a Wild West park complete with rides, an outdoor theater, a sawmill, and a gristmill—said to be the first gristmill built in Tennessee in 100 years.

In 1977, Hershend Enterprises of Branson, Missouri, another Southern tourist town, bought Goldrush Junction and named it Silver Dollar City. They created an Appalachian theme and focused on local crafts and craftspeople. To spice things up, they began adding state-of-the-art amusement park rides, giving them names that reflected the Tennessee mountains.

The smartest thing that these Arkansas travelers did, however, was pull in Dolly Parton as an investor and spokeswoman. In 1986, the park was renamed Dollywood, and the turnstiles have spun ever since. Dolly is the single most popular individual to come from the Smokies, and when it comes to advertising and promoting the place, she is a natural.

The first year that Dollywood opened, it drew 1.3 million visitors, an increase of some 75 percent over the final year of Silver Dollar City. To keep people coming back, Dollywood adds something new every season—a theater, a new ride, or an event—and ceaselessly promotes the park across Tennessee and surrounding states. By 1999, the park had doubled in size from 1986 and hosted over 2.2 million guests annually.

Dollywood doesn't just rake in money; it gives back to the community through the Dollywood Foundation, a nonprofit organization that does various good deeds. With the Imagination Library, for example, children born at the Fort Sanders Sevier Medical Center can get signed up to receive a free book in the mail each month, for a total of 60 books. By 1999, over 100,000 books had been distributed through this program. High school graduates can receive scholarships of up to $1,500 from the foundation.

Why is Dollywood so popular? There are several reasons. First of all, the park offers a quality experience for a wide range of people. Kids love

© DOLLYWOOD PUBLICITY

Smoky Mountain Rampage Ride at Dolly's Splash Country

the rides, and adults enjoy the craftspeople and the live music. The park is kept extraordinarily clean, and the people who work there extend Southern hospitality to all guests. Second, a season's pass costs less than two one-day passes, encouraging locals to return again and again. Finally, people have the impression, rightly or wrongly, that this is Dolly's park—that she selects the rides and picks the craftspeople—and this convinces them that her down-home honesty and sincerity pervades the whole place. Whatever it is, it works. Unlike all its predecessors on this site, Dollywood shows no signs of a name change anytime soon.

Dolly's Splash Country

When it gets hot in the Smokies, this place will satisfy those who enjoy getting flushed through various pipes and slides. This 35-acre water park, although owned by Dollywood, it is a separate organization and is not included in the ticket price for the main park. Admission prices are just over $80 for a family of four. The park is open late May through the first weekend in September. For more information call 865/428-9488 or visit www.dollyssplashcountry.com.

Museums

Carbo's Smoky Mountain Police Museum, 3311 Parkway (the building with bars on the windows), tel. 865/453-1358, takes a curatorial look at the constabulary with badges, guns—official as well as confiscated ones—uniforms, drug exhibits, etc. The centerpiece is the Buford Pusser "death car." (The late Buford Pusser was a legendary West Tennessee sheriff who battled a redneck Mafia and whose deeds were commemorated in the "Walking Tall" trilogy. Pusser was to have played himself in the movies, but died in a suspicious 1974 auto accident.) Admission is $6 for adults and $3 for children 10 and under.

For those who can't make it to Graceland, the **Elvis Museum,** one block south of Ogles Water Park on the Parkway, offers the King's last personal limousine, the first dollar bill he ever earned, guns, musical instruments, clothes, and the original $250,000 "TCB" ring. Admission is $9.75 for adults, $6.50 for kids over 12, and $4.50 for kids 6 to 12.

If Elvis's limo and Buford Pusser's death car only whet your appetite, the **Smoky Mountain Car Museum,** 2970 Parkway, tel. 865/453-3433, will prove delightful. You'll see James Bond's cars from *Goldfinger* and *Thunderball*, as well as vehicles once belonging to Elvis, the ubiquitous Buford Pusser, Al Capone, Stringbean, and Billy Carter. The museum is open varied hours from late spring through December. Call ahead. Admission is $5 for adults and $2 for children 3 to 10.

Patriot Park

Visitors who have never had the occasion to look at a Patriot missile should decamp to Patriot Park, where they'll find one of the four on display in the United States. This free public park in the Old Mill area, near traffic light number 7, also contains flags of all the states displayed in the order in which they were admitted to the Union.

Liquid Refreshment

Mountain Valley Vineyards, 2174 Parkway, tel. 865/453-6334, produces 16 different kinds of wine—mostly sweet and medium sweet. Muscadine wine is the best-selling one, although berry wines run a close second. Visitors can watch wine being made in August and September, and the vineyard is open for tastings all year, seven days a week.

Also on the Parkway, **Ogles Water Park,** tel. 865/453-8741, has an antidote for long hours spent in a car: 10 water slides, a wave pool, and a "lazy river." Open during summer, the park costs $17 for adults and $16 for kids 4 to 11. It's free for children under 4.

ENTERTAINMENT AND EVENTS
Dollywood Venues

Dollywood, tel. 865/656-9620, is the place to see the biggest names in country music: Stars such as Kathy Mattea, John Anderson, Patty Loveless, and the Statlers sing during summer. Dolly herself generally makes one appearance per year—usually at the opening of the season. Weekend concerts begin in May and run through October; the last week of June through the first week in August, every day is show time. The music plays at 2 and 7 P.M., and those who come to the later show do not have to pay to get into Dollywood. All seats are reserved. Call for information and tickets.

Dixie Stampede, at the intersection of Mill Creek Road and the Parkway, tel. 865/453-4400 or 800/356-1676, website: www.dixiestampede.com, has to be the most unusual dinner show in the entire state. More than a thousand patrons sit side by side on five tiers of seats facing a U-shaped, dirt arena. The meal consists of whole rotisserie chickens, ribs, soup, and accompanying dishes, all enjoyed without silverware. The show involves 30 horses; people riding ostriches; people singing, trick riding, roping; and performers dressed as Union and Confederate soldiers. The price for all this is $32.69 for adults and $16.34 for kids 4 to 11. Children 3 and under get in free if they sit on an adult's lap and eat off that person's plate. Owned by Dollywood, Dixie Stampede runs March through December. Call for tickets.

Music Mansion, located on the Sevierville side of Pigeon Forge on the Parkway, tel. 865/428-7469, is another part of the Dollywood empire. It presents an exuberant group of 25 men and women amid scene and costume changes that pay homage to big bands, patriotic music, country music, gospel, and oldies. The star of the show is James Rogers, a versatile entertainer who's been with the Dollywood organization for more than 10 years. Music Mansion stages shows from mid-April through mid-December. Tickets cost $25 for adults; two children ages 4 to 11 get in free with each paying adult. Call for reservations and information.

More Music

Memories Theatre, tel. 865/428-7852, should be the first East Tennessee stop for Elvis fans. It's the home of first-class King impersonators. The theater seats 900 and is open every month except January. It's located on the left coming into Pigeon Forge from Sevierville, before traffic light number 1. Admission is $18.50 for anyone over ago 12; two kids get in free with each paid adult. Check it out on the Web at www.memoriestheatre.com.

Comedy

The **Comedy Barn,** located on the north side of the Parkway between traffic lights 3 and 4, tel. 865/428-5222 or 800/29-LAUGH, packs them in with corny comedy perfected during years of work on cruise ships. A one-man band, live country music, and juggling round out the act. It's open late April through December. Tickets cost $18.50 for adults; kids under 11 get in free. Visit it on the Web at www.comedy barn.com.

Festivals

Pigeon Forge joins Sevierville and Gatlinburg in **WinterFest** November through February. The event differs from year to year but generally consists of concerts, storytelling, and other entertainment. For details about Pigeon Forge events, call 865/453-8574 or 800/251-9100 or go to www.mypigeonforge.com.

WHERE TO STAY

There are lots of lodging choices in Pigeon Forge. As in Sevierville, visitors who expect a true mountain view should ask specifically if they'll be able to see Mount LeConte or Clingmans Dome from the room in question.

For the most up-to-date information, call 800/251-9100 and ask for a copy of the *Pigeon Forge Vacation Planner.* Another good resource is the Pigeon Forge website: www.mypigeon forge.com.

Bed-and-Breakfasts and Inns

Chilhowee Bluff off Wears Valley Road, tel. 888/559-0321 or 865/908-0321, website: www.chilhoweebluff.com, is secluded yet offers ready access to Pigeon Forge and the Townsend side of the Smokies. It includes four rooms with an outdoor hot tub.

Close to Dollywood, the **Evergreen Cottage Inn and Forge Mountain Honeymoon Village,** Old Mill Rd., tel. 865/453-4000 or 800/264-3331, offers two cabins and 11 honeymoon suites in a separate structure. Rooms in the inn go for $69–89, while becoming one of the village people costs $105–120. Look on the Web at www.gocabins.com.

The **Huckleberry Inn,** 1754 Sandstone Way, tel. 865/428-2475, website: www.bbonline .com/tn/huckleberry, is a log house built by hand and containing three guest rooms decorated in country style. All rooms have private baths, and two have fireplaces and whirlpools. The inn serves

a full country breakfast daily. It's 1.2 miles from Dollywood, yet just a half mile off the busy Parkway. Rates are $79–89.

Cabins, Condos, and Chalets

To rent cabins, condos, or chalets, contact **County Oaks Cottages,** tel. 865/453-7640 or 800/662-1022; **Eagles Ridge Resort & Cabin Rentals,** tel. 800/807-4343 or www.eagles ridge.com; **Forge Mountain Honeymoon Village,** tel. 865/453-4000 or 800/264-3331; **Heritage House,** tel. 865/453-8529; **Kimble Overnight Rentals,** tel. 865/429-0090 or 800/447-0911; **Little Creek Cabins,** tel. 865/453-4625 or 800/553-0496; **Mill Creek Resort Club,** tel. 865/428-3498 or 865/ 865/428-4490; **Serenity Mountain Cabin Rentals,** tel. 865/429-8514 or 800/422-2246; or **Wildflower Mountain Rentals,** tel. 865/453-865/2000 or 800/726-0989.

Hotels and Motels

Pigeon Forge offers dozens of lodging options, franchise and otherwise, just a few of which are listed below. Prices vary greatly depending on when you visit and in October can change dramatically from weekday to weekend, so check by phone.

People who see a listing for the **Wonderland Hotel,** 3889 Wonderland Way, tel. 865/428-0779, sometimes ask, "Didn't that place close?" They're thinking of the original Wonderland Hotel, a 1912 establishment that was grandfathered in when the park opened. Time finally ran out for the old hotel, which closed in 1992. This edition of the hotel continues the laid-back tradition of its predecessor—no phones, no TVs, plain furnishings, and rocking chairs on the porch. Rates are $56–72. Although the hotel has a Sevierville address, it is located in Wears Valley between Pigeon Forge and Townsend. Check it out on the Internet at www.smoky.net/wonderland.

River Lodge South, 3251 Parkway, tel. 865/453-0783 or 800/233-7581, is another moderately priced choice.

More expensive options include the **Bilmar Motor Inn,** 3786 Parkway, tel. 865/453-5593 or 800/343-5610; **Smoky Mountain Resorts,** 4034

River Rd. S., tel. 865/453-3557 or 800/523-3919; the **Heartland Country Resort,** 2385 Parkway, tel. 865/453-4106 or 800/843-6686; the **McAfee Motor Inn** 3756 Parkway, tel. 865/453-3490 or 800/925-4443; the **Parkview Motel,** 2806 Parkway, tel. 865/453-5051 or 800/239-9116; the **Vacation Lodge Motel** 3450 Parkway, tel. 865/453-2640 or 800/468-1998; and the **Willow Brook Lodge** 3035 Parkway, tel. 865/453-5334 or 800/765-1380.

Those who don't mind spending even more can try the **Shular Inn,** 2708 Parkway, tel. 865/453-2700 or 800/451-2376.

Camping

Alpine Hideaway RV Park and Campground, 251 Spring Valley Rd., tel. 865/428-3285, offers 96 sites, a pool and cable TV, and all the other "roughing it" amenities. It's open mid-April through early November.

Clabough's Campground, a half mile off the Parkway on Wears Valley Road, tel. 865/453-0729, has 152 sites and all the expected amenities. It is open year-round.

Creekstone Outdoor Resort, located on the Little Pigeon River, tel. 865/453-8181 or 800/848-9097, has 150 sites and full amenities. To get there, turn off the Parkway onto Golf Drive, then turn right on McMahan Road. The campground is open year-round.

Eagles Nest Campground, 111 Wears Valley Rd. (1.5 miles off the Parkway), tel. 865/428-5841 or 800/892-2714, has 200 sites with the works. It's open year-round.

Fort Wear Campground sits a half mile off the Parkway on Wears Valley Rd., tel. 865/428-1951 or 800/452-9835. Open all year, it has 150 sites and all the amenities.

KOA, tel. 865/453-7903 or 800/367-7903, offers 200 sites complete with Kamping Kabins, a heated pool, a whirlpool, and other amenities. Turn off the Parkway onto Dollywood Lane, then drive left on Cedar Top Road. The campground is open April through December.

River Bend Campground, tel. 865/453-1224, has 101 sites. Located between Pigeon Forge and Sevierville, it's open April through November 15.

Park the Winnebago at one of the 175 sites at **Riveredge RV Park,** tel. 865/453-5813 or 800/477-1205. It offers all the amenities. To get there from Sevierville, turn right at traffic light 1, then head west on Henderson Chapel Road. The park is open year-round.

Shady Oaks Campground, tel. 865/453-3276, sits on the Gatlinburg side of Pigeon Forge. It offers 150 sites and quite a few amenities, and it's open year-round. To get there from downtown Pigeon Forge, turn right at Conner Heights Road, the first street past traffic light 8.

The small **Foothills Campground**—with only 46 sites—sits on the edge of town at 4235 Huskey Street, tel. 865/428-3818. It's open April through November.

Z Buda's Smokies Campground, located on the Parkway past traffic light 8, tel. 865/453-4129, weighs in with 300 sites. It's open April through October.

FOOD

Pigeon Forge does not permit the sale of alcoholic beverages in stores or restaurants. Diners can bring their own alcohol to some restaurants, but it's a good idea to call ahead.

Bel Air Grill, 2785 Parkway (next to the Comedy Barn), tel. 865/429-0101, has a '50s and '60s decor and claims to offer the best cheeseburger in the Smokies. Other dishes include steak, shrimp, and chicken.

Chef Jock's Tastebud Cafe, 1198 Wears Valley Rd., tel. 865/428-9781, is far from the madding crowd on the Parkway. This very unassuming place offers a respite from country cooking in the form of sea scallops, pork tenderloin with herbs, and other healthy and tasty dishes. It's open for lunch and dinner Tuesday through Saturday. Reservations are a good idea.

The Old Mill Restaurant, located in the Old Mill complex, tel. 865/429-3463, website: www.old-mill.com, offers dining overlooking the Little Pigeon River. It features country cooking seven days a week for all three meals; breads are made from flour and meal from the nearby mill.

Santo's Italian Restaurant, 3270 Parkway, tel. 865/428-5840, offers fine fettuccine with snow crab, linguine primavera, and other Italian dishes. It's open all year Monday through Saturday.

Smokies Breakfast House, 2751 Parkway, tel. 865/453-0624, is a good place to fuel up for a hike in the mountains with one of 45 different breakfasts. It's open April through December, seven days a week, 7 A.M.–1 P.M.

SHOPPING

The outlet stores here change about as quickly as one can say "Attention, K-Mart shoppers," so there is little point in listing them here. Suffice to say that many outlet malls with acres of parking will beckon for the attention of visitors.

Pigeon River String Instruments, 3337 Old Mill St., tel. 865/453-3789, awaits folk fanciers who need dulcimers, hammered dulcimers, or psalteries. It offers a few guitars and mandolins as

well. See it on the Web at www.pigeon-river.com.

Stages West, 2765 Parkway, tel. 865/453-8086, offers fancy duds—the closest thing to Nashville one will find in these parts.

Arts and Crafts

Jim Gray is perhaps the best known artist in this part of the state. His oils and drawings depict seascapes, Tennessee landscapes, people, wildflowers, and birds. His bronze statues include one of Dolly Parton in Sevierville and one of Andrew Johnson in Greeneville. The **Jim Gray Gallery,** 3331 S. River Rd., across from the Old Mill, tel. 865/428-2202, offers his works in a variety of media. To take an online look, go to www.jimgraygallery.com.

Douglas Ferguson, the founder of **Pigeon Forge Pottery,** tel. 865/453-3883, across from the Old Mill on Middle Creek Road off the Park-

THE BACK DOOR TO GATLINBURG

If you're visiting the Smokies during peak tourist season, here is a less-traveled route to Gatlinburg. From I-40, take Exit 440 and head south on Highway 321 toward Cosby. You can follow this road all the way to Gatlinburg. For most of the way it is a two-lane road.

Coming from Sevierville
From Highway 66 heading south, turn left onto Highway 411 at Sevierville. Less than two miles east of Sevierville, Middle Creek Road goes off to the right. Go 2.2 miles past this road and turn right on Route 416, Pittman Center Road. Drive 5.7 miles to the intersection with Birds Creek Road, which forks off to the right, and drive 4.7 more miles. Birds Creek Road eventually becomes Buckhorn Road, and less than two miles later you'll come to Highway 321. Turn right to Gatlinburg and the park. Note: This is a narrow, two-lane road, not at all suited for RVs.

Coming from Pigeon Forge
As you approach Gatlinburg on Highway 441, look for the Gatlinburg Bypass. It will take you

into Great Smoky Mountains National Park, very close to the visitor's center.

If you miss the bypass, or for some reason need a T-shirt and want to come through Gatlinburg, take the River Road to the right. While a little longer than the main drag, the River Road is mostly lined with motels, not shops and hordes of pedestrians. The River Road rejoins the Parkway on the south end of town, just in time for you to turn right and escape into the park.

Coming from Cosby
If you're coming into town on Highway 321, turn left onto Baskins Creek Bypass, just south of where the Roaring Fork Motor Nature Trail—a one-way road—exits. Turn left onto Cherokee Orchard Road, then right onto Airport Road. This road comes out on the Parkway at traffic light 8. A left turn and two more traffic lights will put you in the park.

If you've rented a cabin or condo on the mountain overlooking Gatlinburg, you can often access it via the Gatlinburg Bypass instead of coming through town. Ask your rental agent if this is possible.

way, came to town in 1937 looking for good clay. The pottery now produces art objects inspired by Smoky Mountains subjects; the biggest sellers are bears and owls. Visitors can watch the artisans at work.

SERVICES AND INFORMATION

Bus Tours of the Smokies, 2756 Middle Creek Rd. #1, tel. 865/428-3014, will come to your door and then head to Cades Cove, the Cherokee Reservation in North Carolina, and several other places.

The **Pigeon Forge Department of Tourism,** 2450 Parkway, tel. 865/453-8574 or 800/251-9100, offers information Monday through Saturday 9 A.M.–5:30 P.M. and Sunday 1–5 P.M. and on the Internet at www.my pigeonforge.com.

Gatlinburg

Gatlinburg is a town that will break your heart. After running the gauntlet of gimcrackery that constitutes Sevierville and Pigeon Forge, motorists on the Parkway enter a serpentine stretch of forest and rushing water. Seemingly at the snap of the fingers, gone are the parking lots, the blaring signs, and the visual clutter of Pigeon Forge. The parkway stays close by the Little River, and the forest closes in on either side. Newcomers to the area believe that they are finally beyond All That.

Then comes Gatlinburg, and you realize that it can get worse.

This was the original Smoky Mountain tourist

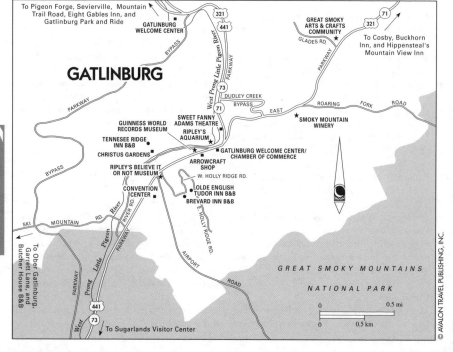

© JEFF BRADLEY

scenic Gatlinburg

town—a place of rocking chairs, rustic accommodations, and hearty food. All but surrounded by Great Smoky Mountains National Park, Gatlinburg has limited space and, mercifully, cannot contain the large outlet malls and thousand-person theaters of Sevierville and Pigeon Forge. Given this situation, and its to-die-for location at the entrance to the most popular national park in the country, Gatlinburg could have been the Aspen of the Appalachians, the Nantucket of the national parks, or the Saratoga of the Smokies.

It didn't happen. Instead, Gatlinburg chose the low road, which in this case is a commercial strip of hucksterism and garish shops whose merchandise is so utterly tasteless that it would make Pee-Wee Herman blush. There are no pedestrian parks here. Visitors are confined to narrow sidewalks where they jostle one another while gangs of 12-year-olds and their mental equivalents lope from the Guinness World Records Museum to Ripley's Believe It or Not, there to gaze in slack-jawed reverie at Tennessee's old electric chair. For the most part, the delightful river that flows through town is fenced off, forcing visitors to gaze down upon the splashing waters or—better yet—buy a postcard of them.

The combination of greed and a total lack of city planning is perfectly symbolized in Ripley's Aquarium, an architectural monstrosity that garishly looms up against the forested mountains. Why, one wants to ask, does a saltwater aquarium belong next to one of the great interior wilderness areas in the country?

That said, Gatlinburg does offer some redeeming features for the visitor. Restaurants here are more upscale than those in outlying towns. The town is small enough that you can walk just about everywhere. Gatlinburg allows its eateries to offer mixed drinks, wine, and beer, and the town has several liquor stores. And its lodges and cabins are as close to the national park as you can get.

Perhaps the best way to approach Gatlinburg is with an anthropological view—to look amusedly at your fellow pilgrims in the Land of the Yahoos. Saint H. L. Mencken said it best: "No one ever went broke underestimating the taste of the American public." This statement that belongs on the Gatlinburg town seal.

TOURISM CORRIDOR

SIGHTS

During the busy season, the best idea is to park the vehicle and leave it, seeing the sights on foot or taking the trolley that makes frequent stops all over town. Rides cost $.25 per person.

Christus Gardens

This River Road perennial, tel. 865/436-5155, website: www.christusgardens.com, is not so much a garden as it is a wax museum. The focus here is 81 wax figures in dioramas depicting scenes from the life of Jesus, culminating in a 40-foot-long depiction of Leonardo da Vinci's *The Last Supper*. Visitors can also see collections of Bibles and other religious texts, 168 coins dating from the 6th century B.C., and oil paintings that interpret nine of the parables. The gift shop offers the pious a souvenir shot glass, no doubt patterned after the ones used at the Last Supper. Christus Gardens is open every day year-round; admission is $8 for adults, $3.25 for kids 7 to 11, and free for those under 6.

> *The gift shop at Christus Gardens offers the pious a souvenir shot glass, no doubt patterned after the ones used at the Last Supper.*

Ripley's Aquarium of the Smokies

Easily the most visible place in town, this aquarium offers a rare chance to view creatures that live hundreds of miles from the Smokies and in a totally different ecosystem. The highlight of the experience is stepping on a moving walkway that creeps along through a clear tunnel in a large tank while bored sharks and extremely paranoid schools of much smaller fish swim beside and above the visitor. One can step off the walkway and gaze rapturously at the sharks from what can only be called a sea urchin's perspective, but the walkway is so slow that most people are content to ride it until the end. All this is accompanied by the sort of music that one hears in movies wherein humans encounter reasonably benevolent aliens. Additional attractions include a tank of piranha, a "tidal pool" with horseshoe crabs, and a shallow tank where visitors can touch stingrays whose stingers have been clipped or surgically removed. Admission is $16 per adult,

$8 for children 6 to 11, and $3 for ages 2 to 5. The aquarium is open every day. Call 888/240-1358 or visit the website at www.ripleysaquariumofthesmokies.com.

Frippery

Orlando, Las Vegas, Hollywood, Niagara Falls, Copenhagen, and Gatlinburg. These are the only places in the world where one can experience the intellectual delights of the **Guinness World Records Museum,** 631 Parkway, tel. 865/436-9100, where 12 galleries depict such wonders as the world's most tattooed lady, the heaviest man, and the obligatory Elvis. The museum is open daily. Admission is $7.95 for adults, $5.95 for seniors and teenagers, and $3.95 for kids 6 to 12.

And there's more! Devotees of shrunken heads and the like will enjoy **Ripley's Believe It or Not,** at traffic light number 7, tel. 865/436-5096, a museum based on an illustrated newspaper feature that those of a certain age may recall. Admission is $8.75 for adults, $5.75 for first-graders through high-schoolers, and free for preschool kids.

Delectables

Longtime visitors to Gatlinburg will remember the candy kitchens. These heavenly smelling places have intricate machines that stretch taffy, measure it out into little finger-sized pieces, lop them off, and wrap them in paper. Fudge and other decadent delights can be had at **Aunt Mahalia's Candies** (three locations on the Parkway), **Mountaineer Kandy Kitchen,** and **Ola Kate's Candy Kitchen.** Kids love these places.

The Smoky Mountain Winery is up Highway 321 a half mile from Parkway traffic light number 3, tel. 865/436-7551. Here visitors can observe the winemaking process and sample the products. Seventy-five percent of the grapes used come from Tennessee. Among the wines offered are cabernet sauvignon and American Riesling. The winery is open year-round 10 A.M.–6 P.M. in good weather; shorter hours in winter.

RECREATION
Ober Gatlinburg
This park, tel. 865/436-5423, is Gatlinburg's ski resort and summertime amusement park. Visitors can drive up the mountain and pay to park, but the best way to go is up the aerial tramway, which departs from downtown and goes 2.5 miles up the mountain. Tram rides cost $7 for adults and $4 for kids 7 to 11. The skiing, while laughable by New England or western standards, nonetheless enthralls the locals, as does the indoor ice-skating, available year-round. The latter is a great idea for rainy days.

Summertime attractions include bungee jumping, batting cages, go-carts, water slides, and an alpine slide. The chairlift that carries skiers in wintertime carries sightseers to the top of a mountain.

© MIKE SIGALAS

Ober Gatlinburg Sky Tram

There is no charge to enter Ober Gatlinburg. All activities are individually priced. Meals are available, but their prices are considerably *ober* what visitors might pay at lower elevations. See what you're getting into ahead of time by visiting www.obergatlinburg.com.

Stables
You can get back in the saddle again for trips ranging from one to four hours at **McCarter's Riding Stables,** tel. 865/865/436-5354, 1.5 miles south of Gatlinburg, close to the Sugarlands Visitors Center. Lead horses are available for children. The stables are open daily, 8 A.M.–6 P.M., from early spring through late fall.

Smoky Mountain Stables, four miles east of Gatlinburg on Highway 321, tel. 865/436-5634, offers guided trail rides lasting one or two hours. It's open from March through Thanksgiving.

Outfitters
Old Smoky Outfitters, 511 Parkway in the Riverbend Mall, tel. 865/865/430-1936, offers fishing, hunting, and historical and nature tours. A half-day trout fishing trip for novices begins at $135 and goes up from there. Overnight backcountry hikes, including all equipment, are also available. See it on the Web at www.oldsmoky.com.

Smoky Mountain Angler, 376 E. Parkway, tel. 865/436-8746, offers access to a six-mile-long private stream where the big fish live. Full-day guided trips with lunch begin at $150 per person ($100 for a half day). The shop offers a good selection of flies and some great advice.

Another option is **Smoky Mountain Guide Service,** tel. 865/436-2108 or 800/782-1061.

The Happy Hiker, tel. 865/436-5632 or 800/HIKER-01, offers gear rentals, shuttles, and lockers. It's located behind the Burning Bush Restaurant on the Parkway, or visit www.happyhiker.com.

ENTERTAINMENT AND EVENTS
Music
Compared to the music halls of Pigeon Forge, the 200-seat **Sweet Fanny Adams Theatre,**

A TOUCH OF CLASS IN GATLINBURG

The visitor can immediately sense something suspicious about the **Arrowcraft Shop,** which stands like an island of serenity at 576 Parkway. First of all, it actually has grass out front. Second, when customers step into the shop, they're not assaulted with the usual riot of Gatlinburg gewgaws. Finally, the place seems more like a museum than a retail establishment, with displays of pottery, weavings, jewelry, and handmade paper.

The items for sale here come from the Southern Highlands Craft Guild, website: www.southern-highlandguild.com, an Asheville-based organization whose purpose is, in its own words, "bringing together the crafts and craftspeople of the Southern Highlands for the benefit of shared resources, education, marketing and conservation." In short, the items for sale in the Arrowcraft Shop are very high quality.

The shop is the tip of a craft iceberg called **Arrowmont School of Arts and Crafts,** which had its origin in the settlement school movement. In the early years of the 20th century, public education in the most remote areas of Tennessee was virtually nonexistent. To fill this need, various religious and other organizations took it on themselves to build and support settlement schools in backwoods communities. Though somewhat patronizing—the organizers wanted to reform the mountain people from their backward ways—these do-gooders had their hearts in the right place.

In 1910, Pi Beta Phi, one of the first national sororities, established a school in Gatlinburg that stressed better health, education, and instruction in the manual arts. As life got better for mountain people, Pi Beta Phi gave up the health-care and educational aspects of the school and shifted the focus from manual arts to crafts. The Pi Beta Phi symbol is an arrow, so leaders named the school Arrowmont. In addition to the Arrowcraft Shop, the school has a 70-acre campus in Gatlinburg.

Over the years, the school began offering summer courses to visitors from all over the world. Courses last from one to two weeks and are designed for all levels of ability. They include subjects such as woodworking, drawing and painting, clay, fiber, and photography. The school offers housing and financial assistance to those who need it. Call 865/436-5860 or visit www.arrowmont.org.

Visitors are welcome at Arrowmont. It has five galleries that are open to the public Monday through Saturday. No admission is charged. Parking—a rare commodity hereabouts—is available on the campus, which can be accessed from a driveway between traffic lights 3 and 4. Tours of the campus can be arranged by calling the school.

The idle mind wonders why the Arrowmont people don't sell their land for what would no doubt be hundreds of millions of dollars and flee a town that has become the antithesis of patience and craftsmanship. Perhaps Pi Beta Phi's mission of reforming the backward is still going on—and in Gatlinburg it's more necessary than ever before.

---

461 Parkway, tel. 865/436-4038, is tiny. The entertainment consists of musical comedy, a sing-along, and a vaudeville-type review six nights a week. A five-member cast performs one show Monday, Wednesday, and Friday, and a seven-member cast presents a completely different show Tuesday, Thursday, and Saturday. Curtain time is 8 P.M. Monday through Saturday May through December, with shows on weekends only in November and December. Admission is $15.50 for adults and $5.50 for kids up to age 12. Any small child who sits on a lap gets in free. Call for reservations.

Fairs and Festivals

Held in July and October in the Gatlinburg Convention Center, the very popular **Craftsmen's Fairs** bring in about 150 craftspeople from all over the United States. The dates fluctuate every year—usually one week in July and one in October—so call865/436-7479 for information. Gatlinburg also joins Sevierville and Pigeon Forge in **WinterFest.** For details about Gatlinburg events, call 865/430-4148 or 800/568-4748.

WHERE TO STAY

The visitor to Gatlinburg will find a massive concentration of places to stay—some 7,500 rooms in all. Listed below are inns and bed-and-breakfasts of note, along with a sampling of hotels and motels.

Long a honeymoon destination—an estimated 10,000 couples tie the knot here annually—Gatlinburg features an enormous number of establishments with whirlpool bathtubs. Indeed, an anthropologist studying the ads for these plumbing extravaganzas might conclude that the marital bath has replaced the marital bed for connubial pleasures.

As in most resort areas, the prices at Gatlinburg hostelries vary according to the season. As a general rule, the lowest prices are offered in winter and the highest during summer and October, when the leaves turn.

Smoky Mountain Accommodations, tel. 865/436-9700 or 800/231-2230, website: www.smokymtnaccom.com, can help find the lodging—motel, condo, cabin, or chalet—that meets your needs. There is no charge for this service. The Gatlinburg Chamber of Commerce, websites: www.gatlinburg.com or www.virtualsmokies.com can offer additional assistance.

> *Smokies towns feature an enormous number of establishments with whirlpool bathtubs. Indeed, an anthropologist studying the ads for these plumbing extravaganzas might conclude that the marital bath has replaced the marital bed for connubial pleasures.*

Bed-and-Breakfasts and Inns

The **Brevard Inn Bed and Breakfast,** 225 W. Holly Ridge Rd., tel. 865/436-7233, consists of the inn and two authentic log cabins. The three guest rooms in the inn have private entrances, their own bathrooms, cable TV, and fireplaces. The cabins have kitchens. The rate is $75.

The **Buckhorn Inn,** 2140 Tudor Mountain Rd., tel. 865/436-4668, is the grande dame of inns in the Gatlinburg area, serving guests since 1938. The inn contains six rooms and has four cottages, all situated on 32 wooded acres six miles from downtown Gatlinburg. The inn centers on a large living room with views of Mount LeConte. It has a grand piano, and guests often sit down and tickle the ivories. The Buckhorn strives to maintain an atmosphere of informal elegance; tables are set with linen, and guests should not show up for meals in jeans and T-shirts. Rooms in the inn offer neither telephones nor televisions. The cottages have TVs as well as limited cooking facilities.

Children must be at least six years old to come to the Buckhorn, and even then they must occupy the cottages. Rates range $105–275 and include breakfast. Sack lunches can be arranged, and guests must make reservations for dinner. Weekends and holidays require a two-night minimum stay. See it at www.buckhorninn.com.

Guests at the **Butcher House Bed & Breakfast,** 1520 Garrett Ln., tel. 865/436-9457, rest above it all at 2,800 feet above downtown Gatlinburg. The four rooms each have a private bath. The house contains Victorian, French, Queen Anne, and American country furniture, and outside is a deck with a wonderful view of Mount LeConte. Rates are $79–109.

The **Cornerstone Inn,** 3956 Regal Way, tel. 865/430-5064, is filled with angels. The owner collects them, and they appear in the three guest rooms, each named for a painting it contains. Each room also has its own bath. Guests get a full country breakfast. Rates range $85–95. Check it out online at www.bbonline.com/tn/cornerstone.

Eight Gables Inn, 219 N. Mountain Trail, tel. 865/430-3344 or 800/279-5716, website: www.bbonline.com/tn/eightgables, is a large building with wraparound porches. It has 12 guestrooms, each with a private bath and its own theme—perhaps centered on a sleigh or four-poster bed. Two suites feature whirlpool baths; breakfast comes in four courses. Rates are $109–165.

Vern Hippensteal is an artist who produces scenes of the Smokies in watercolors, limited-edition prints, and pen and ink sketches. His biggest creation, however, is **Hippensteal's Mountain View Inn,** tel. 865/436-5761 or 800/527-8110, an 11-room inn in the Great Smoky Arts and Crafts Community. Each room has a fireplace, comfortable reading chairs, television, and a private bath with a whirlpool tub. A large common room enables guests to mingle, and many delight in taking in the view from rocking chairs on the wide porches that wrap around the inn. The rate is $135 per night. See www.hippensteal.com for more information.

The **Olde English Tudor Inn Bed & Breakfast,** 135 W. Holly Ridge Rd., tel. 865/436-7760 or 800/541-3798, is within walking distance of most downtown Gatlinburg attractions. The three-story building has an English garden and a waterfall out front. The eight guest rooms and one cottage all have private baths and cable TV. The common room contains a TV and a woodstove, and a large breakfast is served. Rates are $79–150. See www.oldenglishtudorinn.com for more information.

7th Heaven Log Inn, 3944 Castle Rd., tel. 865/430-5000 or 800/248-2923, sits beside the seventh green of the Bent Creek Golf Club outside Gatlinburg. The log structure contains five guest rooms, all with private baths. All have access to a big deck with a hot tub and a large recreation room with a pool table, television, and various games. Unlike some B&Bs—essentially other people's houses—this place was built from the start as an inn. Guests have their own entrances and access to a full kitchen. Breakfast is a five-course affair with homemade bread. Rates run $87–137. Find out more at www.7heaven.com.

Sitting a thousand feet above the town of Gatlinburg, the **Tennessee Ridge Inn Bed and Breakfast,** 507 Campbell Lead, tel. 865/436-4068, offers stunning views of the Great Smokies. The 8,500-square-foot, three-story house has a dining room with glass on three sides. Guests can choose from seven rooms, five of them with whirlpool baths. Breakfast is a full-service, sit-down affair that changes daily, from a full country meal to individual casseroles. Rates range $75–135. See the place online at www.tnridge.com.

Cabins, Condos, and Chalets

The offices that rent cabins, condos, and chalets are usually not on-site; call the agents for full details on their listings.

The accommodations at **Heritage Hollow,** tel. 800/359-6117, are genuine 100-year-old cabins furnished with antiques and country collectible furniture. Equipped with modern kitchens and baths, they have an authenticity that is hard to find in these parts.

You can find other places through **Alan's Mountain Rentals,** tel. 865/436-2512 or 800/843-0457; **Edelweiss Condominiums,** tel. 865/436-7846 or 800/824-4077; **High Chalet Condominium Rentals,** tel. 865/430-2193 or 800/225-3834; **Log Cabins of Gatlinburg,** tel. 865/436-7686 or 800/666-7686; **Masons Mountain Manors,** tel. 800/645-4911; and **Smoky Top Rentals,** tel. 800/468-6813.

Motels

Gatlinburg has fewer franchise motels than any of the other Smokies towns. Most of the motels here are older than their franchise counterparts and have a personality of their own. The good news is that these are often family-run operations that offer friendliness and a level of service not found elsewhere. Some customers return to the same places, even the same rooms, year after year and are greeted like family every time. The bad news is that these places don't always have the kinds of facilities—workout rooms, computer connections, and the like—that some travelers have come to expect. All the more reason to get out of that room and get into the mountains.

The following are just a few of the motels in Gatlinburg. Call 800/568-4748 for a more complete list and ask for the *Vacation Guide.*

The **Fairfield Inn,** 680 River Rd., tel. 865/430-7200 or 800/228-2800, website: www.ffigatlinburg.com, has rooms with balconies overlooking the Little Pigeon River.

A good choice among moderately priced motels is **Brookside Resort** on East Parkway, tel. 865/436-5611 or 800/251-9597. Places that will set you back more include **Edgewater Hotel,** 402 River Rd., tel. 865/436-4151 (in Tennessee 800/423-4532, outside of Tennessee 800/423-

9582); **River Terrace Resort & Convention Center,** 240 River Rd., tel. 865/436-5161 or 800/251-2040; and **Rocky Waters Motor Inn,** tel. 865/436-7861 or 800/824-1111.

Camping

Most of the camping here is for recreational vehicles, those behemoths of the roadways. Tents are permitted, but their occupants cannot escape the sound of air conditioners and the peaceful roar of the occasional generator.

Crazy Horse Campground, 12.5 miles up Highway 321 from Gatlinburg, tel. 865/436-4434 or 800/528-9003, has 207 sites and full amenities. It's open April through October.

Dudley Creek Travel Trailer Park and Log Cabins, just a half mile from downtown G-burg on the Pigeon Forge end of the Parkway, tel. 865/436-5053, has 105 sites with the works and is open all year.

Great Smoky Jellystone Park Camp Resort, 14 miles east of town on Highway 321, tel. 865/487-5534 or 800/210-2119, offers 110 sites. It's open April through November and has all the amenities.

LeConte Vista RV Resort and Campground sits four miles east of town on Highway 321, tel. 865/436-5437. Open March through December, it has all the works spread over 85 sites.

Outdoor Resort, 10 miles out on Highway 321, tel. 865/436-5861 or 800/677-5861, has 150 sites and a wide range of amenities. It's open all year. No tents are permitted.

Trout Creek Campground, three miles out of Gatlinburg on Highway 321, tel. 865/436-5905, has 75 sites. Open April through November, it offers the works.

Twin Creek RV Resort, tel. 865/436-7081 or 800/252-8077, offers 75 sites within the city limits of Gatlinburg on 865/Highway 321. It has all the amenities and is open April through October. No tents are allowed.

FOOD

The **Buckhorn Inn,** 2140 Tudor Mountain Rd., tel. 865/436-4668, outside of Gatlinburg near the Great Smoky Arts and Crafts Community, offers perhaps the finest meals in the area. Typical entrées include poached fillets of salmon and red snapper with champagne dill sauce, and grilled lamb chops with rosemary butter. One frequent appetizer is capellini with prosciutto and fontina cheese in basil sauce. Bring your own bottle. Seating at the inn is limited; overnight guests have first choice, and everyone else must make reservations no later than 10 A.M. on the day they wish to dine. Dinner is served at 7 P.M. and has a fixed price, usually about $30 and worth every penny. To get to the inn, take Highway 321 north out of Gatlinburg. Pass Glades Road on the left, take Buckhorn Road to the left, then go right on Tudor Mountain Road. See the inn online at www.buckhorninn.com.

The **Burning Bush Restaurant** lies about 30 feet from the park boundary at 1151 Parkway, tel. 865/865/436-4669. Patrons can gaze out the windows and watch squirrels cavorting. The food is basic American fare, several notches up from country cooking. Breakfasts come with a glass of LeConte Sunrise, a mixture of fruit juices. The restaurant is open 365 days a year.

Calhouns, 1004 Parkway, tel. 865/436-4100, is a chain offering ribs, prime rib, seafood, and chicken. It serves lunch and dinner seven days a week.

The Greenbriar, 370 Newman Rd., tel. 865/436-6318, lies east of Gatlinburg off Highway 321 in a log structure built by George Dempster, one-time mayor of Knoxville and a member of the Dempster Dumpster family. The restaurant serves dinner only year-round, and diners can choose from entrées such as slow-cooked prime rib or Smoky Mountains strip steak, marinated in olive oil and garlic for several days.

The Little Italian Restaurant, 463 Parkway, tel. 865/436-7880, makes its own sausage, meatballs, bread, and sauces. It serves lunch and dinner every day.

Maxwells Beef & Seafood, 1103 Parkway, tel. 865/436-3738, features fresh seafood and steaks, prime rib, and lamb. Begin with wine or cocktails and finish off with a flambé dessert. Maxwells is open for dinner seven days a week. Visit it online at www.maxwellsinc.com.

TOURISM CORRIDOR

Open Hearth, on the Parkway at the entrance to the Smokies, tel. 865/436-5648, offers fresh trout and salmon, barbecued ribs, and steak along with an extensive wine list. It's open every day all year for dinner only.

The Park Grill, 1110 Parkway, tel. 865/436-2300, occupies a wonderful log building that pays homage to the lodges of the Adirondacks and Yellowstone National Park. The logs came from Idaho, and it took seven trucks to bring them to Gatlinburg. The food—all with Smoky-oriented names—ranges from Moonshine Chicken to Franklin Delano Rib Eye. This place takes no reservations, so get on the list and then go for a stroll. See it online at www.peddlerparkgrill.com.

Smoky Mountain Brewery and Restaurant, located behind 1004 Parkway, is a wonderful place to visit after a long hard hike through the mountains. There are always at least eight microbrews on hand for the tasting. Some nights bring live music, with karaoke on other nights. You'll find pizza, sandwiches, and burgers for lunch and steaks, trout, and ribs for dinner. See www.smoky-mtn-brewery.com for more information.

On the Great Smoky Arts and Crafts Trail

For those whose eyes have glazed over after seeing too much pottery, this is the place. **The Wild Plum Tearoom,** 555 Buckhorn Rd., tel. 865/436-3808, is open for lunch only from March through mid-December. Try one of the combo plates of pasta salad, chicken salad, and fruit, and don't forget the wild plum tea.

SHOPPING

Unlike Pigeon Forge, Gatlinburg has no large outlet malls. Instead, dozens of small shops sell just about anything a visitor could want. Here is a highly idiosyncratic list of favorites.

Armour House, in the Marketplace at 651 Parkway, tel. 865/430-2101 or 800/886-1862, sells Civil War paintings, books, and artifacts. Shop on the Web at www.armourhouseinc.com.

The Happy Hiker, tel. 865/436-5632 or 800/HIKER-01, caters to outdoor enthusiasts by offering all manner of outdoor clothing and

camping gear. It's the place to rent backpacks, sleeping bags, tents, and stoves. Returning hikers can take showers and do laundry. This useful place lies between the Parkway and River Road behind the Burning Bush Restaurant, very close to the entrance to the park. It's on the Web at www.happyhiker.com.

Great Smoky Arts and Crafts Community

The Gatlinburg area has long been known for its arts and crafts. The self-sufficient mountaineers produced quilts, pottery, and other day-to-day items, and through the years the presence of tourists lured other artists to town. When rents for shop space in town became oppressive, a few artists started selling things out of their houses. Thus evolved the **Great Smoky Arts and Crafts Community** on two roads east of town—Buckhorn and Glades—off Highway 321.

The quality of crafts here varies. Some shops deal in high-quality work, but others peddle items better thought of as souvenirs. Despite the watering down of quality, this is a good place to go. Some shops offer leather goods, baskets, quilts, rugs, woodcarvings, brooms, candles, pottery, or stained glass. Others sell wooden toys and puzzles, dulcimers, photographs, and oil paintings. Many craftspeople work in studios beside their shops and sometimes take time to talk to visitors.

Visitors can escape the crowds in town and drive through the woods from shop to shop. The trolley comes here, but using it can be frustrating. Shops are too far apart for walking, but shoppers might have to wait 20 or 30 minutes for a trolley—even if they want to spend only five minutes in each shop.

Highlights along the way include **Ogle's Broom Shop** on Glades Road, which produces fireplace brooms, traditional mountain brooms, and walking sticks. **Alewine Pottery,** on the same road, sells very attractive pieces. Those who want to go home with a great photograph of the Smokies should stop at **A Frame of Mind,** also on Glades Road. Most of these stores are open daily, but during the winter they many reduce hours or open only on weekends.

THE WORLD'S BEST KNIFE STORE

Shopping is a favorite Smokies activity, and its most ardent practitioners are usually female. Although **Smoky Mountain Knife Works** has lots of items of interest to women, this store is the ultimate guy place.

Most men born in the South carry pocketknives, except when they're wearing a bathing suit or pajamas. Knives were an essential part of the frontier as well as the farm, and despite the demonization of pocketknives by public schools, the tradition continues strong today.

Kevin Pipes and John Parker, both native Tennesseans, began their cutlery careers by selling knives from the trunks of cars at flea markets. As business grew, they opened a store in 1978 and later moved it to a larger location. In 1991 Kevin launched what has since become the best knife store in the world.

Smoky Mountain Knife Works sells around 5,000 different types of knives and swords. These include traditional pocketknives from manufacturers such as Case and Remington, fantasy knives

that look like something carried by *Star Trek* Klingons, and all manner of kitchen cutlery.

The Knife Works is more than just a store. Exhibits around the walls display knives from the eighteenth century, the Civil War, and subsequent military conflicts. Collections from manufacturers such as Germany's Boker and Herder, which began making knives in the 1700s, are on display as well. Many of these exhibits, while not always labeled as thoroughly as they could be, are of museum quality. The store also has over 250 wildlife mounts positioned along a stream that flows from the third floor down to the lowest floor in the building.

The company mails out 8 million catalogs a year and sells knives online at www.eknife works.com. The computer inventory list contains 12,000 different kinds of knives.

Located on Highway 66 four miles south of I-40, the store is open daily year-round. For information call 865/453-5871. To get a catalog or place an order call 800/251-9306.

© SMOKY MOUNTAIN KNIFE WORKS

View rare antique cutlery displays from around the world at the Smoky Mountain Knife Works.

TOURISM CORRIDOR

Arts and Crafts in Town

The **Arrowcraft Shop,** tel. 865/436-4604, occupies one of the oldest and most beautiful buildings in town. Built in 1939, it features native hand-split slate. The rooms inside are paneled in chestnut, giving the visitor a glimpse of this hardwood that once dominated nearby forests. The shop sells the work of local and regional artists—not the students at Arrowmont—and is operated by the Southern Highland Craft Guild.

The **Jim Gray Gallery** at the Carousel Mall (traffic light 3), tel. 865/436-5262, and at 670 Glades Road, tel. 865/436-8988, sells works in a variety of media, including oils, drawings, and statues, from one of the state's most talented and famous artists.

The **Vern Hippensteal Gallery,** 452 Parkway, tel. 865/436-4328 or 800/537-8110, features the work of this Gatlinburg resident—watercolors, limited-edition prints, and pen and ink sketches of the Smokies. It's open seven days a week all year long.

INFORMATION

Spread out as a map on the kitchen table, the route to the Smokies looks simple—particularly from the north: Get on I-40, go to Exit 407, and take Highway 66 to the park. It is simple—so simple that millions of people do just that on their way to the most popular national park in the country. The resulting traffic congestion can be truly horrific, especially for children asking "Are we there yet?" On the worst weekends, traffic is bumper to bumper all the way from the park entrance to I-40.

There is a better way. The old blue highways that led generations of visitors to the Smokies are still there and provide a wonderful alternative to the madness of the interstate. Along these routes you can stop for a yard sale, visit a country store, and literally smell the flowers. You can see the old gas stations, restaurants, and other buildings that have not been replicated 500 times across the country. Your trip becomes less of a stressful effort to get to a destination and more of an experience.

© JEFF BRADLEY

Ogles Broom Shop, Gatlinburg

Coming from the West

If your destination is the Gatlinburg entrance to the Smokies, don't get on I-640 at Knoxville. Stay on I-40 until Exit 388, which deposits you on Henley Street, a.k.a. Highway 441. Locals know this road as Chapman Highway. For a good introduction to the region, go left on Hill Avenue and follow the signs to the Gateway Regional Visitors Center. Otherwise, stay on Henley Street and cross the Tennessee River on the high bridge. As you climb away from the river, on the heights to your right stand the remains of Fort Dickerson, a Civil War fortification.

Chapman Highway goes through some Knoxville sprawl for a couple of miles, but then opens up to countryside. As you approach Sevierville, you'll top a hill and there they are—the Smokies in all their glory. At the bottom of the hill you will merge with all the poor devils streaming in along Highway 66.

If your destination is the Townsend entrance to

the Smokies, get off I-40 at Exit 376A and follow I-140 to its intersection with Highway 129, very close to the Knoxville Airport. Follow 129 south until it intersects with Highway 321 in Maryville. Turn left on 321 and follow it into Townsend.

Coming from I-40 East

If your destination is Gatlinburg, get off at Exit 440 and head south on Highway 321 toward Cosby. On your left you will find Carver's Orchard, a great place to get some local fruit and honey. A good place to eat is The Front Porch, just past Carver's on the left.

Coming from I-81 South

If you'd like a one- to two-hour drive through the countryside, get off I-81 at Exit 50, Fall Branch, and take Highway 93 through rolling farmland into Greeneville. This town was the home of President Andrew Johnson, and it contains a good museum about his life and times. From there take Highway 321 for a beautiful drive to Newport, then continue to Cosby and Gatlinburg on the same highway.

The **Gatlinburg Welcome Center,** on the Parkway at the Pigeon Forge side of town, tel. 865/436-0519 or 800/568-4748, is open Monday through Saturday 8 A.M.–6 P.M. and Sunday 9 A.M.–5 P.M. Find it online at www.gatlinburg.com.

TOURISM CORRIDOR

Knoxville

Introduction

The largest city in East Tennessee makes a good beginning or end to a Smokies vacation. Here visitors can enjoy museums, fine restaurants, and a bit of history without enduring hordes of people—unless the University of Tennessee is playing football. On those days, when fans fill up the 104,079-seat stadium, the third largest in the country, Knoxville is best seen from the air.

Children will enjoy the Knoxville Zoo and the Women's Basketball Hall of Fame. When it's time to leave town, Knoxville is a good place to get off I-40 or I-75 in favor of Highway 441, a more leisurely route to the Smokies. Knoxville's official hobby is highway construction, so it might be a good idea to get off the interstates anyway.

Perhaps the most famous writer to come from Knoxville was James Agee. "We are now talking of summer evenings in Knoxville, Tennessee in the time that I lived there so successfully disguised to myself as a child." Those words begin his novel *A Death in the Family,* a wonderful evocation of 1915 life in the Fort Sanders neighborhood.

Agee is part of a long line of creative people to emerge from or do significant work in Knoxville. Clarence Brown, the Metro-Goldwyn-Mayer stalwart who directed more Greta Garbo movies than anyone else, grew up in Knoxville. Actors Patricia Neal, Polly Bergen, and John Cullum also came from Knoxville, and Quentin Tarantino spent his early years here.

Radio stations WROL and WNOX were hotbeds of country music, with Roy Acuff, Chet Atkins, Archie Campbell, Homer and Jethro, and other luminaries making their marks there before moving on to Nashville. Hank Williams stopped at the Andrew Johnson Hotel before taking his last ride in a Cadillac up Highway 11. Don Everly of the Everly Brothers

© JEFF BRADLEY

Old City

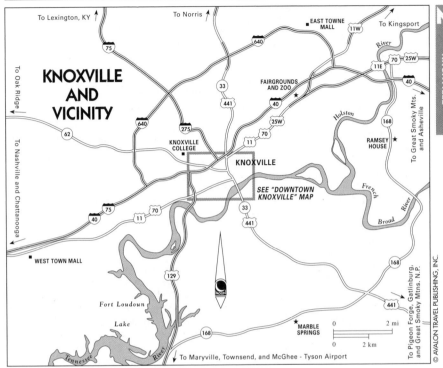

KNOXVILLE
AND
VICINITY

To Lexington, KY

To Norris

EAST TOWNE MALL

To Kingsport

To Oak Ridge

To Nashville and Chattanooga

To Great Smoky Mts. and Asheville

KNOXVILLE COLLEGE

KNOXVILLE

SEE "DOWNTOWN KNOXVILLE" MAP

FAIRGROUNDS AND ZOO

RAMSEY HOUSE

Holston

French

Broad

River

WEST TOWN MALL

Fort Loudoun

Lake

Tennessee

River

MARBLE SPRINGS

To Pigeon Forge, Gatlinburg, and Great Smoky Mtns. N.P.

To Maryville, Townsend, and McGhee - Tyson Airport

0   2 mi

0   2 km

© AVALON TRAVEL PUBLISHING, INC.

wrote "Cathy's Clown" about his West High School girlfriend, and a shy Sevier County girl first faced television cameras in Knoxville, where early morning viewers caught their first glimpse of Dolly Parton. Eva Barber, the country singer for Lawrence Welk, was born here, as was country singer Carl Butler.

Blues brothers Brownie and Sticks McGhee came from Knoxville, and Ida Cox, who penned "Wild Women Don't Have the Blues," lived and died here, and blues violinist Howard Armstrong lived in Knoxville and wrote songs about it.

Novelist and National Book Award winner Cormac McCarthy grew up in Knoxville and used it as the setting for some of his work. And the city is home to the Reverend J. Bazzel Mull, a gospel music disc jockey whose gravelly voice has pushed Chuck Wagon Gang records and tapes on clear channel stations from Alaska to Venezuela.

From its earliest days, East Tennessee's largest

city has served as the pipeline from the north to the south, and vice versa, with people passing through and headed for greatness.

HISTORY
From Fort to Capital

Like many early towns in Tennessee, Knoxville's location was determined by how easily it could be defended from Indians. In 1786 James White built a fort on a hill a few miles downstream from where the Holston and French Broad Rivers combine to form the Tennessee River. When William Blount, a signer of the U.S. Constitution whom George Washington appointed governor of the Southwest Territory, came from Rocky Mount to look for a permanent capital for the territory, White's Fort seemed just right. It just so happened that Blount owned land nearby.

Blount was the kind of man who insisted on

KNOXVILLE HIGHLIGHTS

The **Gateway Regional Visitor Center** is the best place to get tourist information—not just for Knoxville but for surrounding towns and the Smokies as well.

Knoxville Museum of Art, perched above the site of the 1982 World's Fair, presents exhibits that stir the imagination.

Knoxville is a hotbed of women's collegiate basketball. Visit the **Women's Basketball Hall of Fame** or, better yet, go see a University of Tennessee Lady Vols game.

Blount Mansion, the first frame house in a town of log cabins, is the most significant historical site in the entire city.

The **Tennessee Theater,** with its mighty Wurlitzer organ console rising through the floor, shows the glories of past movie palaces.

The **Old City** gives new life to 19th-century warehouses, offering an engaging mixture of shops, clubs, and restaurants.

wearing powdered wigs and silver buckles even on the frontier. Ever the politician, he renamed White's Fort Knoxville in 1791 in honor of Henry Knox, Washington's secretary of war, who doled out money to the Indians in hopes of keeping them in line. In short order Knoxville grew into a booming place with its own newspaper and a college. It became a center for trade, most of it aimed downstream. Adventuresome merchants cut down trees, built flatboats, loaded them with goods such as flour, lime, and cotton, and shoved off. They drifted down the Tennessee, Ohio, and Mississippi Rivers to New Orleans, where they would sell everything, including their boats.

As Tennesseans moved toward statehood, they wrangled and wrote their state constitution in Knoxville. On June 1, 1796, Tennessee became the 16th state, with Knoxville as its capital. Although it was the state capital, Knoxville never had a capitol. The legislature met in taverns and other convivial buildings to work through its business. As the population in western parts of

the state grew, the pressure to move the seat of government closer to the center of the state led to Nashville's designation as the state capital in 1826. Fortunately for Knoxville, the college—by 1840 called East Tennessee University—stayed.

Civil War Siege

When the Civil War broke out, Knoxville was a Confederate lion in a den of Daniels; the city had many Southern sympathizers, but they were surrounded by staunch Unionists. Some historians think that Knoxville was the most evenly divided city in the entire country. Both sides agreed that East Tennessee's largest city was a strategic prize, and, accordingly, a Confederate army under General Felix Zollicoffer occupied the city for the first two years of the war.

In 1863 Union General Ambrose Burnside, the popularizer of sideburns, took over the city when the Confederate army left town. When they returned in the form of General James Longstreet, they found a well-fortified city awaiting them. Longstreet set up his headquarters west of the city in "Bleak House," built and named by an admirer of the Charles Dickens novel. The name proved prophetic. Longstreet began a siege, planning to bombard and starve the city into submission. The loyal Unionist farmers flummoxed these plans, however, by floating rafts full of food down the river at night.

Longstreet finally attacked Fort Sanders, an earthen fort at the western edge of Knoxville, and was repulsed in a brief but bloody battle. When the approach of Union General William Tecumseh Sherman forced Longstreet to give up the siege, Sherman rode into town expecting to find a starving populace. Instead, he and his staff were served a turkey dinner with all the trimmings.

Prosperity

In the years after the Civil War, railroads boomed and so did Knoxville. Its location as a gateway to the South led to a flow of people, goods, and money through the city. East Tennessee University received designation as a land grant college, rebuilt its bombarded buildings, and became the University of Tennessee (www.utk.edu). Knoxville College (www.knoxvillecollege.edu) was found-

BOB RACE

"Great Lakes of the South."

ed in 1875 to prepare young black men and women to be teachers.

Rebuilt railroads and increased steamboat traffic made Knoxville's cash registers jangle. By 1900, the city was the fourth-largest center for wholesale trade in the South, most of this business taking place in what is now the Old City.

With all this prosperity, the city felt a need to show off. This took the form of the 1910 and 1911 Knoxville Appalachian Expositions. The populace had such a good time that in 1913 later they did it again with a federally financed National Conservation Exposition, which drew over one million people. One idea that came from this exposition was the notion that a national park should be established in the East. The ideal place would be the Great Smoky Mountains.

Arrival of the TVA

Knoxville suffered along with the rest of the nation in the Great Depression, but because of that economic calamity the city landed the headquarters of the Tennessee Valley Authority (TVA), a federal agency born of the New Deal (www.tva.gov). It was charged with reducing floods, producing abundant electric power, and, in a grandiose mission statement, assisting in "the development of the natural resources of the Tennessee River drainage basin and its adjoining territory for the general social and economic welfare of the Nation." How successfully TVA did all that is still debated, but the impact on Knoxville was overwhelmingly positive. By the time TVA was finished damming Tennessee rivers, the lakes had almost as much shoreline as Florida has coastline. The once wild Tennessee River that had subjected many old boatmen to harrowing rides became a safe waterway plied by stately barges and a host of pleasure craft.

Knoxville Nowadays

Modern Knoxville's downtown is a relatively compact area between the Old City and the Tennessee River. Like Chattanooga, Nashville, and Memphis, Knoxville has rediscovered its waterfront, and this, plus a renewal of interest in downtown, has made it a good place to visit.

Sights and Recreation

THE LAY OF THE LAND

Knoxville is a city on a hill, or a series of hills, and for visitors it can be divided into five areas: the Gateway area, downtown, Old City, the World's Fair site, and the University of Tennessee (UT). Many of the city's restaurants line Kingston Pike, a four-lane street that heads west from UT and extends for miles in parallel with I-40/75. For decades, this was the main east/west route of Highways 11 and 70. It is now the clogged artery serving most of Knoxville's sprawl.

GATEWAY AREA

Tucked down along the Tennessee River and under a bridge, the **Gateway Regional Visitor Center** is the best place to get tourist information. Exit the interstate at either Henley Street (Exit 388) or the James White Parkway. Once off the interstate, just follow the signs. The center contains a small museum.

Up the hill from the center is a replica of **James White's Fort,** the beginnings of Knoxville. The nearby **Women's Basketball Hall of Fame,** in the building with the big basketball on top, gives visitors a look at this burgeoning sport.

Upstream is the Volunteer Landing Marina, and downstream the **Tennessee Riverboat Company** boards passengers for cruises. Between the two, the **Riverside Tavern** and **Calhouns** will happily quench the thirst of anyone passing through.

DOWNTOWN

The hill that constitutes downtown Knoxville is book-ended by the twin towers of the TVA's headquarters to the north and the Volunteer Landing on the Tennessee River to the south.

Blount Mansion, the seat of government for the nation's first territory, sits above the river on a bluff. This is a good place to begin your tour. History fans will also like the **East Tennessee History Society Museum** on Market Street, which also contains several restaurants and spots to sit down.

Right beside the museum is the most delightful downtown park in the entire state. **Krutch Park** is an inspired blend of greenery and water that offers respite to the footsore tourist. Farther down Market Street is **Market Square,** an open-air place where farmers once sold their produce and a frequent gathering place for Knoxvillians.

Parallel to Market Street is Gay Street, Knoxville's historic main drag. The principal hotel for a long time was the Andrew Johnson Hotel, 912 S. Gay St., and it was here that Hank Williams spent his last day on earth. Two wonderful old theaters hold court here, and both are worth a visit. The **Lamar House-Bijou Theatre,** 803 Gay St., is a former hotel with a theater behind it, while the **Tennessee Theater** is a 1928 movie palace. A stroll north on Gay Street leads to the edge of the Old City. On the way is **Yee-Haw Industries,** perhaps the most remarkable print shop in the entire state.

For a downright medieval experience, go to St. Johns Episcopal Cathedral on the north side of the federal courthouse on Main Street. Walk the labyrinth that's just inside the gates.

OLD CITY

A walk north on Gay Street and right on Jackson Avenue leads into Old City, a collection of turn-of-the-century brick buildings whose offices and warehouses made Knoxville the center of commerce for East Tennessee. The area was also called the Bowery for its various debaucheries that reminded people of the New York City district of the same name. Left to slumber for years, the old buildings became home in the 1980s to an eclectic mixture of eateries, boutiques, antiques shops, galleries, and nightclubs. Here you'll also find the greatest collection of live music in East Tennessee—dance music, jazz, rock, and blues. Simply walking around is exciting. Old City also

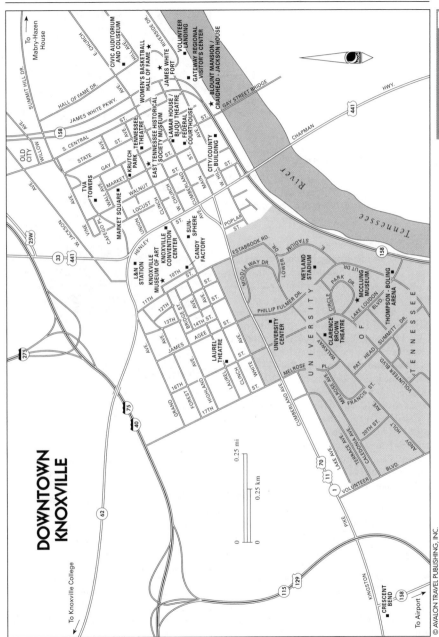

KNOXVILLE

DOWNTOWN KNOXVILLE

To Knoxville College

To Mabry-Hazen House

CIVIC AUDITORIUM AND COLISEUM
WOMEN'S BASKETBALL HALL OF FAME
JAMES WHITE FORT
VOLUNTEER LANDING
GATEWAY REGIONAL VISITOR'S CENTER
BLOUNT MANSION / CRAIGHEAD - JACKSON HOUSE
TENNESSEE THEATRE
LAMAR HOUSE / BIJOU THEATRE
FEDERAL COURTHOUSE
EAST TENNESSEE HISTORICAL SOCIETY MUSEUM
CITY/COUNTY BUILDING
KRUTCH PARK
MARKET SQUARE
TVA TOWERS
SUN SPHERE
CANDY FACTORY
L&N STATION
KNOXVILLE MUSEUM OF ART
KNOXVILLE CONVENTION CENTER
LAUREL THEATRE
UNIVERSITY CENTER
CLARENCE BROWN THEATRE
NEYLAND STADIUM
MCCLUNG MUSEUM
THOMPSON - BOLING ARENA
CRESCENT BEND

HALL OF FAME DR.
SUMMIT HILL DR.
E. CHURCH AVE.
JAMES WHITE PKWY.
HILL AVE.
NEYLAND DR. / RIVERSIDE DR.
GAY STREET BRIDGE
S. CENTRAL AVE.
STATE ST.
GAY ST.
MARKET ST.
WALL AVE.
CAFEGO PL.
UNION AVE.
CLINCH AVE.
W. CHURCH AVE.
MAIN ST.
CUMBERLAND AVE.
W. HILL AVE.
POPLAR ST.
WALNUT ST.
LOCUST ST.
VINE AVE.
JACKSON AVE.
HENLEY ST.
WILLOW AVE.
OLD CITY
S. GAY ST.
W. JACKSON AVE.
ESTABROOK RD.
MIDDLE WAY DR.
STADIUM DR.
LOWER DR.
PHILLIP FULMER DR.
CIRCLE PARK DR.
LAKE LOUDON BLVD.
NEYLAND DR.
MELROSE PL.
MELROSE AVE.
FRANCIS ST.
PAT HEAD SUMMITT DR.
CUMBERLAND AVE.
TERRACE AVE.
CALEDONIA AVE.
LAKE AVE.
20TH ST.
ANDY HOLT AVE.
HOLT BLVD.
VOLUNTEER BLVD.
WALKWAY
VOLUNTEER PIKE
KINGSTON PIKE
To Airport

Tennessee River

UNIVERSITY OF TENNESSEE

CHAPMAN HWY.

10TH ST.
11TH AVE.
12TH ST.
13TH ST.
14TH ST.
AGEE ST.
JAMES AVE.
BRIDGE ST.
16TH ST.
17TH ST.
GRAND AVE.
FOREST AVE.
HIGHLAND AVE.
LAUREL AVE.
CLINCH AVE.
WHITE AVE.

0.25 mi
0.25 km
0
0

62
158
25W
33
441
275
75
40
70
11
1
115
129
158

© AVALON TRAVEL PUBLISHING, INC.

offers several good coffeehouses, and don't miss the mural of famous Knoxville musicians on the side of Sullivan Street Market on Jackson Avenue.

If you're driving, to get to the Old City From I-40, take Exit 388A onto the James White Parkway, then go right on Jackson. During busy weekends, parking can be tight in these parts, so if at all possible try to hoof it.

WORLD'S FAIR PARK

Knoxville was the scene of the 1982 World's Fair, which the world little noted nor long remembered. It's now the site of a new convention center, which helps tie downtown to the city to the west.

Perhaps the oddest legacy of the World's Fair is one of the weirder-looking buildings in the entire state. The 26-story **Sunsphere** looks like an architectural paean to a golf ball or a water tower fresh off the set of *The Jetsons.*

The fair site contains several places to stop. The restored **L&N Station** anchors the upper end of the park. Built in 1905, the station now contains a restaurant and shops.

The Candy Factory, tel. 865/522-2049, will please kids of all ages. This 1919 building was built to house a candy factory and is now home to an unabashed firm named the South's Finest Chocolate Factory, which does all its production here. Visitors can peer through windows to see machines and people busily cranking out the calories. The shop sells more than 100 kinds of candy. Its hours are Monday through Saturday 9:30 A.M.–6 P.M., Sunday 1–5 P.M.

Beside the Candy Factory stands the Knoxville Museum of Art. If touring the museum spurs visitors to add to their own collections, the artists in the **Victorian Houses** at the corner of 11th Street and Laurel Avenue will happily provide. This brightly colored row of houses boasts shops containing original arts and fine crafts. The shops are open Tuesday through Saturday 10 A.M.–5 P.M., Sunday 1–5 P.M.

The Sunsphere looks like a watertower fresh off the set of the **The Jetsons.**

bright lights of Old City

THE UNIVERSITY OF TENNESSEE

Cumberland Avenue dips from downtown to a creek and then climbs a hill to the University of Tennessee. The Knoxville campus is the largest in the statewide system; approximately 19,000 undergraduates and 7,000 graduate students study here. The campus contains 229 buildings spread over 532 acres. A driving tour is the best way to take in the sights.

The Law School is on the right as you drive or walk up Cumberland Avenue from the World's Fair site. On the left, at the corner of Stadium Drive and Cumberland Avenue, is the **University Center,** which houses an art gallery, two restaurants, and an enormous bookstore. Here you can buy books as well as every imaginable item colored orange and white and bearing the UT logo. The center is a good place to find out what's happening on campus—speakers, plays, movies, etc.

The oldest and most architecturally unified part of the campus lies up a hill adjacent to the University Center. This "hallowed hill," as UT's alma mater puts it, has brick buildings in the collegiate Gothic style. The most impressive is the 1919 **Ayres Hall,** which crowns the hill.

UT has a wonderful theater program with its **Clarence Brown Theater** and **Carousel Theater.** The former shows 35mm foreign and art movies on Sunday nights. Museum-goers should check out the **Frank H. McClung Museum,** East Tennessee's main natural history collection, while art lovers should wander over to **Ewing Gallery of Art and Architecture.**

MUSEUMS AND GALLERIES
History
The **Beck Cultural Exchange Center** at 1927 Dandridge Avenue east of downtown, tel. 865/524-8461, website: www.korrnet.org/beck-cec/, houses collections relating to Knoxville's black citizens. Old photographs depicting community events and church life are the bulk of the exhibits. Admission is free, and the center is open Tuesday through Saturday 10 A.M.–6 P.M.

The **East Tennessee Historical Society Museum,** 600 Market St., tel. 865/544-5732, website: www.east-tennessee-history.org/museum, focuses on regional history beginning in the mid-18th century. Exhibits include the surveying equipment used by James White to lay out the original town; "Old Betsy," one of David Crockett's rifles; and early furniture made in East Tennessee. The Civil War section displays uniforms, rifles, pistols, and a regimental flag. The museum is open Monday through Saturday 10 A.M.–4 P.M., Sunday 1–5 P.M. Admission is free.

Every decent university has a museum, and UT's **Frank H. McClung Museum,** 1327 Circle

BOB RACE

the Victorian Houses of the 11th Street Artist's Colony

Park Dr., tel. 865/974-2144, has the best depiction of Tennessee's Indians in the state. Exhibits include life-size murals with scenes from five cultural periods beginning in 10,000 B.C. Children will like the pull-out drawers containing hands-on items they can examine. One of the more remarkable items is a 32-foot-long canoe carved from a single tulip poplar tree. The museum also has an ancient Egypt collection, minerals and fossils from Tennessee, and Civil War items from Knoxville. Admission is free, and the museum is open Monday through Saturday 9 A.M.–5 P.M., Sunday 2–5 P.M. See the museum online at http://mcclungmuseum.utk.edu.

The **Volunteer State Veterans Hall of Fame,** 4000 Chapman Hwy., tel. 865/577-0757, contains more than 2,000 war-related artifacts from the Revolutionary War through Operation Desert Storm. Admission is free, and the Hall of Fame is open Thursday through Saturday 10 A.M.–4 P.M., Sunday 1–4 P.M.

Art
The **Ewing Gallery of Art and Architecture** in the Art and Architecture Building at 1715 Volunteer Boulevard, tel. 865/974-3200, features traveling exhibits as well as those generated from within the university. Admission is free. The museum is open during weekday work hours and on Sunday afternoons during the academic year. See www.sun-site.utk.edu/ewing_gallery for more information.

The **Knoxville Museum of Art,** 1050 Worlds Fair Park Dr., tel. 865/525-6101, occupies a beautiful building. Pink Tennessee marble graces the outside, while inside visitors will find traveling exhibits. Call for information on exhibits. The museum also has a café and a shop and is open Tuesday through Thursday 10 A.M.–5 P.M., Friday 10 A.M.–9 P.M., Saturday 10 A.M.–5 P.M., and Sunday noon–5

P.M. Admission is free. Visit www.knoxart.org for more information.

Specialty

The **East Tennessee Discovery Center,** tel. 865/594-1494, website: www.korrnet.org/etdc, is one of those children's museums without "Don't Touch!" signs. Exhibits include, to list a few, *Rocks, Minerals, and Fossils,* an insect zoo, and a planetarium. To get there, take Exit 392 off I-40 east of downtown. Take Rutledge Pike southeast until it hits Magnolia Avenue. Go right, then turn right again onto Beaman Road. Follow the signs. The museum is open Monday through Friday 9 A.M.–5 P.M. and on varying hours on Saturday. Admission is $3 for adults, $2 for seniors, $2 for children 5 and over, and $1 for kids ages 3 and 4.

The **Women's Basketball Hall of Fame,** 700 Hall of Fame Dr., tel. 865/633-9000, website: www.wbhof.com, offers a state-of-the-art look at this ascending sport. While most of the inductees, alas, are not as famous as they should be, the story of the female version of basketball is well presented here in a striking building. Highlights include old bloomer uniforms; a stretch limousine once used to transport the All American Red Heads, a barnstorming women's team; and a place to shoot hoops. Admission ranges from $6 to $8, and the museum is open seven days a week.

To get there from I-40, take the James White Parkway (Exit 388A) to the Summit Hill Drive exit. Turn left onto Summit Hill Drive. At the light, make a right onto Hall of Fame Drive. Proceed through three lights. At the fourth light, turn left onto Hill Avenue. The Hall of Fame will be on your left, with parking available next to the building.

PARKS AND ZOOS

The **Knoxville Zoo,** tel. 865/637-5331, website: www.knoxville-zoo.com, shelters more than 1,000 creatures representing 225 species, most of which live in re-creations of their natural surroundings. The zoo boasts an extensive large cat collection, and visitors can walk through habitats with names like Gorilla Valley, Cheetah Savannah, and Tortoise Territory. Kids particularly enjoy the petting zoo.

The zoo is open daily 9:30 A.M.–5 P.M. Admission is $7.95 for adults, $4.95 for children 3 to 12 and seniors, and free for anyone younger. To get there, take Exit 392 off I-40 east of downtown and follow the signs.

THEATRICAL JEWELS

Two wonderful old theaters hold court on Gay Street, and both are worth a visit. The **Lamar House-Bijou Theatre,** 803 Gay St., tel. 865/522-0832, website: www.bijoutheatre.com, began in 1816 as a tavern, then saw service as a hotel. In 1909 the two-balconied Bijou Theatre was built onto the back of the hotel, and vaudeville and other live performances of all kinds entertained generations of Knoxvillians. This jewel of a theater is a wonderful place to see or hear anything. Musicians such as Michelle Shocked and Richard Thompson have played here, along with theater groups and classical and jazz artists.

The theater lobby houses the **East Tennessee Hall of Fame for the Performing Arts,** a series of oil paintings of Dolly Parton, Chet Atkins, and others. Visitors can tour the Hall of Fame weekdays 10 A.M.–5 P.M. and perhaps can sneak a peek of the theater itself. Admission is free.

Farther north sits the **Tennessee Theater,** 604 Gay St., tel. 865/525-1840, a wonderful movie palace opened in 1928 in the waning days of silent films. It was on this stage that a young Roy Acuff warbled his songs and played his fiddle. Stage productions and concerts still occasionally take place in this extravagantly decorated theater—performers have included Bob Dylan and Allison Krauss—but movies are the real reason to go. Most are preceded by a brief concert on "the Mighty Wurlitzer," an organ console that rises magnificently from the floor and whose thunderous notes resonate in the chests of theatergoers. Occasionally silent films are shown with organ accompaniment. Call to see what's playing.

KNOXVILLE

HISTORIC SITES

Andrew Johnson Hotel

This tall, thin brick building at the intersection of Cumberland and Gay is no longer a hotel, but at one time its was *the* place to stay in Knoxville. Local historian and author Jack Neely claims that it is the only building that has housed Jean-Paul Sartre, Hank Williams, Amelia Earhart, Duke Ellington, Tony Perkins, Liberace, and Sergei Rachmaninoff, who gave the last performance of his life in Knoxville. The top floor was once the home of radio station WNOX's *Midday Merry-Go-Round,* a live show famous for launching the careers of country music stars.

James White's Fort

Kids love this replica of James White's Fort, 205 E. Hill Ave., tel. 865/525-6514, not far from the Gateway Regional Visitors Center. White built a fort in 1786 and thus provided a place for William Blount to establish the capital of the Southwest Territory. James White's Fort no longer stands at its original location, but his cabin and the buildings that surround it give a vivid picture of Knoxville in its earliest days. The fort is open from March 1 through December 15, Monday through Saturday 9:30 A.M.–4:30 P.M. Admission is $4 for adults, $3.50 for seniors, $2 for children under 12, and free for those under 6.

Blount Mansion

Blount Mansion, website: www.blount mansion.org, possibly the most significant historic building on this end of the state, introduces the visitor to downtown Knoxville. People who have seen grand houses in other parts of Tennessee sometimes find Blount Mansion a bit disappointing. It's a nice house, to be sure, but a *mansion?*

To understand the importance of this house, one has to put it in context. George Washington

> *Local historian and author Jack Neely claims that the Andrew Johnson Hotel is the only building that has housed Jean-Paul Sartre, Hank Williams, Amelia Earhart, Duke Ellington, Tony Perkins, Liberace, and Sergei Rachmaninoff.*

appointed William Blount governor of the Southwest Territory, and for the first two years Blount operated out of someone else's house at Rocky Mount near Johnson City. When it was time to move his capital to Knoxville, he wanted to do it in style. With this aim, he ordered one of the first frame—i.e., not log—houses west of the mountains, a house with so many glass windows that the Indians who saw it called it the "house with many eyes." Knoxville was so raw at this time that it didn't even have a sawmill capable of producing the lumber; it all had to be shipped from points east.

Andrew Jackson walked in this house, and in an office behind the house, Blount and others wrote the state constitution. The office served as the territorial capital from 1792 through 1796, when Tennessee became a state, with Blount as one of its first two senators.

Today's guests can see original Blount family furnishings, a period garden, and occasional demonstrations of activities likely to have taken place here. Visitors to Blount Mansion also get a two-for-one deal. The visitor's center for the mansion is the 1818 **Craighead-Jackson House,** an example of Federal-style architecture. Both are open all year. March through December, the hours are Tuesday through Saturday 9:30 A.M.–4:30 P.M. and Sunday 12:30 –5 P.M. One-hour tours begin on the hour, with the last tour at 4 P.M. In January and February, the mansion is open Tuesday through Friday only. Visitors may arrange a weekend tour by calling 865/525-2375. Admission is $5 for adults, $4.50 for seniors, and $2.50 for children 6–12.

Other Historic Spots

Crescent Bend, 2728 Kingston Pike, tel. 865/637-3163, is a relatively easy-to-find place that consists of a lovely house, formal gardens, and a collection of 18th- and 19th-century English silver and Federal furniture. The house, known as the **Armstrong-Lockett House,** was built in 1834 as the centerpiece of a 600-acre farm. The terraced gardens step down from the house to the Tennessee River. Crescent Bend is open March through December, Tuesday through Saturday 10 A.M.–4 P.M. and Sunday 1–4 P.M.; there's a small admission fee. The gardens are frequently rented out for weddings and other events, so call ahead during wedding season. Admission, which includes a guided tour, costs $4.50 for adults and $2.50 for kids 12–18. Children under 12 get in free.

Farther west lies the **Confederate Memorial Hall,** 3148 Kingston Pike, tel. 865/522-2371, otherwise known as **Bleak House.** Confederate General James Longstreet used this 15-room house as his headquarters while laying his futile siege to Knoxville. Owned by Chapter 89 of the United Daughters of the Confederacy, the house contains period furniture and artifacts. It's open Tuesday through Friday 1–4 P.M. Admission is $5 for adults, $4 for seniors, $3 for children 12–18, and $1.50 those under 12.

Fort Dickerson sits in a commanding position atop a hill, across the Tennessee River from downtown Knoxville. Union General Ambrose Burnside set up earthworks here, and the remnants of these are about all there is to see today, along with a commanding view of Knoxville. To get there, take Henley Street across the Tennessee River and go up the hill. The entrance to the fort is on the right.

The **Mabry-Hazen House,** 1711 Dandridge Ave., tel. 865/522-8661, website: www.korrnet.org/mabry, built by Joseph A. Mabry in 1858, served as headquarters for both sides during the Civil War. The Hazen family lived here until 1987, and the house contains their original furnishings. Joe Mabry and his son—along with their assailant—died in a famous gunfight on Gay Street in 1882. Mark Twain made fun of this event in *Life on the Mississippi.* Now on the National Register, the house is open Monday through Friday 10 A.M.–4 P.M., weekends 1–5 P.M. Admission is $4 for adults and $2 for children 6 to 12. To get there, go east on Hill Avenue to its intersection with Dandridge Avenue. Then follow the signs.

A two-block walk from the Mabry-Hazen House leads you to the **Confederate Cemetery,** where 1,600 Southern troops rest.

Old Gray Cemetery is Knoxville's contribution to the Victorian cemetery-as-garden school of thought. Its 13 acres, dedicated in 1852, were named for the English poet Thomas Gray, of "Elegy Written in a Country Churchyard" fame. The name became Old Gray when the New Gray Cemetery was opened. This is a wonderful place for a walk. Old Gray's lanes lead through a collection of mausoleums and carved angels, all sheltered by large trees. Tennessee Williams's father is buried here, as is the mother of the woman who wrote Little Lord Fauntleroy, and a cousin of Emily Dickinson's.

> *Tennessee Williams's father is buried here, as is the mother of the woman who wrote* Little Lord Fauntleroy

The address of Old Gray is 543 North Broadway. To get there from downtown, walk north on Gay Street, go left at Emory Place, and cross Broadway at the Lutheran church. For information call 865/522-1424 or visit www.korrnet.org/oldgray.

Blount Mansion may have wowed the people in town, but outside of Knoxville, Francis Ramsey hired an English-born master carpenter and cabinetmaker to design and build a home appropriate for the owner of more than 2,000 acres of land. **Ramsey House,** tel. 865/546-0745, was the result, a stately 1795 Georgian stone house—Knox County's first such structure. Knoxville's first elected mayor was born here, and the W. B. A. Ramsey family inhabited the house until 1866. The house is now filled with period furniture, including two Chippendale chairs original to the mansion. It is open April through December, Tuesday through Saturday 10 A.M.–4 P.M., Sunday 1–4 P.M. Admission is $3.50 for adults and $1.50 for children. To get there, take Exit 394 off I-40, go east on Asheville Highway, then turn right onto Highway 168. Cross Strawberry Plains Pike, then turn left onto Thorngrove Pike. Ramsey House is on the left. Visit it on the Web at www.korrnet.org/ramhse.

John Sevier was the first governor of Tennessee, back in the days when Knoxville was its capital. He lived at **Marble Springs,** tel. 865/573-5508, during this time and until his death in 1815. The house is surrounded by seven period structures and contains Sevier family artifacts. Hours are year-round Tuesday through Saturday 10 A.M.–5 P.M., Sunday 2–5 P.M. When a guide is present, admission is $5 for adults and $3 for children and seniors. When the guide isn't around, the admission price drops by half. To get to the house, take, appropriately enough, John Sevier Highway, either from Highway 441 or Highway 129 near the airport.

CRUISES AND RIDING THE RAILS

The **Tennessee Riverboat Company,** tel. 865/522-4630, website: www.tnriverboat.com, offers both a sight-seeing cruise and a dinner cruise. The former lasts one and a half hours, while the latter takes a leisurely two hours. Seeing the sights costs $10.43 for adults and $6.95 for kids (free for children under 3). Dinner cruises cost $25.99 for adults and $14.74 for kids Sunday through Thursday. On weekend nights, the dinner cruise costs $33.80 and $16.90. The 325-passenger boat is hard to miss on the waterfront; it docks at 300 Neyland Drive. The boat runs April through New Year's Eve.

Three Rivers Rambler is an excursion train that departs from Volunteer Landing and chugs up to where the Holston and French Broad Rivers join to form the Tennessee River. At Asbury Quarry outside of Marbledale, the train makes a brief stop while the locomotive is switched from one end of the train to the other for the return trip to Volunteer Landing. The pride of the line is 1925 Baldwin steam engine, and it runs from April through October on Saturdays, Sundays, and holidays. For adults, the ride costs $16.95 or $19.95, depending on which car one chooses. Children ages – 12 are charged $9.95. For information, call 865/524-9411 or go to www.three riversrambler.com on the Web.

MEDIEVAL MEDITATION

The **St. Johns Labyrinth** is one of a growing number of modern-day versions of ancient and medieval floor patterns. Labyrinth walkers use the paths as places to pray, meditate, or just collect their thoughts. This particular one is a copy of the famous labyrinth in Chartres Cathedral. It is open during business hours at the beautiful 1892 St. Johns Episcopal Cathedral, 413 W. Cumberland Ave. (at the intersection of Walnut Street). James Agee was once a choirboy here. No admission price is charged. For weekend hours call 865/525-7347. Visit the cathedral online at www.stjohnscathedral.org.

Entertainment and Events

ON THE STAGE

The University of Tennessee has a very strong theater department, and Knoxville enjoys excellent productions by professional thespians as well as students. The crown jewel is the **Clarence Brown Theater,** built with funds provided by the alumnus and longtime MGM director. Not surprisingly, the theater contains a first-rate 35mm movie projection system, which often shows foreign and art films. For film titles and times only, call 865/974-5455. Adjacent to the Clarence Brown is the in-the-round **Carousel Theater.** For information about plays and tickets at all UT theaters, go to 1714 Andy Holt Avenue, call 865/974-5161, or visit www.clarence browntheatre.com.

FESTIVALS AND EVENTS

The **Dogwood Arts Festival** gets its name from the many dogwood trees that grace Knoxville. Held in April, the festival offers all manner of performing arts, big-name concerts, athletic activities, and other events all over the city. Knoxville suburbanites position lights under their dogwood blossoms and show off their property at night to hordes of slow-driving admirers along "Dogwood Trails," whose intricacies are marked by pink arrows painted onto streets. For information call 865/637-4561 or v i s i t w w w . d o g woodarts.org.

The **Kuumba Festival** is The largest African-American cultural arts celebration in East Tennessee, a four-day celebration of music, dance, arts, and food. For information, call 865/525-0961.

If visitors somehow miss the Fourth of July, then **Boomsday,** held the night of Labor Day, will catch them up very quickly. Said to be the largest fireworks display in the Southeast, it's held on the waterfront. Call 865/693-1020 for details.

The biggest fair on this end of the state is the **Tennessee Valley Fair,** held every year beginning the first Friday after Labor Day. The usual agricultural contests and exhibitions take place, along with live entertainment, usually of the country music persuasion. To get to the fairgrounds, take the Cherry Street exit off I-40 east of downtown Knoxville, go south, then turn left onto Magnolia. Or just follow the crowd. Admission is $7 for adults and $3 for children 6–11. For further information call 865/215-1470 or visit www.tn valleyfair.org.

SPECTATOR SPORTS

Sports are a very big deal at UT. Neyland Stadium is the third largest stadium in the country, seating more than 104,000 people. The Thompson-Boling arena seats 24,535 for basketball games. UT is a member of the Southeastern Conference, and fans enjoy high-level performances from school teams in 17 NCAA sports. The women's basketball team has one of the more successful programs in the country, coached by Pat Head Summitt.

Tickets, at least for the football games, are hard to come by. If you show up the day of the game, however, all manner of helpful people will emerge from parking lots and dark alleys with tickets to sell. Smart consumers wait until five minutes before kick-off before forking over the cash.

To find out who's playing what, call the **UT Sports Information Office** at 865/974-1212. To buy tickets call 865/656-1200 or 800/332-

THE DEATH OF HANK WILLIAMS

Hank Williams, who wrote so many great country songs and lived life as if it were a country song, spent his last day in Knoxville. As recounted in Colin Escott's *Hank Williams, The Biography*, Williams left Montgomery, Alabama, headed for a New Year's Eve show in Charleston, West Virginia. On December 31, 1951, he rode into Knoxville in a Cadillac driven by an 18-year-old Auburn University freshman, Charles Carr. Bad weather had delayed the two, and in an attempt to get to the show on time they caught a plane at Knoxville's airport, but a snowstorm forced the plane to turn back.

Realizing they couldn't make the Charleston show, Williams and his young driver checked into the Andrew Johnson Hotel on Gay Street. Williams had to be carried to his room. Long plagued by back pain that was exacerbated by long car trips, he found relief in morphine shots. That night, allegedly suffering from violent hiccups, he found a doctor who was willing to administer two shots of the opiate and pronounce him fit to travel.

Porters carried an inanimate Williams back out to his Cadillac, and he and Carr set off at 10:45 P.M. up Highway 11 West. Carr drove quickly and was pulled over for speeding near the town of Blaine. The arresting officer expressed concern about the comatose figure in the back of the car but was assured that Williams had been sedated.

Carr discovered that Williams was dead after pulling off the road in Oak Hill, West Virginia. Biographer Escott suggests that Williams died either in Knoxville or shortly after leaving town. His last single, "I'll Never Get Out of This World Alive," reached number one on the country charts. Williams was 29 years old when he died.

VOLS from anywhere in Tennessee. Or try the website: www.utsports.com.

NIGHTLIFE

Knoxville manages to offer something for just about everyone. If you're looking for an alcohol-fueled night out, here's a handy short list, sorted by the tenor of the evening you can expect to experience. These reviews were compiled by Adrienne Martini, entertainment editor and gal about town for *Metro Pulse*. Available free all over town, it's the best source for what's happening.

Danceteria

Knoxville isn't the center of the clubbing universe, but **Fiction,** 214 W. Jackson Ave., tel. 865/329-0039, website: www.fictionfx.com, is as close as we come. Pounding bass and drums—as well as a seriously stocked bar and flashy light show—will keep your head spinning even if you never venture out onto the dance floor. A word of caution: Fiction has a strict dress code that warns dancers to dress "funky, not junky." However, costumes like that little French maid number you've had hanging in the closet are encouraged.

Bluesy and Boozy

Something in the Tennessee soil has grown healthy blues scenes on both ends of the state. While Memphis may win in terms of sheer volume and variety, Knoxville has one truly remarkable club, **Sassy Ann's,** 820 N. Fourth Ave., tel. 865/525-5839, which always has something blue going on. Located in a restored Victorian house in a historic neighborhood, this multi-story club is a comfortable place to catch either a homegrown or nationally known acts. Come on Sundays and you might get to blow your own horn . . . or harmonica.

Diver Down

While the Strip—the stretch of Cumberland Avenue that fronts the UT campus—is best known for its cookie-cutter bars, the **Long Branch,** 1848 Cumberland Ave., tel. 865/546-9914, is the best place to find something just a little bit more dangerous. Curl up with a cold longneck in one of the many dark corners and wait to see what will unfold in this great dive. A brash band might be rocking it out upstairs or a bunch of bikers might be tearing it up downstairs—you just never know. And that's part of its charm.

Smells Like Indie Spirit

Get soaked in the sweat of some of the hippest, hottest indie bands in the country at **The Pilot Light,** 106 E. Jackson Ave., tel. 865/524-8188, website: www.thepilotlight.com. It's loud. It's dark. It's small. And it's perfect for catching every last breath the singer (or the T-shirted guy next to you) utters. On Sunday nights, check out the Light's selection of indie films, which can range from an obscure Buñuel to an even more obscure Bresson. But while the Pilot Light's offerings may seem a bit hipper-than-thou, the atmosphere usually isn't.

Rainbow Rooms

A night at one of these gay clubs is one of the most fun diversions in town—no matter what your orientation. **The Electric Ballroom,** 1213 Western Ave., tel. 865/525-6724, is the granddaddy of the scene yet still young at heart. From the huge dance floor to the requisite drag shows to karaoke, the ballroom can meet almost any need. **The Rainbow Club,** 131 S. Central St., tel. 865/522-6610, the new guy on the scene, offers a more casual vibe. Its Lipstick Lounge, a small room off the main dance floor and separated from the hordes by some fabulous curtains, hosts some of the highest-energy drag shows around, as well as nationally known divas including former Weathergirl Martha Wash.

Adventure in High Cheese

Michael's, 7049 Kingston Pike, tel. 865/588-2455, isn't for everybody—but if you're looking for some action, this West Knoxville nightspot is the best place to make your move. Sure, you can groove to '70s and '80s-era dance tunes, but the prime activity is scoping out Mr. or Ms. Goodbar. You can simply smell the hormones wafting through the cologne-clogged air.

Beer Bash

Barley's Taproom and Pizzeria, 200 E. Jackson, tel. 865/521-0092, is the place to plant your rear on a stool. With well over 20 different beers on tap (and dozens more in bottle form), you're sure to find something to quaff. Most nights Barley's offers up some of the better acoustic acts around, and there's never a cover. While the room can sometimes get a bit clogged with young hippies, there's always space out on the patio.

For a more authentic, low-key, blue-ish-collar Knoxville experience, **MacLeod's,** 501 Market St., tel. 865/546-2103, can't be beat. This small, smoky bar is where all our movers and shakers move and shake when they want to have a cold one or three after office hours.

Frat Party

The Strip—Cumberland Avenue at the UT campus—is the place to go to tank up before the big game or to drown your post-scrimmage sorrows. But for the college and post-college crowd with cars, **The Spot,** 6915 Kingston Pike, tel. 865/588-8138, is like a second home—one with more beer, presumably. The bands generally are decent and draw the set list from a large repertoire of cover tunes. Seriously—you never can get enough of "American Pie" or Dave Matthews, can you?

High-Brow Highballs

For the martini and cigar crowd, either the West Knoxville **Baker-Peters Jazz Club,** 9000 Kingston Pike, tel. 865/690-8110, or the Old City **Lucille's,** 100 N. Central St., tel. 865/546-3742, should toothpick your olive. Baker-Peters wins in terms of historical import—its building housed an infirmary during the Civil War—but Lucille's frequently gets the crème de la crème of the university's musicians, including the world-renowned Donald Brown. Either way, you can fulfill your Rat Pack dreams.

Where to Stay

BED-AND-BREAKFASTS AND INNS

Hotel St. Oliver, 407 Union Ave., tel. 888/809-7241 or 865/521-0050, contains 28 rooms filled with antiques and reproduction antiques. It's located in a downtown structure just off Market Square. When local leading lady Patricia Neal comes to town, this is where she stays. Rates range from $55 to $180.

The **Maple Grove Inn,** on 16 acres west of Knoxville at 8800 Westland Drive, tel. 865/690-9565 or 800/645-0713, website: www.maple groveinn.com, is a 1799 house whose eight rooms all offer private baths. Two master suites feature fireplaces and whirlpool baths. Guests have access to a swimming pool and tennis court. Rates run $125–250 on weekends and $95–200 during the week for two people. Dinner is available for guests Thursday through Saturday nights.

Maplehurst Inn, 800 W. Hill Ave., tel. 800/451-1562, website: www.maplehurstinn.com, sits discretely in a riverside neighborhood between downtown Knoxville and the University of Tennessee. More like a small European hotel than a bed-and-breakfast, this place is small enough to allow you to enjoy the interesting guests and large enough to let you comfortably escape the bores. Eleven rooms with private baths on four separate floors overlook the Tennessee River. Rates range from $79 to $150 per night.

Masters Manor Inn, 1909 Cedar Ln., tel. 877/866-2667 or 865/219-9888, website: www.mastersmanor.com, is located in the Fountain City neighborhood in North Knoxville, in a mansion that once anchored the Karnes plantation. The six rooms have private baths, private phones, and modem ports. Rates range from $80 to $200.

Mimosa Bed and Breakfast, 512 Mimosa Ave., tel. 865/577-1744, offers two guest rooms that share a bath. Mimosa Avenue is on the Smokies side of the Tennessee River. Rates are $95 per night.

Mountain Vista, on the road to the airport yet close to UT at 3809 Vista Road, tel. 865/970-3771, consists of a seven-acre estate and a big porch looking straight at the Smoky Mountains. Six full bedrooms have private baths, and the inn offers access to a heated pool—glassed in for all-year use—as well as a laundry. The rate is $120 for two people.

Wayside Manor Bed and Breakfast lies south of Knoxville in the little town of Rockford at 4009 Old Knoxville Highway, tel. 865/970-4823 or 800/675-4823. The 13 rooms here include a separate two-bedroom cottage, Dove's Nest, as well as a separate five-bedroom house, Eagles Lodge, which comes with fireplaces and in-room whirlpool baths. Outside are a tennis court, swimming pool, and creek, plus spots for shuffleboard, croquet, basketball, and volleyball. Rates range $89–225.

HOTELS AND MOTELS

Like most larger cities, Knoxville is blessed with the usual national chain hotels downtown—Hilton, Hyatt, and Radisson—and the usual motels stretched along the interstates. Keep in mind that hotel rooms are very difficult to find when the University of Tennessee plays a home football game. For a list of weekends to avoid, visit www.govols.com/mens/football.

CAMPING

North of Town

Open all year, the 98-site **Fox Inn Campground,** tel. 865/494-9386, has all the amenities you'll need. To get there, take the Highway 61 exit off I-75 and go about a quarter-mile east.

In Heiskell, **Jellystone Park Camp-Resorts,** 9514 Diggs Gap Rd., tel. 865/938-6600 or 800/BET-YOGI, offers 77 sites and everything from a pool to a restaurant. It's open year-round.

Escapees Raccoon Valley, 908 Raccoon Valley Rd., also in Heiskell, tel. 865/947-9776, has 76 sites plus a pool and laundry. The park is open all year. Take Exit 117 off I-75, then go west on Raccoon Valley Road. See www

.resortparks.com/members/resorts/493.htm for more information.

East of Town

The following campgrounds are quite a ways out of Knoxville, but they strike a good compromise for those wanting to see K-town and the touristy areas of the Smokies.

Knoxville East KOA, 241 KOA Dr., tel. 865/933-6393, offers 200 sites and is open all year; this place has all the amenities. Take Exit 407 off I-40 and go north. The website is www.koakampgrounds.com/where/tn/42159.htm.

Smoky Mountain Campground, tel. 865/933-8312 or 800/684-2267, weighs in with 246 sites and is open all year with all the amenities. It's off I-40 at Exit 407. Go south on Highway 66 for about 100 yards, then drive a half mile east on Foretravel Drive.

Food

Knoxville has more good places to eat than the rest of East Tennessee combined. The following lists only a sampling, and an idiosyncratic one at that. Note that barbecue places warrant their own category. These reviews were compiled by "Ally Carte," the restaurant critic for *Metro Pulse,* Knoxville's weekly newspaper. For her latest culinary opinions, visit www.metropulse.com.

BARBECUE

Even though Knoxville's dining scene has grown to include all manner of fancy cuisine, our hearts still hold a special place for large slabs of meat, slow-cooked and expertly sauced. If you need just a quick hit of the 'cue, stop by **Buddy's Bar-B-Q,** a little chain that, like kudzu, has taken over most of the city. With locations at 121 West End Avenue, tel. 865/675-4366; 8402 Kingston Pike, tel. 865/691-0088; 3700 E. Magnolia Avenue, tel. 865/523-3550; 4500 N. Broadway, tel. 865/687-2959; 4401 Chapman Highway, tel. 865/579-1747; and 5806 Kingston Pike, tel. 865/588-0528, it's sure to be near wherever you may find yourself. Be sure to get a side of the green-onion-spiked hush puppies.

Calhoun's, with locations at 400 Neyland Drive, tel. 865/673-3355; 10020 Kingston Pike, tel. 865/673-3444; 4550 City Park Drive, tel. 865/673-3366; and 6515 Kingston Pike, tel., 865/673-3377, serves much more than barbecue, but it is their ribs that just keep sticking to ours. Plus, Calhoun's brews its own fabulous beers. Named after local touchstones like Thun-der Road, they're the perfect way to wash down ribs, fried catfish, or white bean chili. All locations are open seven days a week for lunch and dinner. The original Neyland Drive location is right on the waterfront and has one of the city's best views.

Corky's, 260 N. Peter's Rd., tel. 865/690-3137, may be one of the best things Knoxville has imported from Memphis. Here you can sample their dry-rub style of 'cue, based on a multi-spice powder that's rubbed into the meat before slow cooking. Try the pulled pork sandwiches if you want a small glimpse of barbecue heaven. Corky's is open for lunch and dinner seven days a week.

Spooky's, 130 Northshore Dr., tel. 865/330-0110, is where the locals go (and take out-of-town guests) when they just can't resist the call of slow-cooked, rich and smoky ribs and soul food. It's open for lunch and dinner every day except Sunday, when owner Clark "Spooky" Frazier gets to have his day of rest.

TOP OF THE HEAP

Mango, 5803 Kingston Pike, tel. 865/584-5053, an upscale, urbane, and sleek eatery, proves that Knoxville has grown into a real live city that welcomes excursions from our down-home norms. Open for dinner every night except Sunday, Mango brings fusion fare to the art-drenched Bearden area, with dishes like grilled pork tenderloin with potato pancakes in an espresso-chipotle barbecue sauce or calamari tempura with a ginger-apricot glaze and a green curry chutney.

Just down the street from Mango is **By the Tracks Bistro,** 5200 Kingston Pike, tel. 865/558-9500. While this is a new location for By the Tracks—it used to be housed in a very intimate building next to the rail lines—the excellent food and stellar service haven't changed at all. Expect to be treated like royalty at this cozy yet well-appointed restaurant and don't forget to save room for the masterful and rich crème brûlée.

The place to celebrate is the **Jockey Club,** located in the L&N Station at World's Fair Park, tel. 865/523-9990. Owner David Duncan has transformed this formerly dilapidated 1905 train station into an amazing restaurant, filled with both grand architecture and fine European-inspired cuisine. The wine list reads like a pedigree, the wait staff is impeccable, and the food will make your tongue sing. Nothing is spared to make a night at The Jockey Club memorable and entertaining. Multi-course dinners, which can take up to three glorious hours, are offered Tuesday through Saturday. Reservations are required.

Not to be outdone in terms of elegance and high cuisine is the more established **Orangery,** 5412 Kingston Pike, tel. 865/588-2964, Knoxville's first multi-star restaurant. Chef David Pinckney has created sumptuous dinner dishes—olive oil poached halibut with saffron-infused sun-dried tomato sauce, grilled buffalo tenderloin with foie gras and a zinfandel reduction—that are inspired without being too stuffy. The Orangery is also the place to scope out local celebrities, like Mary Costa and Patricia Neal, and to overhear the latest dish about politicos' peccadilloes.

Old high-end haunts are still doing quite well, both in terms of business and quality. **The Copper Cellar** at 1807 Cumberland Avenue, tel. 865/673-3411, and in West Knoxville at 7316 Kingston Pike, tel. 865/673-3422, is still the most popular place to go for a good slab of prime rib or a well-aged steak and all the traditional fixings. Both locations are open for lunch and dinner seven days a week, for those who want to experience simple and good food without all the folderol of a gourmet establishment.

The **Regas Brothers Cafe,,** 6901 Kingston Pike, tel. 865/588-5358, open for lunch and dinner seven days a week, offers small plates like cornmeal-crusted oysters, big salads, and grilled meats in a fresh, modern atmosphere.

EASIER ON THE WALLET

Knoxville is chock full of eateries that serve excellent food for moderate prices. One of the newest entries is **City Brew,** 414 S. Gay St., tel. 865/292-BREW, the perfect place to grab a bite before a show at the Tennessee or Bijou, or a night checking out Old City's clubs. City Brew, as the name implies, is primarily a brewpub, and while the beers are well balanced and tasty, the food also deserves some attention. From the inventive salad dressings to homemade veggie and non-veggie burgers to spicy pork tenderloin, City Brew's lunch and dinner offerings should please every palate.

Riverside Tavern, 950 Volunteer Landing Ln., tel. 865/637-0303, is one of the trickiest restaurants to get to (hint: go straight down the hill from the Women's Basketball Hall of Fame) but is well worth the navigational headache. As the name would imply, it's smack on the banks of the Tennessee River, and the food is just as good as the view. Any of the offerings from the rotisserie grill or the wood-fired oven are sure to please. The tavern is open seven days a week for lunch and dinner.

Knoxville, being a fair hike from most major bodies of fishable waters, isn't really a seafood town. But **Chesapeake's,** 500 Henley St., tel. 865/673-3433, is the place to get fresh fish, which is flown in weekly. The atmosphere is reminiscent of the basement of an upscale Maryland restaurant, complete with sailing-themed objets d'art and the occasional drift net. But the food, from crab cakes to salmon fillets, is cooked to perfection. Open for lunch and dinner daily.

If steak is your passion, run (don't walk) to **Ye Olde Steak House,** 6838 Chapman Hwy., tel. 865/577-9328, located deep in the heart of South Knoxville. The Steak House has been a haven for meat purists since 1968 and knows just how to flame-grill your cut to absolute perfection. Open for dinner every night.

For the best burger you've ever had, head to

North Knoxville's **Litton's,** 2803 Essary Dr., tel. 865/688-0429, located in Fountain City just across from the duck pond. Bring the family for lunch or dinner, any day of the week, and try your best to leave room for some equally yummy desserts.

While Knoxvillians love traditional, meat-based fare, there's also a growing appreciation for meatless cuisine. While the menu at **Sunspot,** 1909 Cumberland Ave., tel. 865/637-4663, isn't strictly vegetarian, it is full of inventive meat-free dishes and some of the most interesting tabletops you're likely to find in the area. Ask for the Elvis table. Sunspot is open daily for lunch and dinner.

Another entry into our lexicon of more health-conscious dining spots is downtown's **Tomato Head,** 12 Market Square, tel. 865/637-4067, home of the best pizzas in town (try one with owner Mahasti's basil-heavy pesto). Unique sandwiches include the Cheddar Head, a delightful combination of marinated tofu, melted cheddar cheese, grilled onions, fresh tomato, and crisp spinach, served on a homemade wheat bun. Tomato Head is open for lunch Monday through Saturday and dinner Tuesday through Saturday.

Knoxville also has a thriving Asian community and some thriving Asian restaurants. The **Korea House,** 1645 Downtown West Blvd., tel. 865/693-3615, serves over 20 authentic Korean dishes, including *bulgogi,* a marinated rib eye thinly sliced and cooked to order on your personal tabletop grill. Korea House is open for lunch and dinner every day except Monday, with a special buffet on Sundays.

Tomo, 112 S. Central Ave., tel. 865/546-3308, is a Japanese sushi bar located in the heart of the Old City. Along with the expertly prepared rice and fish are several tempura dishes that are simply delightful. Tomo is open for dinner every day except Monday.

If you're looking for romance, **Naples,** 5500 Kingston Pike, tel., 865/584-5033, is the place to take that special someone. Cozy booths line the walls of this intimate Italian place with a well-stocked wine cellar. Image you and your sweetie slurping a strand of spaghetti like the pups from *Lady and the Tramp.* Open for dinner seven nights a week and for lunch on weekdays.

If you'd rather get to your lover's heart with some hands-on dining, Old City's **Melting Pot,** 111 N. Central Ave., tel. 865/971-5400, is the city's only fondue place. Spear a tasty cube of bread and run it through some melted cheese or jab a tender chunk of chicken for a trip through some bubbling court bouillon. Don't forget to stick around for the dessert course, a chocolate fondue so rich and delicious that you'll fall in love—with the food, if not each other. Open for dinner daily.

Not to be missed is **King Tut's,** 4123 Martin Mill Pike, 865/573-6021, the best place in town to get dinner and a show. While the great menu is mostly Middle Eastern and features a nightly theme (Egyptian Night on Wednesdays is usually most interesting and scrumptious), it is owner Mo Girgis's floorshow that really makes the place memorable. You just never know whether he'll be egging you to toss Nerf balls or to join him in a chorus of "Rocky Top" during your meal. Open for breakfast, lunch, and dinner Monday through Saturday.

DOWNRIGHT REASONABLE

If you're feeling a bit cash poor, Knoxville has plenty of cheap-but-good eats to choose from—and not just those that are under Golden Arches.

For something both exotic and inexpensive, head to the **Falafel Hut,** 601 James Agee St., tel. 865/522-4963, located near the UT campus in the Fort Sanders area. A falafel wrap, filled with deep-fried chickpea and garlic patties, tomato, lettuce, and a spicy yogurt sauce, is the best use for $3 you'll find. While the service can be a bit distracted and the decor minimal at best, you just can't beat the made-with-care food. Open Monday through Saturday for lunch and dinner.

Indian food, with all of its curries and dips, is often a great way to eat well for little. Knoxville has two restaurants to meet your tandoori needs. **Kasmir,** 711 17th St., tel. 865/524-1982, is close to campus and does a thriving take-out business. It's open for lunch Monday through Saturday and for dinner Monday through Sunday, with a special buffet on weekends. **Sitar,** 6004

Kingston Pike, tel. 865/588-1828, is located in West Knox. It does a thriving lunch buffet business and is open for lunch and dinner daily. Both restaurants use fresh, natural ingredients as well as lush spices that enhance every dish that comes out of the kitchen.

When you want to feel well taken care of and be fed only the finest, healthiest (but never dreary) dishes available, head downtown to **Crescent Moon,** 705 Market St., tel. 865/637-9700. Every day brings a new mashed potato special that is sure to please, as well as innovative rollups that will stick to your ribs. Try the smoked turkey with creamy dill sauce or the Fungi and Mold, a

tofu and portobello mushroom offering. Open for lunch on weekdays.

When you're ready to chuck the diet, head to the **Marble Slab,** 4835 Kingston Pike, tel. 865/766-0290. Here you'll find the finest in frozen desserts. Waffle cones (choose from vanilla sugar, vanilla cinnamon, and honey wheat) are baked fresh in the store, and the ice cream comes with your choice of mix-ins, including nuts, candies, and fresh fruit. Special flavors roll out each season, and it's not Thanksgiving until you've had pumpkin ice cream with graham cracker mix-ins in a cinnamon cone. Open from noon to at least 10 P.M. daily.

More Practicalities

SHOPPING

As in most cities, Knoxville's big stores have fled to shopping malls. In their place, however, have sprung up interesting communities of shops. Try the Old City area and Homberg Place near the corner of Kingston Pike and Homberg Place, west of the University of Tennessee.

Fine Arts and Crafts

Jim Gray is perhaps the best-known artist in this part of the state. His oils and drawings depict seascapes, Tennessee landscapes, people, wildflowers, and birds. His bronze statues include one of Dolly Parton in Sevierville and one of Andrew Johnson in Greeneville. The **Jim Gray Gallery,** 5615 Kingston Pike, tel. 865/588-7102, website: www.jimgraygallery.com, offers works in a variety of media from this talented artist.

In addition to sugary creations, **The Candy Factory** in the World's Fair Park contains several galleries.

The **Victorian Houses** at the corner of 11th Street and Laurel Avenue also have shops containing original arts and fine crafts. Given the changing tastes of the public and the vagaries of the artistic existence, shops come and go, but the quality remains high.

West of downtown is **Hanson Gallery Fine Art & Craft,** 5706 Kingston Pike, tel. 865/584-

6097, website: www.hansongallery.com, offering oils, Thomas Pradzynski's Parisian street scenes, serigraphs, lithographs, and gifts.

In Farragut, the **Homespun Crafts and Antique Mall,** 11523 Kingston Pike, tel. 865/671-3444, is a large assembly of artists and dealers selling antiques, jewelry, pottery, and all manner of creations. It's located near Exit 373 off I-40/75.

Other Notable Shops

Yee-Haw Industries, 413 South Gay St., tel. 865/522-1812, website: www.yeehawindustries.com, uses letterpress, a type of printing seldom used anymore, to crank out wonderful folk art posters. Typical is *Hank Williams Secret Theory #29,* which reads as follows: "Ole Hank was a drinking man. I heard stories that he had a hollow leg. They say that his woman cheated on him. I think that if Hank was around today he would probably play jazz and he would probably kick Jr. in the ass. He was a man of double vision. He saw the light brother amen."

Book Eddy, 2537 Chapman Hwy., tel. 865/573-9959, website: www.bookeddy.com, is a book lover's dream come true—85,000-plus used books on every subject imaginable. It's located one-half mile south of downtown on Henley Street/Chapman Highway.

If you're looking for something old in the Old City, **Jackson Antique Marketplace,** 111 E. Jackson Ave., tel. 865/521-6704, offers some 24,000 square feet of antiques.

SERVICES AND INFORMATION

The **Gateway Regional Visitor Center,** tel. 800/727-8045 or 865/523-7263, is the best place to get tourist information. Exit the interstate at either Henley Street (Exit 388) or the James White Parkway. Once you're off the interstate, just follow the signs. The Knoxville Convention and Visitors Center maintains a website at www.knoxville.org.

Metro Pulse is a free weekly paper that keeps close tabs on the entertainment scene. You can find it all over town or at www.metropulse.com.

East Side of the Smokies

The towns on this end of the park afford the traveler a chance to see beautiful countryside and to catch a glimpse of rural Tennessee and North Carolina—without enduring hordes of fellow tourists. An excellent way to travel in this region is via Highway 25/70, from Asheville downstream along the French Broad River. This beautiful river cuts through the Appalachian Mountains from east to west. Until the coming of the railroad, this valley was the main route for wagons and drovers through the mountains. Along the way, you'll pass through Del Rio, the home of a real life opera singer and as a fictional teacher who continues to inspire people.

For visitors approaching the Smokies down I-81, Greeneville is a good place to get off the interstate and begin experiencing the real Tennessee. This town was the home of Andrew Johnson, the 17th president of the United States.

It has an excellent museum devoted to his life and times.

Highway 321 from Greeneville to Newport and then to Cosby is a delightful drive past prosperous farms and apple orchards. Visitors can stop and buy whatever fruits or vegetables are in season. The hamlet of Cosby offers hikers access to the park without traffic jams. Dandridge, northwest of Newport, was named for one president's wife and saved by another first lady.

All these towns offer hospitality and a down-home feel that is increasingly rare in this part of the world. They are a good way to begin or end a Smokies vacation.

HARTFORD

At Exit 447 on I-40, Hartford is the first Tennessee town that the traveler from North Carolina encounters. Once a logging center, Hartford is now enjoying a revival thanks to white-water

© GREAT SMOKY MOUNTAINS NATIONAL PARK

rafting on the Big Pigeon River. The town is also the home of **Mountain Mama's,** a legendary stop for through hikers on the nearby Appalachian Trail. It retains the feel of an old-time general store and serves three meals every day.

Hikers often leave the trail and detour here for a meal, a shower, and a bunk. They pick up packages and generally take it easy. Most are happy to talk about their trek to visitors. Call 423/625-1073 for more information.

Nearby is the **French Broad Outpost Ranch,** a dude ranch offering horseback riding, rafting, and other activities. Eight-day packages are available, as are three- and four-day stays. Call 800/995-7678 or visit www.frenchbroadriver.com for more information.

For a list of rafting companies, see "Rafting in the Mountains" in Chapter 2.

Exit 451 is where the fabled Appalachian Trail crosses I-40. It is also the home of **Standing Bear Farm,** tel. 423/487-0014, located 100 yards from the trail and adjacent to national forest land. Guests can choose from a 12-bed bunkhouse or a more private cabin that sleeps four. The emphasis here is on old-time, rustic living, with woodstoves and outhouses for toilets. There are no Internet connections here. Guests should call ahead for directions.

COSBY

This small community was once considered "the Moonshine Capital of the World," a distinction that locals are only now beginning to acknowledge with pride. Cosby retains a small-town feel that long ago departed from places such as Gatlinburg and Pigeon Forge. This is a good place to stay—close enough to enjoy the national park—yet far from the hordes of people.

A One-of-a-Kind Place

Halfway between Cosby and Newport stands **The Fort,** tel. 423/487-2544, a singular establishment up Dark Hollow Road, an address right out of a bluegrass song. Consisting primarily of a doublewide mobile home on the side of a hill, The Fort, a.k.a Fort Marx, is alleged to occasionally serve the product that made Cosby fa-

EAST SIDE OF THE SMOKIES HIGHLIGHTS

The Fort, near Cosby: A one-of-a-kind drinking establishment that will probably never pay dues to a chamber of commerce.

Rafting on the Big Pigeon River: The whitest water you will see in Tennessee this side of the Ocoee River. Kids love it.

The Front Porch: This restaurant on Highway 321 halfway between Cosby and Newport is perhaps the only place in the state where patrons can eat portobello mushroom steaks and listen to live bluegrass music.

Tinsley-Bible Drugs, Dandridge: Enjoy lunch where you half expect to see Barney Fife wooing Thelma Lou in an adjoining booth.

Ramp Festival: Two days later, others will know you've been there.

mous. "Good to the last drop" takes on a whole new meaning here. Hamburgers, fried rabbit, and other delectables are available—the specialty is Moonshine Cherries. The Fort is open every day except Sunday from 4 P.M. "until everyone goes home."

To get to the Fort from Cosby, go north on Highway 321/32 to Wilton Springs Road. Turn right and drive one mile to Dark Hollow Road, which goes off to the right just before a bridge. Drive one mile and look up the hill on the right. And don't get in any arguments inside.

Sights

The first stop in Cosby, particularly for music lovers, should be **Musicrafts,** tel. 423/487-5543. To get there from I-40, take Exit 440 and follow Highway 321/73 to the intersection with Highway 32. Take Highway 32 for less than a mile and turn right into a small driveway. Founded almost 40 years ago by Lee and Gene Schilling, this very rustic center publishes books, releases folk music recordings, and distributes the music of others. It also sells dulcimers, hammered dulcimers, and other instruments. The center is open daily from 10 A.M. until "5 or so" and may

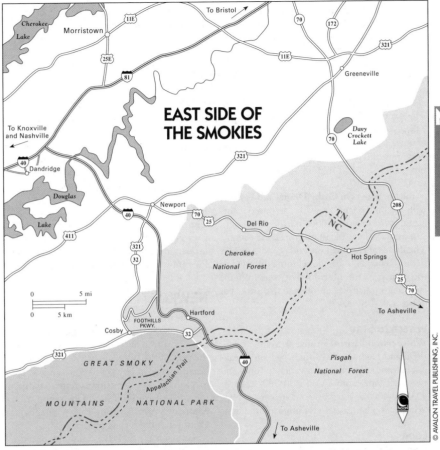

EAST SIDE OF THE SMOKIES

EAST SIDE

close during cold winter weekends.

Cosby is also home to several apple orchards. **Carver's Orchard,** on Highway 321 about 3.5 miles beyond the Cosby post office, tel. 423/487-2419, grows more than 100 varieties of apples—old favorites as well as exotics such as Ginger Gold, Jena Gold, and Fuji. Apple harvesting begins in June and extends well into the fall. Visitors are welcome to watch cider being pressed, taste it, and buy apples, honey, molasses, pumpkins, and Indian corn. Carver's is open seven days a week year-round.

Deerfoot Quilts, located in a log building at 3892 Highway 321, tel. 423/487-3866, offers high-quality quilts—usually 80 to 100 locally made ones are in the store at any given time—plus clothing and quilting supplies.

Festivals

Perhaps the best time to visit Cosby is during one of its festivals. The **Dulcimer and Harp Festival,** run by Musicrafts, begins the second Friday in June. Other, smaller gatherings are held Memorial Day, the Fourth of July, and Labor Day weekends. Each takes place on Saturday and is characterized by traditional mountain music, covered-dish meals, old-time dancing, and other events. For information call 423/487-5543.

EAST SIDE

The longest-running gathering in Cosby is the **Ramp Festival,** a celebration of the ramp, a pungent, onionlike plant has been described as "the gift that keeps giving"—in one's breath and through one's pores. Ramps are eaten in omelets, straight, or as side dishes along with barbecue and chicken. The festival, held the first Sunday in May, is a one-day affair consisting of music, crafts, selection of the Maid of Ramps, and plenty of handpicked bluegrass music. Call 423/487-3492 or 423/623-5410.

> *Ramps, the pungent, onion-like plant is "the gift that keeps giving"— in one's breath and through one's pores.*

Fall brings the **On Cosby Drama and Festival,** with local musicians, fireworks, an outdoor theatrical performance, antique tractors, and crafts. The music includes bluegrass, gospel, and country. The drama, performed on Friday and Saturday nights, centers on a topic seldom addressed in these parts: the forced removal of locals from the land that now makes up the national park. For details, call 423/487-5700.

Where to Stay

Whisperwood Farm, located at Middle Creek Road and Highway 321, offers bed-and-breakfast accommodations and a variety of one- and two-bedroom cabins. Call 800/962-2246 or 423/487-4000 or visit www.gocabins.com or www.whisperwoodretreat.com for more information.

Food

Cosby Barbecue Pit, on Highway 321 near the Cosby post office, tel. 423/487-5438, offers ribs, pork barbecue, hamburgers, and steaks. It's open seven days a week except December through March, when it is open only on weekends.

The Front Porch, on Highway 321 halfway between Cosby and Newport, tel. 423/487-2875, is worth a visit all by itself. This restaurant features a trained culinarian—a rarity in these parts—and this evidences itself in portobello mushroom steaks, rib-eye steak, and dry ribs. Patrons can also enjoy live bluegrass and occasionally blues. Open only Friday through Sunday for lunch and dinner, the restaurant also serves enchiladas, chimichangas, and other Mexican dishes, as well

as vegetarian versions thereof. Italian food is available, too. Brown bagging is permitted.

Get seats early for dinner on Friday and Saturday; the music takes off at 8:30 P.M. and soars until 10:30 or 11. There is no cover charge, although diners are expected to order at least $6 worth of food, and the band is very likely to pass the hat. Eating ribs while listening to bluegrass is about as down-home as you can get. But note that Sunday night's atmosphere is more akin to that of a coffeehouse. The music begins at 6:30 P.M.

Information

The best website for information on Cosby is www.cockecounty.com. Another source of information is the Smoky Mountain Regional Information Center at 423/487-5700.

NEWPORT

Anyone who has eaten canned vegetables or made pasta sauce from canned tomatoes has probably had an inadvertent brush with Newport. About the turn of the last century, the Stokely family, headquartered in Newport, began canning tomatoes and shipping them downstream to the growing cities of Knoxville and Chattanooga. The company grew so strong that it bought Van Camp, an Indiana food producer.

Although the Stokelys mainly produced comestibles, one branch of the family turned to food for the mind. The late James Stokely, son of the first president of the family firm, married Wilma Dykeman of Asheville, North Carolina. Together they wrote books about the causes of racism and about people who worked to overcome it. On her own, Dykeman published a series of novels, as well as a history of Tennessee. Her writings, both fiction and nonfiction, illuminate the state in a manner that few writers can match. Jim Stokely, their son, continued the literary tradition as coeditor of *An Encyclopedia of East Tennessee.*

As in Cosby, Newport and surrounding Cocke County used to be home to entrepreneurs who

MOONSHINE

The little town of Cosby claims to be the Moonshine Capital of the World, a title disputed by places in North Carolina, Virginia, and who knows where else.

What is clear, however, is that a great deal of illegal whiskey was distilled around here. Locals claim that merchants in nearby Newport sold more canning jars than anywhere else in the country—and that those jars were not used for storing homemade tomato juice.

Cocke County residents, many of them of Scotch-Irish descent, had made whiskey ever since their arrival, but demand for the fiery product grew during Prohibition, which began in 1919. The moonshiners could make all the whiskey they wanted, but getting it to thirsty cities was harder. Two developments in the 1930s made things much easier: good highways and fast cars.

Cocke County was an excellent place to make 'shine. Heavily vegetated hollows provided cover, and each one had a clear-running stream to provide water as well as a cooling function for the distillery. The formula was simple: Combine 100 pounds of cornmeal with 50 or so pounds of sugar in a barrel. Fill it with water. Throw in yeast. The yeast devoured the sugar and corn, transforming them into alcohol. Depending on the time of year, this "mash" was ready to distill in four or five days.

The mash was poured a batch at a time into a distillery—known as a still—and heated by a fire until the alcohol became vapor. (Water boils at 212° Fahrenheit, while alcohol vaporizes at a lower temperature.) The vapors were channeled though a condenser—often a coil of copper tubing surrounded by cold creek water—where they turned back into a liquid. That liquid was moonshine, a fiery drink un-mellowed, as are commercial whiskeys such as Jack Daniel's, by spending years in a wooden barrel.

The art of moonshining was to regulate the heat to maximize the purity of the alcohol coming out of the condenser. Sophisticated stills used steam pipes to heat the mash. A 50-gallon barrel of mash could produce six gallons of white lightning. The bigger the still, the more whiskey could be made, but going big time also increased the chances of getting caught.

Even after the end of Prohibition, agents of the federal Bureau of Alcohol, Tobacco, and Firearms—known to Appalachians as revenue men or revenuers—diligently worked to combat moonshining. Legal whiskey generated a vast amount of federal tax dollars, and illegal spirits cut into Washington's income stream.

However, Cocke County was a difficult place for revenuers to work. In a small place like Cosby, any out-of-towner instantly fell under suspicion. And the local population was ill inclined to inform on friends and relatives in the whiskey business.

Oddly enough, the creation of Great Smoky Mountains National Park was a boon to the moonshiners. Having a still on one's own farm was a risky venture; it was hard to claim with a straight face that you didn't know it was there. Locating a still in remote corners of the park, however, made things easier. If the revenuers closed in, the crew could literally head for the hills and escape arrest.

Manufacturing the whiskey was just half of the equation; the next challenge was getting it to market. Revenuers often had the upper hand here; they knew roughly where the moonshine was coming from and where it was going, so all they had to do was apprehend the 'shine when it came through.

But moonshine runners had all manner of tricks. A fast car and nerves of steel were a good start. A heavily loaded car will sit lower than usual, a sure tip-off to federal agents, so backwoods mechanics would reinforce the springs to compensate. Some runners went the slow route; they put their precious cargo in a beat-up truck under a load of corn or manure. Getting caught often meant going to prison, but a successful run guaranteed much-needed cash.

Cocke County whiskey made its way to Knoxville, Asheville, and sometimes Atlanta. *Thunder Road,* the 1958 Robert Mitchum movie and song about running moonshine, had the still in Kentucky, but it could have originated in Cosby just as easily.

could transform corn into a much more portable and potable product. At one time it was said that more Mason jars were sold in Newport than anywhere else in the country.

While driving along Main Street away from I-40, look for the stone building to the right at traffic light number 9. It's the **Rhea-Mims Hotel,** at one time one of the more famous hostelries in these parts. The round stones prominent in the walls are said to be grindstones from Cherokee Indian mills.

At the corner marked by traffic light 3, turn onto Highway 321 to see the **Cocke County Museum,** tel. 423/623-7201, and Newport Chamber of Commerce. Here you can get information about the past and present. The former includes artifacts from Ben Hooper, a local boy who became governor of the state, and from Grace Moore, an East Tennessee diva. The museum is open Monday through Friday by appointment only. Admission is free.

A far different kind of music was played and sung by "Pappy Gube" Beaver, a Newport native who performed on Knoxville radio stations and released several records. According to an article in Barry McCloud's *Definitive Country,* Beaver gave up "singing for the devil" and became a minister noted for his tent revivals. There, his enthusiasm led him to stand on his head and climb poles, truly an example of that old-time religion.

The nearby community of Bybee is the birthplace of the late Buster Moore, half the husband-and-wife team of Bonnie Lou and Buster, whose homegrown bluegrass and country music graced local television in Appalachia for decades.

Where to Stay

Christopher Place, tel. 800/595-9441 or 423/623-6555, website: www.christopher place.com, sits amid 200 scenic acres. Four rooms and four suites await guests, who can enjoy a pool, a tennis court, and a casual dining room. Although listed in Newport, this elegant place is located on the east side of I-40.

Most of Newport's other lodging lies along I-40. Here the weary traveler will find the **Best Western Motel,** tel. 423/623-8713 or 800/528-1234; **Family Inns,** tel. 423/623-6033 and

423/623-2626; and the **Holiday Inn,** tel. 423/623-8622.

Just off I-40 and open all year, **Newport KOA,** tel. 423/623-9004, offers 75 sites, hookups, laundry facilities, a swimming pool, fishing, and a recreation hall.

TMC Campground, 112 Carson Springs Rd., tel. 423/625-0433, is also open all year-round. It has 210 sites, hookups, a store, a pool, and pretty much the works.

Food

A visit to **The Grease Rack,** tel. 423/623-9279, gave one diner a sense of what it must have been like to go to a speakeasy. The parking lot of the former garage—thus the name—was full of cars and pickup trucks, yet the door was locked. After a tentative knock, someone inside peered out the peephole, then the door opened, revealing a honky-tonk bar with country music blaring away. All the patrons turned to inspect the visitor. "Is this a restaurant?" "Sure," came the reply. "Just follow me." In the back was a large, windowless room filled with all manner of folks—couples, families, and singles. Steak and seafood is the fare here, in generous portions. The knock-at-the-door business is a means of complying with Cocke County's peculiar liquor laws.

The Grease Rack is open for dinner Wednesday through Saturday. To get there from the interstate, go to traffic light 12, then drive right on Lincoln Avenue for 0.7 miles. At the blinking yellow light, drive 0.3 miles on Morrell Springs Road. To see a lively side of Cocke County, secure a table when a University of Tennessee football game is being televised on a Saturday night.

The **Fox and Hounds** on Fox and Hounds Lane, tel. 423/623-9161, is a bit more sedate and is considered Newport's premier restaurant. Steaks, prime rib, and seafood make up the menu, served for lunch and dinner Monday through Saturday. To get there, get off I-40 at Exit 432B and go north on Highway 25/70 for about a mile and a half. The driveway to the restaurant is between Slammer's and Knight's Auto.

The **Log Cabin Inn,** 2477 Elkway, tel. 423/623-5959, features a buffet of country cooking for dinner Thursday through Saturday and for lunch on Sunday.

Newport is also home of one of the best Thai restaurants in East Tennessee. The **Thai Kitchen,** 323 Village Shopping Center, tel. 423/623-2752, serves traditional Thai food for lunch Monday through Friday and dinner Monday through Saturday.

Just outside of town, on Highway 160 between Morristown and Newport, Greek-American food is the order of the day. **C. J. Papadops,** 551 Briar Thicket Rd., tel. 423/623-0933, serves lamb and Greek salads as well as steak, lasagna, and spaghetti. This place is open for dinner Thursday through Sunday.

Information
Visit the **Newport/Cocke County Chamber of Commerce,** 803 Prospect St., tel. 423/623-7201, or call the tourism office at 423/625-9675. Online visit www.cockecounty.com.

DEL RIO

Before the railroad arrived, farmers in East Tennessee could get the best prices for their goods in the Carolinas. And the easiest products to ship were those that could transport themselves. In *Touring the East Tennessee Backroads,* Carolyn Sakowski estimates that every year drovers herded some 150,000 to 200,000 hogs to the Carolinas along the French Broad River through what is now Del Rio. A healthy hog, it seems, could hike 8 to 10 miles per day, a porcine procession that stopped every night at designated stock stands along the way. "It was not uncommon," she writes, "for ten to twelve herds numbering from 300 to 1,000 or 2,000 animals apiece to stop overnight and feed at the stands."

The most famous person from Del Rio is opera singer Grace Moore, who was born here in 1901 and lived here until 1906. "The Tennessee Nightingale" made her debut at the New York Metropolitan Grand Opera Company in 1927. She appeared in *La Bohème, Tosca,* and *Romeo and Juliet,* to name a few. She went on to star in a series of movies; *One Night of Love* is the most famous. She died in a plane crash outside Copenhagen in 1947, at the height of her fame.

Del Rio is more famous now as the setting for *Christy,* a novel published in 1967 by Catherine Marshall and based loosely on the experiences of her mother. The book tells of a religious 19-year-old who goes to a remote corner of Tennessee—Cutters Gap in the book—to teach in a mission school in 1912. A television series based on the novel renewed interest in the story, and for a few seasons it was performed as an outdoor drama in Townsend, Tennessee.

Christy has developed something of a cult following, as seen on the website: www.members .tripod.com/~Constance_2/. Devotees who don't mind dirt roads can make the pilgrimage to see the community on which the novel was based.

There is not a great deal to see; only the foundations of the original buildings remain, but in warm weather this is a good place for a picnic. To get there, get off Highway 25/70 at Del Rio. Head south on Highway 107, then turn right on Old Fifteenth Road. Go 4.3 miles and turn right at the Sand Hill Church of God. Two-tenths of a mile later, go right up a hill at a fork onto Chapel Hollow Road. Continue for one mile until you see the signs. Farther up the road from the site is the home of Larry Myers, a keeper of the Christy flame.

Down-home music is offered every Saturday night at **Hillbilly's Music Barn** in Del Rio. No admission is charged, and no drinking is allowed. Local artists perform bluegrass and old-time music. Patrons, if they feel so inclined, are welcome to get up and do some clogging.

To hear the music, take Highway 107 until it becomes a dirt road. At that point, go right for about three-fourths of a mile on Blue Mill Road, which is asphalt. Look for the Hillbilly's sign and turn left. Cross a creek and drive a quarter of a mile. Hillbilly's is on the left. For more information, call 423/487-5541.

HOT SPRINGS

Just over the North Carolina line, this small town on the French Broad River has seen better days. Once known as Warm Springs, it was an important stop on the road from Cumberland Gap to

© JEFF BRADLEY

Christy Mission site

the markets of Charleston. In those days, huge droves of cattle, hogs, and even turkeys would come down the road.

With the coming of the railroad, the livestock drives halted, but more and more health seekers began to come to town. People had been coming to the springs since Cherokee days, but now local residents earnestly began to market them. The hot-water-cure business grew exponentially. The local hotel lured flatlanders with promises that the springs would "bring the bloom back to the cheek, the luster to the eye, tone to the languid pulse, strength to the jaded nerves, and vigor to the wasted frame."

Entrepreneur James Patton of Asheville bought the springs and built the massive, 350-room Warm Springs Hotel in 1837. Soon, everyone who was somebody was coming to town. In fact, the daughter of the springs' second owner met her husband Frank Johnson—son of President Andrew Johnson—in the hotel's majestic ballroom.

The railroad arrived in the early 1880s, but the Warm Springs Hotel burned down shortly thereafter. Northerners moved in and built the Mountain Park Hotel in 1886. They discovered an even hotter spring on their property and shrewdly changed the town's name from Warm Springs to Hot Springs—to advertise both the change in ownership and the upgrade in amenities.

The Mountain Park Hotel was smaller (200 rooms), but it featured 16 marble pools, landscaped lawns, and those Victorian-era standbys—croquet and tennis courts. By the time World War I rolled around, however, hot springs were out of fashion, and the hotel gladly accepted the chance to serve as a prison camp for 517 German officers and 2,300 German merchant marines captured at the start of the war. So pleased were these resort-dwelling POWs with their accommodations and treatment that many of them returned after the war to live around here.

By war's end, the hotel and springs had lost their grasp on the public imagination, and the hotel conveniently burned to the ground in 1920. Two later hotels were built on the springs; neither held a candle to the previous two, and both also burned to the ground.

While nothing remains of the old hotels, and the springs themselves are on private property, the French Broad River still attracts a number of folks to the area, as does the Appalachian Trail, which runs right through town. The privately owned springs have reopened as **Hot Springs Spa & Resort,** 315 Bridge St., tel. 800/462-0933 or 828/622-7676. In keeping with the hyperbolic spirit of the springs' previous promoters, the current owners claim that "the Goddess of Health waved her magic wand" at these springs. It'll cost you and a friend $15–25 an hour for a private soak in the goddess-blessed water. The spa also offers massage. You can rent a two-couple cabin, complete with Jacuzzi, for $125 a night or tent camp for just $10 a night. Setting aside the question of the water's curative powers, this is a nice, reasonably priced spot to enjoy a hot relaxing soak and the company of friends. And this poignant combination can be a blessing in itself.

Greeneville and Vicinity

Greeneville is most associated with Andrew Johnson, who moved here in 1825 as a teenage apprentice who was running away from a North Carolina tailor. At that time the town was the center of a rich agricultural area, one that readily grew tobacco and other crops. The farmers and merchants were "self-made men," and their pride was exceeded only by their independence.

Just how independent they were is evidenced in 1861, when Tennessee voted to leave the Union. This action, driven by interests in Middle and West Tennessee, found little support in the eastern part of the state. Nine days after secession, 26 East Tennessee counties sent delegates to Greeneville to discuss seceding from the secessionists. They asked the state legislature to let them form a separate state. Permission was denied.

The divisiveness continued, a situation best exemplified by the Greeneville murder of Confederate General John Morgan. Morgan had led a band of mounted troops on an unauthorized raid deep into Kentucky, Ohio, and Indiana. Depending on how one viewed it, the raid was either a daring feat that gave the Yankees a taste of their own war, or a bunch of thugs on a spree of terror.

After one of his forays, the general came to Greeneville for some needed rest and found hospitality at the spacious Dickson-Williams House, the home of a local doctor and his wife. Someone—no one ever found out just who—slipped off and informed a nearby Union general that Morgan was in town. The general led Union forces into town and surrounded the house. According to one Southern account, Morgan leaped out of bed and ran into the back garden, where he was captured. As he stood there, a Union soldier shot him dead, snatched up his body, and rode off with it draped across his horse. After parading the late general around the Union camp, the soldier unceremoniously dumped the body in a ditch. This incident, probably magnified in the telling, further inflamed passions in this divided town.

The divisions that once split Greeneville still show in the Civil War monuments that stand in the courthouse yard. One is a rhapsodic paean to Morgan, while the other commemorates Union soldiers.

Modern Greeneville is the seat of Greene County and a center of the tobacco business. In recent years the town has acknowledged its heritage and abundance of historic buildings. Most conveniently for the visitor, most of Greeneville's historic sites follow Business 321 off Highway 11E. Here stand the old homes, bed-and-breakfasts, the General Morgan Inn, and the Andrew Johnson National Historic Site. The best guide to the town is "A Walk with the President." This brochure is available at the General Morgan Inn, the Andrew Johnson National Historic Site, and the Greeneville/Greene County Area Chamber of Commerce at 115 Academy Street.

SIGHTS

Drive south through town on U.S. 321, on your right you'll see the **Cumberland Presbyterian Church,** a Greek Revival church with a tall steeple. It was used as a hospital and a stable during the Civil War. On the day that General Morgan was killed, the church was shelled, and you can still see a cannonball from the skirmish imbedded in the front wall.

The block across from the Cumberland

ANDREW JOHNSON

Poor Andrew Johnson. For decades he was known primarily for being impeached and in recent years has suffered the indignity of being mentioned in the same paragraphs as Monica Lewinsky and Kenneth Starr. All this notoriety, plus the fact that he followed the greatest president of all time, siphons interest away from this remarkable man. And that is unfortunate, for Andrew Johnson was a complex individual. His rise from a poor childhood to the highest office in the land is an embodiment of the American dream.

Even more so than Abraham Lincoln, Andrew Johnson came from humble beginnings. He was born in Raleigh, North Carolina, in 1808, and his childhood was one of poverty. He never spent a day in school and by age 10 was apprenticed to a tailor. The young Johnson got in a dispute with his master about how long he should serve, and he fled to Greeneville, Tennessee, riding into town on a wagon at age 16.

Keenly aware of his lack of education, Johnson strove to improve his mind. He had once worked in a shop where a man read aloud to the tailors, and in Greeneville he hired people to read to him. He entered a local debating society and honed his public speaking, eventually becoming an orator who could hold a crowd for two or three hours and, typical of hard-knuckled Tennessee politics, sarcastically belittle an opponent as well as take care of any hecklers in the process.

Johnson was a good tailor who prospered in Greeneville. In 1829, he and a working-class slate ran for aldermen in an election that pitted them against wealthier candidates. Johnson's group won, and the victory launched his political climb. If anything can characterize Johnson's politics, it was a willingness to stand up for the common man and woman. His supporters—small farmers and shopkeepers typical of East Tennessee—distrusted the wealthy plantation owners who controlled politics in Middle and West Tennessee, and Johnson never forgot those who elected him. A Democrat, he served as mayor, state representative, state senator, and congressman. During

his five terms in Congress, always intent on educating himself, he read for hours in the Library of Congress, possibly spending more time there than any representative before or since.

In 1853 he was elected governor of Tennessee, and for two terms he supported public education and the construction of railroads. He also brought about the purchase of Andrew Jackson's home, the Hermitage. Johnson followed his gubernatorial terms with election to the U.S. Senate in 1857. In the critical 1860 election to select his fellow senator, he and his supporters backed a Democrat who favored secession—a so-called War Democrat. Nonetheless, when the issue of secession arose in Tennessee, Johnson argued long and loudly against it. When his state left the Union, Johnson traveled to Washington and became the only Southern senator to keep his seat.

In reward for Johnson's loyalty, in March 1862 President Lincoln appointed him military governor of Tennessee, the first Southern state to fall to Union armies. Johnson proved a stern figure in this post, jailing ministers for preaching pro-Confederate sermons and earning the contempt of many Tennesseans from the Mississippi to the mountains. His two years as military governor ended when Lincoln picked him as his running mate on the 1864 ticket. Lincoln, a Republican, and Johnson, a Democrat, ran together on the Union Party ticket.

Johnson had been vice president for only 42 days when John Wilkes Booth fired his pistol into the box at Ford's Theatre. Lincoln had always argued that the Southern states should be treated with compassion, and Johnson was left to carry out Lincoln's policies. Ulysses Grant, who followed Johnson into the White House, expressed an interesting assessment in his autobiography of his predecessor: "He would have proven the best friend the South could have had, and saved much of the wrangling and bitterness of feeling brought out by reconstruction under a president who at first wished to revenge himself on Southern men of

President Andrew Johnson achieved a series of firsts in his remarkable political career.

wished to rid himself of Stanton, Congress passed the Tenure of Office Act, which stated that a president could not remove an officeholder who had been approved by the Senate without that body's consent. Johnson, wanting to let the courts decide this constitutional matter, and confident that he would win, ordered Stanton to resign anyway.

The House of Representatives now had what it considered a smoking gun. Not willing to let the courts settle the issue, it impeached Johnson on several charges based on his violation of the Tenure of Office Act. Put on trial before the U.S. Senate, he was saved from conviction by only one vote. He ended his term in bitterness, refusing to attend U.S. Grant's inauguration in 1869, but returned to Greeneville in triumph. The man who had been detested as military governor was now considered a hero in Tennessee as well as in the rest of the South.

Out of office for the first time in 30 years, and in no way content to rest on his laurels, Johnson jumped right back into politics. Running for the U.S. Senate in 1869, he lost by a vote of 55-51— in those days the Tennessee senate elected U.S. senators—and in 1872 he lost a three-way race for Congress. Still the old campaigner fought on. In 1875, the Tennessee senate, after putting itself through 55 ballots in a period of days, elected Johnson once more to the U.S. Senate—the only ex-president to serve in that capacity. Johnson took enormous satisfaction in his election to the group that had tried him, and he rose in a special session on March 20 to attack President Grant in a speech. He ended his address, as he had done so many times over the years, with a ringing appeal to support the Constitution. He was heartily applauded by his colleagues. He has not been so lauded by historians; a 1996 poll rated him a failure, a fate shared by his successor as well.

Back in Tennessee during a Senate recess, Johnson had a stroke while visiting his daughter. He died three days later, on August 1, 1875, at 66 years of age. He was buried on Signal Hill in Greeneville after a funeral attended by thousands.

better social standing than himself, but who still sought their recognition, and in a short time conceived the idea and advanced the proposition to become their Moses to lead them triumphantly out of all their difficulties."

This Moses might have wanted to lead, but Congress was in no mood to follow. With the Great Emancipator gone, the radical Republicans in Congress showed no restraint in their attack on the man who was left to carry out Lincoln's reconciliatory policies. They began to look for reasons to remove him from office.

Johnson had inherited Lincoln's secretary of war, Edwin Stanton, who proved extremely disloyal to his new boss. Knowing that Johnson

Presbyterian Church contains **Bicentennial Park and Big Spring,** the water source that caused Greeneville to be located here. The same block contains what might be called the **Lost Capitol of the Lost State of Franklin.** The real capitol stood for years beside Greene County's present courthouse on Main Street. During Tennessee's centennial celebration in 1896, however, the old log building was shipped off to Nashville, where it was displayed, dismantled, and promptly lost. A few years ago, interest in the Lost Capitol of the Lost State was rekindled, and a suitable replacement building was found.

Crossing Church Street and looking to the right, the **General Morgan Inn & Conference Center,** 111 North Main St., tel. 800/223-2679 or 423/787-1000, is worth a look, even if you have no intention of staying there. (For information on spending the night, see "Where to Stay," below.) This complex came about when Greeneville, like so many towns in Tennessee, tried to revitalize its downtown. Four buildings that had been "railroad hotels" stood close to each other. Chief among these was the Hotel Brumley, which operated from 1920 to 1981. Created with a combination of local and federal money, the General Morgan Inn came into being on the site and opened in 1996.

Just off the lobby, Brumleys restaurant retains the name of one of the old hotels. Above the bar, an etched-glass scene depicts nymphs cavorting on wine glasses. In the old days, this picture was considered so naughty that on Sundays curtains were drawn so as not to give offense. This now-quaint prudishness still prevails.

General Morgan had his sleep, and shortly thereafter his life, interrupted while he was a guest at the **Dickson-Williams Mansion,** which stands behind the General Morgan Inn. Begun in 1815 as "the showplace of East Tennessee," this home and its extensive gardens once occupied an entire city block. Guests in the home included the Marquis de Lafayette, Andrew Jackson, James K. Polk, and Henry Clay. The house then passed out of the family and began a decline that so often overtakes such mansions. After being a school, a tobacco factory, an inn, and a hospital,

it was finally bought by the city. It's open by appointment only. For further information, call 423/639-0695.

Returning to Main Street and turning left onto Depot Street, you'll find Johnson Square and the **Andrew Johnson National Historic Site.** The log cabin replica of the president's birthplace is not part of the park, which includes three separate units. Begin at the Visitor Center Complex, which contains Johnson's original tailor shop, a museum, and park headquarters. The museum displays a coat that Johnson stitched, as well as a poster from a disgruntled employer in North Carolina offering a reward for his runaway apprentice.

Across the street sits a two-story brick home where Johnson and his family lived from 1838 to 1851. Oddly enough, Johnson bought the property on which the house stands from the heirs of Abraham Lincoln's second cousin. Two rooms here are open to the public. They contain a genealogy of the family as well as changing exhibits.

The Homestead on South Main Street, the second unit, was Johnson's home from 1851 until his death in 1875. Due to astute real estate dealings, Johnson was one of the wealthier people in Greeneville, and this house reflects his prosperity. Vandalized by both Union and Confederate sympathizers during the Civil War, the house now contains Johnson family furniture and items given to him while he was president.

The final unit is the Andrew Johnson National Cemetery, where the 17th president and his family are buried. To get there, follow the signs down West Main Street from the Homestead.

There is no charge to visit the Visitor Center Complex or the cemetery. Tours of the Homestead, offered on the half hour, cost $2 for adults and are free for anyone under 18 or over 62. For more information, call 423/638-3551 or see www.nps.gov/anjo.

The **Old Greene County Gaol,** which stands behind the current Greene County Detention Center on Main Street, was built in 1804–05. Water from an adjacent creek was periodically channeled through a trough in the jail's stone floor to flush out the contents. In 1838 the jail was moved to its present locale, and a half-century later its brick second story was added.

Named for the man for whom the county and town were also named, the **Nathanael Greene Museum of Greene County History,** on West McKee Street off Main Street, tel. 423/636-1558, contains an eclectic mixture of town memorabilia. Visitors can see a suit made by tailor-turned-president Andrew Johnson, tickets to Johnson's impeachment trial, and other relics of Greeneville and Greenevillians. The museum is open Tuesday through Saturday 10 A.M.–4 P.M. Wheelchair access is limited; admission is free.

RECREATION
Parks
Kinser Park, tel. 423/639-5912, located along the Nolichucky River has a nine-hole golf course, a driving range, tennis courts, a water slide, and a playground. To get there, take Highway 70 south about five miles. Turn left onto Old Allen's Bridge Road, drive about three miles, then turn right at the fork in the road near the University of Tennessee Tobacco Experiment Station. Drive about a mile to the park entrance. Kinser Park is open from March 15 to October 15, and possibly later if weather permits.

Cherokee National Forest
Cherokee National Forest offers a number of recreation areas; all offer picnicking, hiking, and wilderness activities. For further information, visit the Nolichucky Ranger District Office, 120 Austin Ave., Greeneville, tel. 423/638-4109, website: www.southernregion.fs.fed.us/Cherokee.

The forest's **Paint Creek Recreation Area** lies in a mountain cove beside a creek south of Greeneville. Dudley Falls is a popular place for swimming and picnicking, and the area is fun to simply explore. To get there, take Highway 70 south for about 14 miles. Look for the Forest Service signs and follow them for three more miles.

Farther up the ridge lies **Horse Creek Recreation Area,** where you can swim in the creek free of charge. Nature trails are also available, including one paved for accessibility. To get to

© JEFF BRADLEY

East Tennessee Bridge

EAST SIDE

Horse Creek take Highway 107 north from Greeneville for six miles, then turn right and follow the signs for two more miles.

Old Forge Recreation Area lies at the foot of Coldspring Mountain. It's very popular with horseback riders. Visitors can swim in the stream or hike on the nearby Appalachian Trail. Take Highway 107 north of Greeneville for six miles, then turn right and follow the signs to Horse Creek Recreation Area. From there, you'll take a Forest Service road to Old Forge.

At the bottom of Meadow Creek Mountain lies the **Houston Valley Recreation Area,** where hikers can climb to the Meadow Creek fire tower. Farther down the road, boaters can enjoy the French Broad River. From Greeneville, take Highway 70 south to the intersection with Highway 170. Turn right, then drive about eight miles. Look for the campground on the left, just before Burnett Gap.

Close by the Appalachian Trail, **Round Mountain Recreation Area** lies at an elevation of 3,400 feet. It offers great views, particularly during the fall color season. Take Highway 70 south from Greeneville for about nine miles. Turn right on Highway 107 and continue about 13 miles to the intersection with Highway 25/70 at the Del Rio post office. Remain on Highway 107 for about six miles, until the pavement ends and the road becomes gravel. It then climbs Round Mountain for about six miles. Look for the sign to the campground.

To get to **Round Knob Recreation Area,** take Highway 350, the Jones Bridge Road, south from Greeneville toward the Camp Creek community. Continue on a country road there for two miles, then turn right onto Forest Service Road 88 for five miles.

EVENTS AND FESTIVALS

The **Battle of Blue Springs,** a Civil War reenactment, takes place west of Greeneville in Mosheim (MOSS-hime) on the third weekend in October. Spectators can see authentic military and civilian campsites, the firing of full-scale cannons, cavalry maneuvers, a battle with about 200 participants in period dress, a battlefield

hospital, and a period church service. To get there, take Exit 23 from I-81 and follow Highway 11 east to Mosheim, where signs lead to the battlefield. Admission is $3 per person; free for children under 12. For further information, call Earl Fletcher at the Mosheim Town Hall, tel. 423/422-4051, or visit www.members.tripod.com/bluesprings2/.

The **Iris Arts and Crafts Festival** takes place in May. Traditional and contemporary crafts are available, plus food. Some crafts are demonstrated. For further information, call the Greene County Partnership at 423/638-4111.

WHERE TO STAY
Bed-and-Breakfasts and Inns

The **Big Spring Inn,** 315 N. Main St., tel. 423/638-2917, is a bed-and-breakfast. It's located in a turn-of-the-last-century, three-story Greek Revival house, surrounded by 100-year-old trees and gardens in Greeneville's Historic District. The six rooms in the inn, most with private baths, are named for prominent Greeneville women. The rate is $86 per night per couple. The inn is open April through October. To see it, go to www.virtualcities.com/ons/tn/e/tne3001.htm.

The **General Morgan Inn & Conference Center,** 111 North Main St., tel. 800/223-2679 or 423/787-1000, offers perhaps the most luxurious accommodations on this end of the state. The Presidential Suite, which goes for $235 a night, has a bathroom with heated floor tiles, a fireplace, and a Chippendale-style canopied bed. More modest rooms go for $89 per night. The inn has 82 rooms in all. See www.greene.xtn.net/com/genmorgan/ for more information.

Hilltop House on Route 7, tel. 423/639-8202, is a spacious old bed-and-breakfast on a bluff overlooking the Nolichucky River valley. Decorated with English antiques, the house features afternoon tea and lawn croquet. The innkeeper—a former landscape architect for the U.S. Forest Service—arranges weekends centered on quilting, fishing, hiking, or gardening. The rate is $70 for two people, with dinner available at $10–12 per person.

Nolichucky Bluffs, 400 Kinser Park Ln., tel.

423/787-7947 or 800/842-4690, offers a B&B and cabins overlooking the Nolichucky River about seven miles south of Greeneville. The B&B has three rooms, all with private baths and one with a whirlpool bath. The cabins have stoves or fireplaces. Rates are $95–110 per night.

Motels

Try the **Charray Inn,** 121 Seral Dr., tel. 423/638-1331 or 800/852-4682, or the **Holiday Inn,** 1790 E. Andrew Johnson Hwy., tel. 423/639-4185 or 800/465-4329.

Camping

Kinser Park has 108 campsites, some with full hookups. It is open from March 15 to October 15. See "Parks" under "Recreation," above.

The **Davy Crockett Birthplace State Historical Area** offers 75 campsites along the Nolichucky River. It's open year-round.

The following **Cherokee National Forest** campsites are available on a strictly first-come, first-served basis; no reservations are taken. They are generally open, depending on the weather, from May through mid-November.

Paint Creek offers 21 sites. **Horse Creek** has 10 sites. **Old Forge's** has nine tent sites near a waterfall. **Houston Valley** has 10 sites, and **Round Mountain** has 16 sites. Directions to each site are listed under "Cherokee National Forest" under "Recreation," above. For further information contact the Nolichucky/Unaka Ranger District Office at 120 Austin Avenue in Greeneville or call 423/638-4109.

FOOD AND INFORMATION

Food

Augustino's Restaurant, 3465 E. Andrew Johnson Hwy., tel. 423/639-1231, specializes in Italian cuisine.

Brumleys is the in-house restaurant at the General Morgan Inn & Conference Center, 111 North Main St., tel. 800/223-2679 or 423/787-1000. It offers continental and Southern cuisine.

Not surprisingly, the **Butcher's Block,** 125 Serral Dr., tel. 423/638-4485, features beef—

from 8- to 32-ounce steaks. It also offers seafood, barbecue, and chicken.

Pal's, with burgers and hot dogs, operates out of 1357 Tusculum Blvd., tel. 423/638-7555.

Stan's Bar-B-Q, 2620 E. Andrew Johnson Hwy., tel. 423/787-0017, is one of the more up-scale barbecue places on this end of the state. It serves pork, ribs, chicken, and beef. Try the dry ribs with a Memphis rub.

Information

To learn more about Greeneville and Greene County, contact the **Greeneville/Greene County Area Chamber of Commerce,** 115 Academy St., Suite 1, tel. 423/638-4111, website: www.greeneville.com. Or drop by during business hours.

TUSCULUM

This little town east of Greeneville is home to Tusculum College and is well worth a stop. Home to approximately 1,700 students, the Presbyterian-affiliated college serves as a cultural center for Greeneville and outlying areas. The name allegedly comes from that of Cicero's home outside Rome.

Tusculum College resulted from the merger of Greeneville College, founded in 1794, and Tusculum Academy, a private school founded in 1818 by father and son ministers the Reverend Samuel Doak and the Reverend Samuel Witherspoon Doak. The latter engineered the academic merger and saw that his institution's name won out over that of Greeneville College. Tusculum has a museum studies program, and the campus contains two museums worthy of a stop

Andrew Johnson was a trustee of the college, which served as his official presidential library. The present-day **Andrew Johnson Museum and Library** occupies an 1841 building with several exhibits pertaining to the president: most of the books from his home, some carpet from the White House, the bed in which he died, and personal items such as a collar box and some of his wife's possessions. The library is open Monday through Friday 9 A.M.–5 P.M. Admission is free, and the building is wheelchair accessible. See http://ajmuseum.tusculum.edu/ for more information.

The elder Samuel Doak, an important religious leader in upper East Tennessee, lived the last years of his life in a large house whose construction began in 1818. Academy classes were taught there until the next building, now called Old College, was erected. The **Doak House Museum** contains college-related artifacts, Doak family artifacts (1830–1865), and educational and religious artifacts and documents from northeastern Tennessee. The museum is open Monday through Friday, 9 A.M. to 5 P.M. by appointment. Call 423/636-8554 or 800/729-0256, ext. 251, for more information or visit http://doakhouse.tusculum.edu/.

The other noteworthy building on campus is Virginia Hall, one of only three buildings in the South designed by Chicago architect Louis A. Sullivan.

To find out what plays, concerts, or other collegiate activities are taking place at Tusculum College, call 423/636-7304 or visit www.tusculum.edu.

A pleasant place to eat is **Ye Olde Tusculum Eatery**, tel. 423/638-9210, across the road from the college. Lunch is mostly sandwiches—with specials such as portobello mushrooms—while dinner brings forth steak, chicken, seafood, and Italian dishes.

Next door the **Three Blind Mice** gift shop, tel. 423/639-0180, has artwork and craft pieces from local as well as national artists. It's closed on Sunday except in November and December.

DANDRIDGE

Dandridge is a town whose historic buildings, though on the National Register, are still inhabited, where cute little shops have not invaded, and where the drugstore still has a lunch counter.

As far as anyone knows, it is the only town named for Martha Dandridge Custis Washington, wife of George. Created in 1793, Dandridge became the seat of Jefferson County. Troops moved back and forth through the town during the Civil War. One night a Union gen-

eral stayed in a local house. Events the next day caused him to depart in haste, leaving a bottle of very good brandy. The following night Confederates stayed in the same house and made humorous toasts with the brandy until it was gone.

Dandridge may have been named after Martha Washington, but another president's wife once saved the town. When the Tennessee Valley Authority was planning Douglas Dam on the French Broad River, it looked like curtains for Dandridge—the town would soon be underwater. A local grande dame bombarded senators with letters of protest, to no avail. Finally, she sent her poems and pleas to Eleanor Roosevelt, who prevailed on Franklin to issue a presidential decree ordering that a dike be built to save the town. Newcomers still get a surprise when they climb what looks like a big hill behind the town and top it to see a great expanse of water.

The **Jefferson County Courthouse** contains one of those wonderfully eclectic museums that fill Tennessee. Here, in corridors that lead to offices of assorted bureaucrats, one can gaze for free on a hornet's nest, a German World War II helmet, Vietnamese sandals, the remnants of a moonshiner's still, Civil War bullets, and the marriage license issued to one David Crockett. The courthouse is generally open Monday through Friday 8 A.M.–4 P.M. and Saturday 8–11 A.M.

Across the street sits **Tinsley-Bible Drugs,** tel. 423/397-3444, a store with old furnishings and new merchandise. The action takes place at the six-seat lunch counter and nearby booths, where a cheeseburger is inexpensive but the accompanying dose of small-town life is priceless. Here you will see county officials—including one dignified gent addressed as "judge"—giggling high school girls, and assorted others.

Where to Stay

The Barrington Inn, 1174 McGuire Rd., tel. 888/205-8482 or 865/397-3368, is out in the country between Dandridge and New Market, but a mere 2.5 miles off I-40. The inn offers three rooms in a restored farmhouse and three more in a

Dairy House. All rooms have sitting areas as well as private bathrooms. Rates range from $65 to $125. Perhaps the best reason to stay here is for the food, which is described below. Dinner is available to guests every night by prior arrangement. See the inn online at www.bbonline.com/TN/Barrington.

Goose Creek Farm Bed and Breakfast, tel. 865/397-6166, is a restored farmhouse on 12 acres. Located next to a barn and former milking parlor, it contains three bedrooms. Rates begin at $80. See www.bbonline.com/tn/goosecreek for more information.

Mill Dale Farm Bed & Breakfast occupies a 19th-century farmhouse with period furniture. It's located one mile north of I-40. See www.bbonline.com/tn/milldale for information.

Take Highway 139 west out of Dandridge for a pleasant drive to the **Mountain Harbor Inn,** 1199 Hwy. 139, tel. 865/397-3345. Located right on Douglas Lake, the inn offers views across the water to the mountains. All 12 rooms have quilts hanging on the walls, microwave ovens, coffeemakers, refrigerators, and private baths. Rates are $65–125. See www.mountainharborinn.com for more information.

Cabins

Deep Springs Settlement gives visitors a chance to experience the old ways of cabin living, with wood stoves, oil lamps, and rocking chairs on the porch. This place also holds a plowing festival and a molasses festival. Contact 865/397-1460 or www.deepspringssettlement.com for more information.

Where to Camp

Douglas Lake Campground is the closest to Dandridge. It offers 100 sites with full hookups, a Laundromat, boating, fishing, and swimming. To get there, go east on Highway 9 out of town. Turn right on Oak Grove Road.

Fancher's Campground lies on the French Broad River (Douglas Lake) upstream from Dandridge. It has 324 sites, boating, swimming, and fishing. It also has a lot of noise from the traffic on I-40. To get there, take Highway 9 east out of town, cross the river, and look for the sign. Call 865/397-3510 for more information.

Food

The Barrington Inn, 1174 McGuire Rd., New Market, tel. 888/205-8482 or 865/397-3368, is one of the better restaurants on this end of the state; the proprietors used to run a restaurant in Key West. Dinner is offered to non-guests Thursday through Saturday. The menu includes entrées such New Zealand crown rack of lamb, beef Wellington, ground ostrich wrapped in veal, and lobster and shrimp croustade. These cost from $13 to $28 per person.

Cowboys on the Water, 1435 Hwy. 139, tel. 865/397-2529, has a name that doesn't make sense—until diners understand that "Cowboy" was the founder of this very informal and fun place. You'll find fishing and western gear on the walls and sawdust and peanut shells on the floor, but it's the food on the plates that keeps people coming back: shrimp, clams, flounder, catfish, crab legs, steak, and burgers. Open every day for dinner only.

Dandridge Seafood Restaurant on Meeting Street, tel. 423/397-2315, offers catfish, flounder, shrimp, and orange roughy, as well as steaks.

Or try the restaurant at **Mountain Harbor Inn,** 1199 Hwy. 139, tel. 865/397-3345. It's open Friday through Sunday; reservations are a good idea. Prime rib is the specialty of the house—10 ounces for $18—while grilled chicken breast and char-grilled fish are available as well. Lunch is served Friday and Saturday and includes a wide choice of sandwiches, salads, and pastas.

If you want a burger and the Tinsley-Bible Drugs lunch counter doesn't satisfy, go to the Dandridge Exit (Exit 417) of I-40 for a selection of franchise restaurants.

Information

The Jefferson County Chamber of Commerce can be reached at 865/397-9642 or www.jefferson-tn-chamber.org.

EAST SIDE

Asheville

Introduction

The economic and cultural center of western North Carolina, Asheville never served as a fort or an outpost as did Knoxville, its East Tennessee counterpart. No, Asheville has by and large made its living off the kindness of strangers—tourists, to be exact. In fact, so time-honored is Asheville's tradition of tourism that its minor-league baseball team is named the Asheville Tourists. The team's bear mascot, Ted E. Tourist, wields a bat in one paw, a suitcase in the other.

Many of the famous names associated with Asheville—George Vanderbilt, Zelda and F. Scott Fitzgerald—came here only seasonally or for a "mountain cure." The best-known novel by the most famous Asheville-born novelist, Thomas Wolfe, is about growing up in the home his mother ran for visiting out-of-towners.

HISTORY

Named for early North Carolina governor Samuel Ashe, Asheville serves as the seat of Buncombe County, one of the few counties in America whose names have passed into the language. In the early 19th century, when pressed to state his point after a rambling, inconclusive speech about a topic of interest to only a few folks back home, Felix Buncombe, a Revolutionary War veteran and early congressman from the area, replied, "I was just talking for Buncombe." Thereafter, whenever a congressman's mouth ran ahead of his thoughts, he might be asked if he, too, was "talking for Buncombe." By the start of the 20th century, the phrase had transmogrified into "talking bunk" and was heard in the public statements of Henry Ford and others.

But while the county's name became a household word, Buncombe County's seat, Asheville, remained just a stop on the road from Greeneville, Tennessee, to Greenville, South Carolina—a place where drovers and their herds of cattle, hogs, or turkeys spent the night before moving on. In 1792, the Buncombe County courthouse was built at the

Wall Street

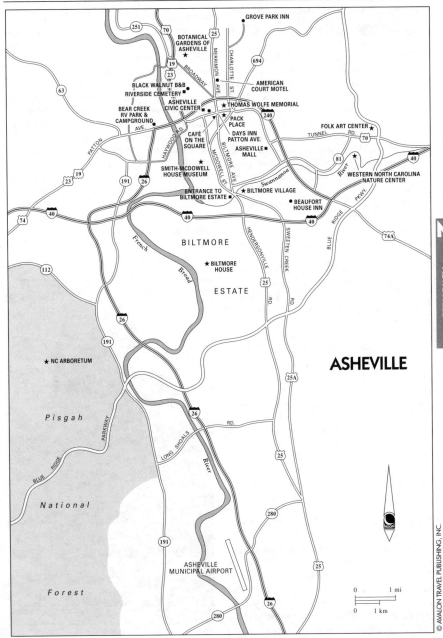

GROVE PARK INN

251
70
25

BOTANICAL
GARDENS OF
ASHEVILLE
★

694

19
23

CHARLOTTE ST

MERRIMON AVE.

AMERICAN
COURT MOTEL

BROADWAY

63

BLACK WALNUT B&B
RIVERSIDE CEMETERY

ASHEVILLE
CIVIC CENTER

★ THOMAS WOLFE MEMORIAL

BEAR CREEK
RV PARK &
CAMPGROUND

240

AVE.

PACK
PLACE

PATTON

HAYWOOD RD.

CAFÉ
ON THE
SQUARE

DAYS INN
PATTON AVE.

FOLK ART CENTER ★

TUNNEL   RD.

70

McDOWELL ST.

ASHEVILLE
MALL

BILTMORE AVE.

23 19

★ SMITH-McDOWELL
HOUSE MUSEUM

191   26

81 ★

40

ENTRANCE TO
BILTMORE ESTATE ■

Swannanoa

River

WESTERN NORTH CAROLINA
NATURE CENTER

★ BILTMORE VILLAGE

74

40

BEAUFORT
● HOUSE INN

40

BILTMORE

HENDERSONVILLE

SWEETEN CREEK

BLUE RIDGE PKWY

74A

French

★ BILTMORE
HOUSE

112

Broad

ESTATE

25
RD.

26

191

25A

★ NC ARBORETUM

ASHEVILLE

25

Pisgah

PARKWAY

26

RD.

25

National

LONG SHOALS

River

280

191

BLUE RIDGE

25

Forest

ASHEVILLE
MUNICIPAL AIRPORT

0   1 mi

0   1 km

26

280

MOON

ASHEVILLE

© AVALON TRAVEL PUBLISHING, INC.

ASHEVILLE HIGHLIGHTS

Biltmore Estate and Winery: The largest privately owned home in the world, with all the accessories, including incredible gardens. Also home to one of the East's top wineries.

Biltmore Village: Where the craftsfolk who made and maintained the estate once lived; now a charming and busy shopping area

Pack Place: Education, Arts and Science Center: Museums, galleries, shops, and live performances—a perfect urban Saturday, all in one place.

Thomas Wolfe Memorial: The former boardinghouse where the author was raised, now equipped with a museum.

present-day location of Pack Square, and the little country town began to grow around it. In 1797, David Crockett—born over the mountains in Limestone, Tennessee—was married in Asheville to a local woman.

Long after Crockett lay famous and dead at the Alamo, Asheville lay low. Wealthy Charleston and Savannah planters, trying to avoid the malaria-plagued summers back home, came for the crisp air and "curative" sulfur springs. Zebulon Vance, North Carolina's beloved Civil War and post-Reconstruction governor and long-time senator, was born and raised in the area, but the war itself largely passed Asheville by. A Confederate armory here manufactured Enfield-type rifles early in the war, but the plant was moved to Columbia, South Carolina, in 1863. The Battle of Asheville was a minor and fleeting Confederate victory against Union raiders from Tennessee, occurring on April 6, 1865, only a few days before the end of the war.

The coming of the railroad in 1880 marked the period of Asheville's greatest growth. Within 20 years, two men who would put Asheville on the map came to town. In 1889, George Vanderbilt rolled into Asheville. Grandson of the steamboat and railroad baron Cornelius Vanderbilt, he proceeded to build the largest privately owned house in the world—his country

house, mind you—which he called Biltmore. About the same time, E. W. Grove, who had made his money in the patent medicine business, moved in from St. Louis; in 1913 he completed construction on the Grove Park Inn, which was and still is the finest hotel in the region.

Oddly, a good bit of Asheville's growing prosperity came from others' misfortune. Prominent doctors in the East began recommending Asheville to patients suffering from tuberculosis or any ailment that required fresh air and rest. The new railroad made it easy to get to Asheville, and the health seekers poured in. The city responded with the construction of hotels, sanitariums, and over 100 boardinghouses. One of the latter establishments was run by a Julia Wolfe, whose son Thomas was to scandalize the town with his semi-autobiographical novel, *Look Homeward, Angel.*

an old church in Asheville

© MIKE SIGALAS

Many of the sick recovered and decided to stay on. Some call the 1920s Asheville's golden era, and not without reason. Relics from this time period include the art deco City Hall, L. B. Jackson's Gothic skyscraper, and Edwin Wiley Grove's Arcade. What is now the University of North Carolina at Asheville arrived in 1927.

The town suffered terribly from the 1929 stock market crash. In a time when everybody was tightening up their purses, Asheville—a town built on discretionary spending—was hit hard. Most of the regular vacationers were too broke to visit. And around the same time, advances in medical science offered new treatments for tuberculosis, eliminating the need for the mountain cure.

Predictably, land prices tumbled. Many who had speculated on North Carolina real estate lost all they had. The city itself fell so deeply that it would take some 40 years to pay off its debts.

Since that low point, however, the city has come back.

Beginning in the 1970s, fueled partly by students and residual alumni at UNC, downtown developed into a regional center for the "alternative" subculture. Now, like Athens, Austin, Berkeley, and most other college towns in America, Asheville is known for its nightclubs, galleries, espresso bars, and acupuncturists. For those visiting from larger cities, downtown will either seem comfortingly familiar or too much like home. But for many Easterner.alt types, Asheville's collision of bohemia and Appalachia strikes a perfect midway point between home and Haight Street.

In addition to those who school here and stick, Asheville, with a population around 62,000, attracts a lot of up-on-Friday/down-on-Sunday tourists. The main draw by far is the Biltmore Es-tate; though George Vanderbilt is no longer with us, his house still pulls in the crowds. The Blue Ridge Parkway also funnels nature lovers of all kinds into the city, and having Great Smoky Mountains National Park just 40 miles away doesn't hurt, either.

However, the high level of tourism—and the city's traditional catering to the out-of-towners who sustain the local economy—doesn't set well with everyone. In May 2001, beating drums and waving signs, scores of Asheville residents—many of whom had weeks earlier paraded peacefully in a pro-hemp rally—marched from Aston Park to the Vance Memorial (without the proper permits) to protest the city's community calendar.

The "Take Back the Streets" marchers claimed that festivals and other events put on by the city unfairly catered to tourists. Police and sheriff's deputies intervened and made arrests. Word spread among the deputies that one of the protesters had fired a pistol. Indeed, one was shot in the foot, apparently by a pistol he was carrying in a backpack. The remaining protesters marched on the jail until turned back by the Buncombe County sheriff brandishing a riot gun.

Protest marches and gunplay aside, *most* Asheville residents are very glad to have visitors, and the town is highly equipped to guide them through the city and the region. The Chamber of Commerce Convention and Visitors' Bureau is bursting with brochures, maps, and courteous people. Several signs direct motorists to the bureau, which is located off I-240 at 151 Haywood Street. It's open 8:30 A.M.–5:30 P.M. on weekdays and 9 A.M.–5 P.M. on weekends—later during tourist season. Call 828/258-3916 for information.

ASHEVILLE

Sights and Recreation

ATTRACTIONS
Biltmore Estate and Winery

This monument to unbridled spending often affects visitors in one of two ways. Either they lust after the money and power that could build such an edifice, or they decry a system in which one person could accumulate—much less *inherit*—such a fantastic pile of money. Sometimes visitors do both: first lust, then decry.

Others take the historical angle. In one sense, the Biltmore Estate is a shrine to the industrial-powered American economic explosion in the 19th century. Biltmore sprang from the millions made by Cornelius Vanderbilt in steam boating and railroads—rushing forty-niners to the goldfields of California, hauling goods in from the ships of New York City, and pulling natural resources out of the inland areas for shipment overseas. During the post–Civil War Gilded Age, Cornelius's son William greatly expanded the family empire, as did William's older sons. But William's youngest son, George, apparently saw no reason to be an industrial baron when he could be a baron of the more traditional sort. His fortune assured, he spent his time traveling the world with an eye toward finding the place to create his own kingdom. His travels brought him to the Blue Ridge, and he decided it would be nice to have a cozy little fiefdom in the mountains. At 26, the same age at which Brian Wilson

Church of St. Lawrence

© MIKE SIGALAS

created *Pet Sounds,* George Vanderbilt began his own masterpiece. Like Brian, George had solid financial backing.

Completed in 1895, the house took five years and the efforts of a thousand workers to build. It has over 255 rooms. The original estate totaled 130,000 acres, though now it's been whittled down to a mere 8,000—a little cramped, but still enough to provide the house some privacy. The distance from the front door of the mansion to the street is three miles, which could make getting the morning paper a bit hellacious in cold weather. No wonder these people needed servants.

And these are not just any 8,000 acres. Remember 1992's *Last of the Mohicans?* That was filmed here. Remember the scene in *Forrest Gump* where Forrest runs cross-country through the cornfields of the American Midwest? That was filmed here, too. This is a large, diverse place. The grounds were laid out by Frederick Law Olmsted, who, on a less-ambitious day, also designed New York's Central Park.

Biltmore is open every day except Thanksgiving and Christmas. The Reception and Ticket Center is open from 9 A.M.–5 P.M. daily January through March and 8:30 A.M.–5 P.M. daily April through December. Expect to pay around $31 for a one-day adult admission, but look for online specials at www.biltmore.com. "Behind the Scenes" tours cost extra.

If you have but one day to spend at Biltmore, arrive early and well rested. Spend the extra money and rent an audio-tour headset. You've got to part with a good bit of cash to get in anyway, so you might as well know what you're looking at. Most find the experience to be a bit of a cross between touring the Louvre and watching *Citizen Kane* in 3D. You'll need around an hour and a half to take in the residence.

After leaving the house, check out the mountain view from the South Terrace. Then walk down and explore the Azalea Garden, Spring Garden, Walled Garden, and Conservatory. There you'll find **A Gardener's Place,** featuring estate-grown plants, garden accessories, books, and gifts, as well as the seasonally operated **Conservatory Café.**

Over by the stables you'll find the **Stable Shops,** including a bookshop, Christmas store, candy store, bakery, and ice cream store.

You'll need to drive to get to the 96,500-square-foot dairy converted into a winery, but the chance to go wine-tasting in the former Confederacy should never be lightly passed by. In fact, the Biltmore Winery is the most visited winery in all the United States. The wine list is extensive (non-alcoholic sparkling drinks are also available) at both the winery and the Wine Shop. **The Bistro,** also located here, is open daily from 11 A.M.–9 P.M.. It features estate-raised beef, lamb, and trout; pizza, pastas, and desserts; and Biltmore wines. A children's menu is available.

The **Deerpark Restaurant,** open for lunches most of the year, sits between the house and the winery. It gives you the chance to dine outside while enjoying a luncheon buffet and Biltmore Estate wines. Children 9 and under dine free when accompanied by a paying adult. Other on-grounds spots to eat include the **Stable Café,** open daily 11 A.M.–5 P.M. for lighter meals. For the most formal lunches on the estate, look to the **The Dining Room.** You'll need to make reservations to eat here, and you can do so at the Reception and Ticket Center, the Twelve-Month Pass Desk in the Stable Hallway, and the winery Passholder Desk.

Other than looking and eating, there's lots more to do here, including hiking, rafting, carriage rides, horseback riding, and mountain biking. Which is why you'll want to arrive early. But if you don't or can't, then come after 3 P.M., and they'll validate your ticket for the next day.

Biltmore received some exciting news in fall of 2000 when researchers from Appalachian State University, digging at a mound near the estate's entrance, found bone, pottery shards, weapons, and other evidence of a 6,000-year-old Connestee trading village. Here, apparently, tribes from the Midwest, southern Ohio, and the Gulf Coast met at the crossroads of two major trading routes and did business. The Connestee people (who predated the Pisgah, who themselves predated the Cherokee) set up shop here and apparently exchanged mica for imported flint, copper, shells, and pottery.

The village site promises to be one of the

WILLIAM DUDLEY PELLEY AND THE SILVER SHIRTS: ASHEVILLE'S WOULD-BE FUHRER

A sheville has over the years attracted creative geniuses, New Age gurus, and not a few political radicals. In William Dudley Pelley, the Land of the Sky got all three.

Writing Sensation

Born in 1890 and raised in poverty in a small Massachusetts town, Pelley rose to fame with short stories published in *Colliers, Red Book,* and *The Saturday Evening Post.* At the end of WWI, a publisher sent him to report on the Russian revolution. The atrocities he witnessed and his interviews with revolutionaries convinced him that a cabal of wealthy Jewish bankers loomed behind all the bloodshed. Anti-Semitism twisted his thinking from then on.

Pelley returned to the United States in 1919, a troubled man. His marriage crumbled. He headed to California to cash in on his reputation as a writer, tapping out screenplays. Over the next decade, he wrote the stories and/or scripts for at least a dozen silent films, including star-making vehicles for Lon Chaney and western stars Tom Mix and Hoot Gibson. In his spare time, he penned two popular novels.

The Aliens Make Contact!

But more changes lay ahead. According to Pelley's account, on May 29, 1928, alone in his Pasadena bungalow, he experienced a spiritual awakening of sorts, an out-of-body experience in which his soul sailed into a spiritual realm normally forbidden to humans, and then returned so that he could write about it.

And write he did. Published in 1929 in *American Magazine,* and later as a pamphlet, Pelley's article "Seven Minutes in Eternity," sold nearly 100,000 copies.

Pelley Comes to Asheville

Ready to turn his newfound "spiritual" angle into a publishing empire, Pelley left Hollywood for Asheville in 1930. He opened Galahad College at the old Asheville Women's Club building on the corner of Sunset Parkway and Charlotte Street and established the Galahad Press publishing house (later the Pelley Publishing Company) in the former bank building beside the Biltmore depot. He published papers and magazines, most-notably *Liberation,* which preached a Darwin-meets–H.G. Wells theory that humanity descended from the interbreeding of apes and extraterrestrials from the Sirius 2 system. Sirian "Masters" had passed on these revelations to Pelley, making him the first (by some accounts) to claim to "channel" extraterrestrials.

The Not-So-Great Dictator

But being a spiritual "Contactee" brought social obligations. As the Depression deepened, Pelley, through his writings, began advocating the establishment of a national cooperative that would operate without banks or money. The two-time winner of the O. Henry Award for Short Fiction sat over his Asheville desk, plotting his own Fascist paramilitary organization. He named his troops the "Silver Shirts" in homage to Hitler's Brown Shirts and Mussolini's Black Shirts. In place of Hitler's swastika, Pelley himself designed a logo featuring the letter "L"-for "Loyalty" (to the United States) and "Liberation" (from the "bankers").

Keeping Asheville as his base and publishing center, Pelley traveled in a touring car, giving addresses largely in the depressed, rural areas of the Midwest and Northwest. Anti-Semitism was on the rise in these areas, and he won the friendship of a handful of politicians, and such Midwest-born celebrities as Charles Lindbergh and Walt Disney.

Students, blue-collar workers, and disillusioned WWI vets signed up for the "Silver Legion." Chapters opened around the country. They held rallies and marched in parades, wearing uniforms modeled after Hitler's storm troopers.

Public Response

The Silver Shirts' emergence raised concern among many Americans, including, understandably, the American Jewish community. A New York congressman attempted to ban the Silver Shirts uniform from public display. Novelist Sinclair Lewis, with whom Pelley had once been compared as an artist, wrote the cautionary novel *It Can't Happen Here,* featuring a Pelley-like character and warning of the Fascist threat to America.

However, many Ashevilleans who observed Pelley and his followers up-close simply laughed them off. In 1934, the Asheville *Times* published an editorial calling the Silver Shirts "a ridiculous expression of social unrest and egotism." The group's manifestos, the paper suggested, "should receive hearty laughter rather than quaking fear."

Pelley versus F.D.R.

Pelley soon found himself before a subcommittee on Un-American Activities. Undeterred, he ran for president in 1936 in the State of Washington as head of his euphemistically named "Christian Party" ticket, and the exposure tripled the Silver Shirts' ranks. Some now estimated the number of active Silver Shirts at 100,000, and the ranks of supporters and sympathizers stood much higher. Pelley planned to run in all 48 states in 1940, and some worried that he controlled enough working-class votes to—with many opposed to a third term for Roosevelt—swing the next election away from F.D.R.

Roosevelt supporter Walter Winchell was called upon to condemn Pelley's organization over the airwaves. Not long before the election, Roosevelt ordered the F.B.I. to investigate Pelley again. They seized Pelley's Asheville printing presses, and arrested a number of Silver Shirts on various charges. After months of expensive legal wrangling, the charges were dismissed, but the Silver Shirts had lost their money. Pelley never received his printing presses or building back. He did not run for president in 1940, and Roosevelt won an unprecedented third term and led America into war against Pelley's would-be compatriots, Hitler and Mussolini.

But Pelley did not give up. After the attack on Pearl Harbor, copies of Pelley's antiwar *Roll Call* magazine began to show up in the dufflebags of U.S. servicemen in fields of war, questioning the government's honesty in reporting the losses suffered at Pearl Harbor. Roosevelt called for Pelley's arrest on charges of sedition. Pelley had by now left Asheville for Indiana, but the Buncombe County sheriff swore out the warrant for Pelley's arrest. He was caught and brought back to Asheville for violation of the Espionage Act, was tried, convicted, and sentenced to 15 years in maximum security prison.

New Age Sage

In 1952, Pelley was paroled on the condition that he participate in no "political activities of any nature." Now based with his second family in Noblesville, Indiana, he created the Soulcraft

(Continued)

ASHEVILLE

WILLIAM DUDLEY PELLEY AND THE SILVER SHIRTS: ASHEVILLE'S WOULD-BE FUHRER (cont'd)

Publishing House, and published such titles as *Beyond Grandeur: Design for Immortality,* and *Know Your Karma.* For those in tune with the New Age pantheon, Pelley's associations are telling. Back in the 1930s he had served as teacher of Edna Ballard, whose large "I AM" cult derived many of its tenets from Pelley's teachings, and in fact began as a group of Pelleyites looking for leadership during their leader's incarceration. In his post-prison era, Pelley was a close associate of fellow "psychic contactees" George Hunt Williamson and George Adamski.

Over his remaining 14 years, Pelley achieved fame with a new audience. Directly and indirectly, his teachings have fed the ideas of many New Age devotees and UFO-enthusiasts since the 1930s. They've trickled down in modified form to such sects as "Heaven's Gate," which hit the headlines in 1997 after dozens of its members staged a mass suicide in Southern California, not far from the Pasadena bungalow where 70 years earlier, Pelley first wrote of his alleged enlightenment at the hands of extraterrestrials.

The uniquely 20th-century American career of this journalist/novelist/screenwriter/publisher/Fascist and E.T. channeler ended when Pelley died peacefully in Indiana in 1965.

most significant archaeological findings in this part of the country. At publication, research was only beginning, and it's expected to last at least 10 years.

Biltmore Village

Beyond the gates of the Biltmore estate, a village was constructed in 1898 to serve the needs of the Vanderbilts, their servants, and their guests. Twenty-four of the original buildings remain, including three designed by Richard Morris Hunt: All Souls Church, Biltmore Railway Station, and the Biltmore Estate Office. The village is a charming place to eat lunch, walk around, and visit the many small, often-touristy shops that surround the historic buildings. It is located off Highway 25 East, west of the downtown area.

Downtown Asheville Historic District

Approximately 170 buildings, some built as early as 1840, make up the largest collection of historic architecture in Asheville. Since the late 1980s, Asheville residents have made a concerted effort to bring the area back to its former glories—and they've largely succeeded. Centering on Pack Square, historic structures include the Spanish baroque **Church of St. Lawrence,** 97 Haywood St.; the Neo-Georgian **Battery Park Hotel** at

Battle Square; and the art deco **S&W Cafeteria** at 56 Patton Avenue.

MUSEUMS, GALLERIES, AND HISTORY

Pack Place: Education, Arts and Science Center

Located at 2 South Pack Square, this complex contains museums, galleries, shops, and live performances. The museums include the **Colburn Gem and Mineral Museum; the Health Adventure,** a health and biology museum; the **YMI Cultural Center,** featuring African American and African exhibits and commissioned by George Vanderbilt in 1893; and the **Asheville Art Museum.** The art museum's permanent collection focuses on 20th-century American art, including paintings, sculpture, prints, and various handicrafts. Admission is $3 per museum, or $6.50 for all the museums in Pack Place.

Botanical Gardens—Asheville

Occupying 10 acres of the campus of the University of North Carolina at Asheville, 151 W. T. Weaver Blvd., 828/252-5190, these gardens contain 26,000 plants native to Appalachia, a sculpture garden for the blind, and a log cabin.

Located off Highway 25 North near Merrimon Avenue, the gardens are open all year. No admission fee is charged.

Folk Art Center

Located off the Blue Ridge Parkway at Milepost 382, this center, tel. 828/298-7928, features craft demonstrations, exhibits, and the 100-plus-year-old Allanstand Craft Shop, featuring the work of the Southern Highland Craft Guild. The guild calls the center home, and its presence guarantees the quality and authenticity of the handcrafted items sold there. No admission is charged.

Riverside Cemetery

As cemeteries go, tree-shrouded Riverside, 58 Birch St., tel. 828/259-5800, is a pleasant place to visit. Locally born author William Sidney Porter, a.k.a. O. Henry, is buried here. So is Asheville-born Thomas Wolfe, proving that while you can go home again, it's not always healthy when you do. Incidentally, Wolfe's famous homeward-looking angel isn't here at Riverside. It's over at a cemetery in Hendersonville.

Smith-McDowell House Museum

Located at 283 Victoria Road, tel. 828/253-9231, this 1848 brick house is home to a local history museum that illustrates in detail the texture of Victorian-era life in Asheville. The home features a double porch supported by short white columns. It originally faced the old Buncombe Turnpike. A small admission fee is charged. Call for hours.

Thomas Wolfe Memorial State Historic Site

For anyone who has read the painful story of *Look Homeward, Angel,* this house (52 Market St., tel. 828/253-8304) is a required stop. Though he changed the name to Dixieland, this was the real boardinghouse, run by his mother, that inspired him. A fire nearly brought the building down a couple of years ago, but at press time, plans were well underway to refurbish and reopen the home, which is one of Asheville's top attractions. Just next door, in one of those "What-the-$!#!-were-they-thinking?" anomalies of modern life, the too-big, too-slick Radisson Hotel Asheville stands here spoiling the ambience like a storm trooper at a hoedown. It clearly belongs out next to an airport somewhere, but here it stands, dwarfing Wolfe's childhood home.

Western North Carolina Nature Center

Western North Carolina used to be the scene of various "See the Bear" roadside exhibits, at which unlucky bruins dwelt in filthy cages. Legislation now forbids such abuse of the state's largest animal, but here at the nature center, 75 Gashes Creek Rd., 828/298-5600, you can still see bears in an environment more like their natural one. Occupying seven acres, the center is home to a selection of wild and domestic animals, including a bear, a cougar, a golden eagle, deer, skunks, snakes, foxes, and more. Kids will enjoy the small petting zoo. A small admission fee is charged.

NIGHTLIFE AND EVENTS
Nightlife

Downtown has most but not all of the nighttime action in Asheville. The **Asheville Civic Center,** 87 Haywood St., tel. 828/259-5544, features the Thomas Wolfe Auditorium, one of Asheville's largest venues. Folks say that Elvis and Dylan both played here (though never together). The Asheville Symphony plays here throughout the year. Call 828/254-7046 for information.

The much more intimate **Grey Eagle Music Hall,** 185 Clingman Ave., tel. 828/232-5800, features a great mix of nationally and locally renowned artists. Previous performers have included folk greats like Arlo Guthrie and Guy Clark and bluegrass legends Del McCoury and Doc Watson. The doors open every day but Sunday at 4 P.M., though shows rarely get underway before 9. Tuesdays are open-mike night. To get there from Pack Square, take Patton Avenue west past the Federal Building. Follow the signs to Clingman Avenue, cross Clingman, make a right, and then turn right again until you've looped around onto Clingman.

Other local favorites include the family-friendly **Asheville Pizza & Brewing Compa-**

ny, 675 Merrimon Ave., tel. 828/254-1281; the versatile **Be Here Now,** 5 Biltmore Ave., tel. 828/258-2071; the Irish-themed **Jack of the Wood Pub,** 95 Patton Ave., tel. 828/252-5445; the hip **New French Bar,** 1 Battery Park Ave., tel. 828/252-3685; and uptown jazzy **Tressa's,** 28 Broadway, tel. 828/254-7072. For the college set, **Vincent's Ear,** 68 N. Lexington Ave., tel. 828/259-9119, is a cut above most other student bars. It brings a lot of college-circuit acts to town. Gays and lesbians looking to drink and dance with same favor the well-established, "private" **O. Henry's,** 59 Haywood St., tel. 828/254-1891. A small membership fee is required.

Events

Asheville is stuffed with people who are thankful they're there, and a town like that just loves to celebrate. Probably Asheville's top annual event, and by some accounts the largest street festival in the Southeast, **Bele Chere** offers road races, mountain music and dancing, cooking, craft demonstrations, games, and lots of other shenanigans, all on the (closed) streets of downtown Asheville in late July. The **North Carolina International Folk Festival/Folkmoot USA,** also in July, offers international dance and music in the Thomas Wolfe Auditorium. August sees the **Mountain Dance and Folk Festival,** tel. 828/258-6107, held annually here since the 1920s and featuring old-time and bluegrass music and mountain dancing. For a complete listing of events, contact the Asheville Chamber of Commerce at 828/258-3858. Christmas brings a host of events including **A Dickens Christmas in the Village,** tel. 828/274-8788, and alcohol-free **First Night Asheville,** tel. 828/259-5800, yet another excuse to celebrate in the streets. Is this a great town or what?

Practicalities

WHERE TO STAY
Bed-and-Breakfasts and Inns

Beaufort House Victorian Inn, 61 Liberty St., tel. 800/261-2221 or 828/254-9334, website: www.beauforthouse.com, is a historic 1894 home with big bay windows and pleasant views of the mountains. Recently ranked number one of all western North Carolina inns, it offers rooms for $125–235. The **Black Walnut B&B,** 288 Montford Ave., tel. 800/381-3878 or 828/254-3878, website: www.blackwalnut.com, also over 100 years old, sits right in the historic district. You may recognize it from its role in *28 Days,* the Sandra Bullock detox epic. Rooms run $95–200, including a full gourmet breakfast served by candlelight in the formal dining room.

Outside of town, the **Sourwood Inn,** 810 Elk Mountain Scenic Hwy., tel. 828/255-0690, website: www.sourwoodinn.com, sits on 100 mountainous acres. The hotel features 12 rooms with wood-burning fireplaces, plus a cabin. Rates run $140–175, including breakfast.

Hotels and Motels

If Biltmore House is the place to see in Asheville, **Grove Park Inn and Spa,** 290 Macon Ave., tel. 800/438-5800 or 828/252-2711, is definitely the place to stay. Built in 1913 by E. W. Grove, who served as his own architect and contractor, the inn reflects its mountain setting inside and out. The original portion of the inn was built of massive boulders; the fireplaces inside can easily burn 10-foot logs. F. Scott Fitzgerald used to stay here while visiting his wife/nemesis, Zelda, in a local mental hospital. With later additions, the inn now offers 510 rooms, which run $135–425. Suites run into the $625 range.

Open seasonally for years, the Grove Park Inn is nowadays open year-round. In February 2001, the inn's new 40,000-square-foot spa opened, providing all manner of luxuriating for those with the time and money.

For something much, much less expensive but still dependable, **American Court Motel,** 85 Merrimon Ave., tel. 828/253-4427, is a reasonably priced, non-chain alternative, just $69 in high season. Nothing fancy—it's a basic 1950s motor inn—but you won't get Tom's sort of friendly service at a Motel Six. **Days Inn Patton Avenue,** 120 Patton Ave., tel. 828/254-9661, sits within walking distance of Pack Square Plaza and the Civic Center.

Camping

Thirteen miles south of town on State Road 191, the eight-acre **North Mills River** campground, tel. 828/891-3016, is run by the National Forest Service, which means it's both basic and cheap. Sites run $5 a night. No showers or hookups are available. For more amenities, try **Bear Creek RV Park and Campground,** 81 S. Bear Creek Rd. For $20–26 a night you'll get full hookups at most sites and even cable TV hookups. Fifty tent sites are available.

FOOD

Asheville contains more good restaurants than you can shake a fat pincher at; the ones listed here are only a sampling. For starters, **Café on the Square,** 1 Biltmore Ave., tel. 828/251-5565, is in the running for the Middle of It All award. Local folks have named it the Best Downtown Eatery repeatedly over the years. It offers pastas, grilled meats, and seafood. The **Laughing Seed Café,** 40 Wall St., tel. 828/252-3554, is a less expensive vegetarian option on an agreeable side street. It's just upstairs from the Jack of the Wood Pub.

If you've been up in the Smokies and are dying for some good, spicy food, **La Paz,** 10 Biltmore Plaza, tel. 828/277-8779, offers fine southwestern cooking, margaritas, and patio seating (in season) in the Biltmore Village.

Malaprop's Bookstore and Café, 61 Haywood St., tel. 828/254-6734, is something like the Arnold's Drive-in of the patchouli and piercing set. The crowds just add to the urban feel. You'll find inexpensive sandwiches here. **Zambra,** 85 Walnut St., tel. 828/232-1060, offers Spanish cuisine, a tapas menu, a large assortment of wines, and a quiet environment. **Barley's Taproom and Pizzeria,** 42 Biltmore Ave., tel. 828/255-0504, offers live music Thursday through Saturday, featuring everything from jazz to folk to bluegrass. (Eating spinach and feta pizza while listening to "Foggy Mountain Breakdown" is a quintessential Asheville experience and not one to be missed.) The beer selection is tops, with over 40 to choose from, and all the req-

M

ASHEVILLE

© MIKE SIGALAS

Laughing Seed Café

uisite pizzeria recreational garnishes—darts, pool tables, and so on—make an appearance.

The perennial favorite barbecue in these parts is undeniably **Little Pigs BBQ,** 1916 Hendersonville Rd., tel. 828/684-0500, with other locations at 100 Merrimon Avenue, tel. 828/253-4633, and 384 McDowell Street, tel. 828/254-4253.

If you'd just like to pick something up and picnic, or eat as you stroll, head over to Biltmore Avenue, where you'll find the **Asheville Wine Market,** 65 Biltmore, tel., 800/825-7175 or 828/253-0060, website: www.ashevillewine.com, continually voted the top wine shop in Asheville in newspaper reader polls. It features a strong selection of wines, cheeses, and all the other ingredients for a pleasant do-it-yourself gourmet meal, including Carolina smoked trout. Next door, **Laurey's** makes sandwiches, soups, and desserts and will even lend you a picnic basket. Just across the street, the **Blue Moon Bakery** specializes in fine breads, soups, salads, and sandwiches. They also offer a Sunday brunch.

If coffee (and maybe a light breakfast) is all you want, **Beanstreets Coffee,** 3 Broadway, tel. 828/255-8180, is generally considered to brew the best in town.

SHOPPING

Just walk around Biltmore Village or downtown, and you'll find plenty of places with unique crafts and fascinating items just a-beggin' to be purchased. **World Marketplace,** 10 College St., tel. 828/254-8374, website: www.worldmarketplace.org, is a neat nonprofit shop that tries to funnel some of the disposable income floating around Asheville out to the Third World, where it can do wondrous things. The volunteer workers are happy to tell you about the various Third World–made products for sale here. Of local interest is the **Appalachian Craft Center,** 10 N. Spruce Rd., tel. 828/253-8499, where you can buy authentic handicrafts made by local craftspeople—not by Asian sweatshop workers. **Mast General Store,** 15 Biltmore Ave., 828/232-1883, website: www.mastgeneralstore.com, is an authentic, nostalgia-filled shop, with old-time can-

© MIKE SIGALAS

Shopping Daze, outside Malaprops bookstore

dies and some honest-to-goodness quality clothing and footwear—perfect for mountain living.

Finding Cherokee-made goods in town is tricky. Local merchants would love to carry them, but instead you'll need to make the drive up to the Qualla Boundary Reservation.

SERVICES AND INFORMATION

The Asheville Convention and Visitors Center, 151 Haywood St., tel. 800/257-1300 or 828/258-6111, will load you up with maps, brochures, and other information. Or try the **Asheville Gifts and Welcome Center,** 14 Battery Park. A good informational website is www.go asheville.com.

The paper of record in Asheville is the *Citizen-Times,* website: www.citizen-times.com. *Mountain Xpress,* a free weekly, does a good job reporting on the local entertainment scene. You'll find it all over town and online at www.mountainx.com.

Cherokee and Vicinity

Introduction

Just south of Great Smoky Mountains National Park on Highway 441, the parkland whose every use is closely supervised by the U.S. federal government butts directly up against a land where Uncle Sam holds little sway—the Qualla Boundary Cherokee Reservation.

The reservation lies in the southwestern section of North Carolina, arguably the most unspoiled section of the Southern Appalachians. The millions of visitors to Great Smoky Mountains National Park do not clog the roads here. The inns in the mountains are quiet, and in some places you can view landscapes that have not changed since before the Cherokee themselves arrived.

The Cherokee Reservation's residents—formally known as the Eastern Band of the Cherokee to distinguish them from their exiled cousins in Oklahoma—descend from the 1,000 or so individuals who refused to leave their homeland. Through sheer willpower, they keep their ancient culture alive, even today.

One of the most inspirational tracts of virgin timber in the East, the Joyce Kilmer Memorial Forest—named for Joyce "Only God Can Make a Tree" Kilmer—is found here. The waterfalls are the most striking in the region, and nowhere else in the country can you find so many kinds of precious stones. For those seeking natural beauty, outdoor activities such as whitewater rafting and hiking, or simply some relief from the pressures of modern life, the Cherokee region is hard to beat.

HISTORY

Despite its glittery casino future and recent cement-tepee past, Cherokee's deepest roots reach back centuries, through the ages when this place was the Cherokees' *world*. The Cherokee thrived in the richly forested land, where towering chestnut trees covered mountains spilling with waterfalls and laced with trout-rich streams. Bison, bear, and deer roamed the valleys. With a language that would outlive their dominance, the Cherokee gave names to the mountains and rivers that reflected the beauty they saw.

Main Street, Ghost Town in the Sky, Maggie Valley

© MIKE SIGALAS

CHEROKEE AND VICINITY

Then the outsiders came. Searching for a city of gold that the Indians kept telling him was farther away, Hernando De Soto and over 600 soldiers filed through this area in 1540, plundering Cherokee crops and forcing Indians to carry their gear as they pushed onward. Euro-Indian relations hit a low point in 1838 when Andrew Jackson sent U.S. troops to the area. They rounded up every Cherokee they could find—over 15,000—and forced them and their one thousand African American slaves to walk and/or take boats to Oklahoma. The four different trails the Cherokee took to the new "Indian Territory" are now collectively called the Trail of Tears. Some

4,000 Cherokees—mostly the elderly and children—died in the move, as did many of their slaves and dedicated Baptist missionaries.

Heartened by the virtual disappearance of the "savages," a different type of people began to arrive further east in southwestern North Carolina. The men wore high boots, the women wore silk dresses, and most families brought slaves. These were planters from places like Charleston and Savannah who came to the mountains to escape the summertime heat and fevers of the Low Country. They bought large pieces of land and built second homes, most of them larger than the homes the local folks used all year. Their

CHEROKEE AREA HIGHLIGHTS

Museum of the Cherokee Indian, Cherokee: Great collection of Cherokee artifacts, covering Cherokee history from prehistory to present.

Great Smoky Mountains Railroad, Dillsboro: With stops in Dillsboro, Bryson City, and Andrews and a variety of creative trips, it's a classy operation.

Harrah's Cherokee Casino: What the heck—it's here.

Highlands: At a 3,835-foot elevation, this appealing town was designed as a delightful vacation getaway.

Maggie Valley Opry House, Maggie Valley: Local-born bluegrass star Raymond Fairchild puts on a fun, authentic show.

Oconaluftee Indian Village, Cherokee: A fascinating and well-interpreted replica of a Cherokee community circa 1750.

Rafting the Nantahala Gorge: Shoot the rapids between stone walls from 500 to 1,500 feet high. The best rafting in the Smokies.

***Unto These Hills* Outdoor Drama:** A cast of 130 depicts the history of the Cherokee people from the point of first contact with Europeans to their 1828 removal. Powerful, entertaining, and a painless if heart-wrenching history lesson.

High Churches and society ways came with them, setting sophisticated architectural standards that still hold sway in such towns as Highlands. During this time, certain villages began to experience a seasonal variance in population, a common circumstance nowadays, but a novel one then.

The Civil War impoverished the planters and curbed the summer-long mountain pilgrimages. But the arrival of the railroad brought another wave of outsiders—people who had done a little better with the war financially—northerners. They were determined to make more money from the natural resources in the region. As the timber and minerals rode the rails out, money flowed in, enabling the mountain people to prosper a little themselves. Naturalists and tourists began to come in greater numbers, and the locals scurried about building inns and mountain hotels to make them comfortable.

In the early 20th century, as more and more Americans moved off farms and into cities, they began to miss their connection with nature. The government took steps not only to preserve the natural beauty of remote areas such as southwestern North Carolina but also to provide places of enjoyment and recreation for visitors. In the 1930s and 1940s, the TVA constructed a series of dams on the region's rivers, providing electrical power as well as beautiful lakes. Great Smoky Mountains National Park protected the highest of the mountains, while the Nantahala and Pisgah National Forests ensured that the resources of the area would be managed carefully. In fact, up to 70 percent of the land in some counties fell into the hands of Washington, D.C., preserving manifold delights for visitors.

ORIENTATION

Like well-defined characters in a good play, the towns on this side of the park all have their specialties. **Cherokee** has gambling and Indian Heritage sites. **Maggie Valley** offers the most lodging and the best Appalachian music. **Waynesville,** the biggest town this side of Asheville, is small-town cosmopolitan with its walkable Main Street and numerous bed-and-breakfasts. **Dillsboro** is a quaint train town, home to the historic Jarrett House Inn and a depot for the Great Smoky Mountains Railroad. **Bryson City** serves as gateway to the best white-water action in the entire Smokies region.

Cherokee

The Eastern Band of the Cherokee, who populate the Qualla Boundary Reservation, descend from the thousand or so Cherokee who evaded President Andrew Jackson's great 1838 removal of Native Americans from the path of "American progress." About 300 of them held U.S. citizenships and demanded their rights as American citizens; the rest lay low in Tennessee and North Carolina towns or hid out in the mountains.

© MIKE SIGALAS

Unto These Hills, an outdoor drama depicting the history of the Cherokee people

Today's boundary population is over 6,300, and tribal enrollment is 10,000.

The Cherokee who live here today find themselves dwelling on some prime real estate. Few other reservations, if any, enjoy proximity to so many tourists. It's no wonder that Harrah's gladly moved in to build and operate the tribe's casino. Next to the gates of Disney World in Orlando, this is about as good a location as Harrah's could ask for.

If you're interested in Cherokee culture and history, you'll want to take in the Museum of the Cherokee Indian, the Oconaluftee Indian Village, and perhaps the outdoor drama *Unto These Hills*. But be prepared for some disheartening roadside scenes, including the much-lamented presence of Plains Indians tepees and headdresses, "Injun"-themed miniature golf, and war dances for hire. The folks up here need to make a living somehow, and it'll be a while before every last rubber tomahawk has been beaten into a slot machine.

Maggie Valley

Unlike old-time mountain communities such as Dillsboro and Waynesville—founded in horse-drawn centuries and designed to accommodate foot traffic—Maggie Valley is a more pedestrian-unfriendly strip of tourist-related businesses. Maggie Valley didn't get a post office until 1904 and didn't *really* get going until after World War II. It was shaped by the automobile and the needs and wants of those who drove to the national park. Even today, for all its hundreds of rooms, Maggie is home to just 300 year-round residents.

But this is not necessarily a bad thing. For all its attempts to gussy itself up, the town always seems about one step away from being pure country. Therein lies its charm. Just travel a couple of hundred yards from Highway 19's restaurants and motels, and suddenly you're in a beautiful, rural Appalachian valley. In fact, a number of outfits in Maggie Valley rent brookside cabins amid mountain laurels and hemlocks but within walking distance of restaurants and shops.

Maggie also offers some good barbeque, a homegrown amusement park or two, and a couple of must-sees for any enthusiast of Appalachian culture: the **Maggie Valley Opry House** and **The Stompin' Grounds.**

One note: Maggie has just one main street, but that street has two names, Highway 19 and

PREGNANCY AMONG "THE PRINCIPAL PEOPLE"

According to contemporary accounts by European explorers, pregnant Cherokee women were habitually given an herbal potion that included, among other things, slippery elm bark to make the birth canal smooth. While pregnant, women were forbidden to eat squirrel meat, since squirrels run up trees when frightened, and a squirrel-influenced baby might head upward rather than down. Eating speckled trout was also banned, to prevent birthmarks.

a cozy cabin at Pioneer Village, Maggie Valley

Soco Road. Most locals use the former and give directions by landmark ("It's on 19 past Ghost Town"). Where possible, however, we've taken the post office's lead and included the Soco Road address as well.

Dillsboro

Known as the home depot for the **Great Smoky Mountains Railroad** and as a cute mountain village (pop. 100) loaded with local crafts, Dillsboro is a child of the old Western North Carolina Railway, which arrived hereabouts in 1882. William Allen Dills founded the town as a stopover for travelers up from Asheville. He built the Mount Beulah Hotel on Main Street—which operates today as the Jarrett House, still a worthwhile lodging and restaurant.

Waynesville

Waynesville was founded by officers and soldiers who received land grants following the American Revolution. Many had served under General "Mad" Anthony Wayne, and they named their settlement in his honor.

A couple of generations later, at the end of the War Between the States, Waynesville wit-

nessed the surrender of the last Confederate force in North Carolina—the bedraggled Army of Western North Carolina—on May 6, 1865. For a long time, Tarheels argued that the very last shot of the Civil War fired on land occurred here on May 10, 1865, but later records determined that Confederates down in Brownsville, Texas, held out three days longer, so Waynesville was stripped of this particular glory. The railroad reached here in 1883, bringing some of the town's first tourists.

Today, this pretty town (pop. 10,000) features a pleasant downtown area with brick sidewalks and several small shops in old buildings.

Bryson City

Calling itself "the Outdoor Adventure Capital of the Smokies," Bryson City (pop. 1,100) offers great, uncrowded access to the park, yet plenty of shops and restaurants to keep you from feeling deprived. It's also close to the Nantahala River Gorge, the most popular area in the region for white-water rafting, most often with outfitters at the Nantahala Outdoor Center, Nantahala Rafts, or Wildwater Ltd. Rafting.

Sights and Recreation

MUSEUMS AND GARDENS

Located on U.S. 441 at Drama Road in downtown Cherokee, the newly renovated **Museum of the Cherokee Indian,** tel. 828/497-3481, houses a great collection of Cherokee artifacts covering Cherokee culture from prehistory to present. Fascinating multimedia exhibits tell the Cherokee story. The museum is open year-round; admission runs $3.50 for adults.

Oconaluftee Indian Village on Drama Road off U.S. 441 (near the Mountainside Theatre), tel. 828/497-2315 or 828/497-2111, is also very worthwhile. The village is a replica of a Cherokee community circa 1750. The guided tour includes live demonstrations of Cherokee crafts and skills, including beading and the proper use of a blowgun. You'll also see replicas of Cherokee buildings, including average homes and the Council House, the political center of the village. (You'll see the headquarters for the pleasant **Cherokee Botanical Garden and Nature Trail** as you exit the village.) Presented by the nonprofit Cherokee Historical Association, the village is open 9 A.M.–5:30 P.M. from May 15 until October 25. Admission is not cheap: $12 for adults, $5 for children 6–12, free for children under 6. But you can buy a package ticket that includes entrance to the village and the museum and a discount on tickets to *Unto These Hills.*

In Waynesville, the **Shelton House Museum of North Carolina Handicrafts,** 49 Shelton St., tel. 828/452-1551, is set in the old Shelton House, a two-story home built between 1876 and 1880 and now listed on the National Register of Historic Places. The museum contains Civil War and Native American artifacts and displays of such handcrafted goods as woodcarvings, quilts, pottery, musical instruments, and weavings. Located at the corner of Shelton and Pigeon Streets, the museum is open May through October, 10 A.M.–5 P.M. Wednesday through Saturday, 2 P.M.–5 P.M. on Sunday. Admission is free.

AMUSEMENTS
Harrah's Cherokee Casino

In most parts of the country, Indian casinos offer all the depressing aspects of Las Vegas without any of its glitzy visual hyperbole or $5.95 lobster dinners in trade. No matter what the billboards

Harrah's Cherokee Casino

© MIKE SIGALAS

CHEROKEE

claim, they all tend to resemble the most smoke-filled, godforsaken corner of the seediest one-off casino in Reno.

Harrah's Cherokee Casino, tel. 800/427-7247 (HARRAHS), is several cuts above the others, largely because the Cherokee wisely selected Harrah's experienced and well-financed casino makers to build and run the whole show. Harrah's offers vacationers a place to help compensate Cherokees for taking their land, one coin roll at a time. Vegas-style childcare-video games and free pizza—is thoughtfully provided at Planet for Kids.

The 60,000-square-foot, 2,300-machine casino cost $80 million to build in the 1990s, but it already *clears* $120 million annually. Major additions, including new restaurants and a 15-story, 252-room hotel, are already underway.

In return for allowing this little bit of Vegas in Appalachia, each registered tribal member receives payments totaling around $5,000 a year. And so far at least, this figure grows annually. But the benefits go well beyond individual payments. The tribe has built a dialysis center and plans to create a $12 million wellness center with casino profits. What's more the Harrah's complex provides employment for some 1,900 people.

Great Smoky Mountains Railroad

With stops in Dillsboro, Bryson City, and Andrews, the Great Smoky Mountains Railroad, tel. 800/872-4681, is a classy and creative operation.

You might remember the railroad, in fact, from its role in the Harrison Ford/Tommy Lee Jones film *The Fugitive*. Though none of the current trips include collisions with busfuls of convicts, the railroad does offer a number of different trips with a variety of themes. It operates both steam and diesel trains on most routes, with the steam trips running about $5 more than the diesel trips. (The prices quoted below, unless otherwise noted, are for the steam trips.) Kids 2 and under ride free; those 3–12 ride for roughly half the adult fare.

The **Tuckasegee River** trip ($31) leaves from Dillsboro Depot, heads west to Bryson City, lays over for an hour there, then returns to Dillsboro. Along the way, you'll thread the pitch-black, 836-foot Cowee Tunnel.

Other trips take in the Nantahala Gorge (Bryson City departure, $31), Red Marble Gap (Andrews departure, $26, diesel only), and the Fontana Trestle (Dillsboro departure, $31). You can also take a seven-hour Raft 'n' Rail trip that includes rafting (Bryson City departure, $64) and Gourmet Dinner trips (Dillsboro

CHEROKEE

© MIKE SIGALAS

Great Smoky Mountains Railroad car, Dillsboro

departure, $54, diesel only). For youngsters and parents of same, every summer for a week or so, the railroad swings a deal with Sir Topham Hatt and brings in that oft-cheeky tank engine, Thomas, direct from the Isle of Sodor and the VCRs of every parent in America. The 30-minute trips (Dillsboro departure—steam only, of course) cost $10 a ticket (for both adults and children). Be sure to call ahead for reservations. The gift shop at the GSMR station at Dillsboro, incidentally, offers one of the world's largest selections of Thomas items.

Ghost Town in the Sky

Located high above Maggie Valley, Ghost Town in the Sky, tel. 800/446-7886 or 828/926-1140, website: ghosttowninthesky.com, is not a true abandoned old town but is actually a small aging amusement park—and a funky, homegrown bit of Americana. Built in 1960 at the height of the *Gunsmoke-Bonanza* era, Ghost Town is a tribute to the East's fascination with the West, as delineated in dime novels, Saturday morning se-

rials, and early television shows. The plywood Ghost Town brings to mind the mid-20th-century Western craze—think Roy Rogers, Howdy Doody, and wagon-wheel chandeliers—far more than it does the American West of the 1880s. Unless, of course, you're six years old.

And that's the key to Ghost Town. For young children and their parents, it can be a real hoot.

Admission, like the mountain itself, is a bit steep: $20.95 for everyone over 10, $13.95 for kids over 3 (kids 2 and under get in free). But these prices include unlimited use of the carnival-like rides and shows. Getting *up there* is half the adventure. You can take the minivan tram, a 3,364-foot double incline railway (with grades up to 76.9 percent), or a two-seat 1962 Italian chairlift—a dramatic and novel way to arrive anywhere, much less a Western ghost town. You'll arrive at the park's Mining Town area, but to hit the bulk of the park, you've still got some climbing to do, or you can take another tram.

Ghost Town is divided into four themed areas: Mining Town (the lowest), Western Town, In-

Ghost Town in the Sky

dian Village (with Cherokee dancers), and Mountain Town. For older kids, the Red Devil roller coaster, the only real thrill ride up here, is a big draw. The short, looping metal coaster seems all the higher by being some 5,000 feet up a mountain. There's also a small train, a kiddie area, and a handful of carnival rides that don't fit the park theme. Thus, you might find yourself deep in Appalachia, swinging back and forth in a huge Viking ship, high above a re-created midwestern town.

Parents, depending on their philosophies, will either want to catch or avoid the hourly gunfights on Main Street. Double, I suppose, for the cancan shows in the saloons. The park considerately allows guests to bring in coolers packed with picnic goodies and will even transport your cooler to the Picnic Area, where it'll be waiting for you when you're ready to eat. The town itself dishes up some fair grub, including ice cream, funnel cakes, and that staple of the 19th-century American frontier diet—pizza. If nothing else, parents can enjoy the views of the surrounding mountains.

Soco Gardens Zoo

The animals you'll find at Soco Gardens Zoo, 3758 Soco Rd., Maggie Valley, tel. 828/926-1746, aren't specific to the Smokies, but are rather largely exotics: a jaguar, alligators, llamas, monkeys, ostriches, and so on—including a number of species that haven't seen the top of a mountain since working their way down Mount Ararat.

As at every zoo, the reptile shows are very popular at Soco. If you're planning to hike the Smokies, you can get a good, safe eye-to-eye with a cottonmouth and a copperhead ahead of time, to better identify them in the wild. Years ago, somebody lost a leg here to one of the park's alligators. Fortunately—for the zoo's insurance company at least—the victim was another alligator, theretofore known as Tripod. You can still see him today, unless things have taken a grimmer turn and he's now known as Pogo.

The zoo is open 10 A.M.–6 P.M. during spring and fall, 9 A.M. to 7:30 P.M. during summer (closed winters). Admission is reasonable: $6 for ages 13–65, $5 for seniors, $3 for kids 12 and under. The zoo is wheelchair accessible.

SHADES OF GRAY: SLAVEHOLDING AND REBELLION IN THE CHEROKEE NATION

From the colonial period through the 1838 forced removal to Oklahoma, most members of the "Five Civilized Tribes"—the Cherokee, Seminole, Creek, Choctaw, and Chickasaw—blended steadily with the white society around them, adopting the Christian faith, European-style clothing, and the white American lifestyle. Intermarriage was common.

Roughly 10 percent of all Cherokees owned African American slaves. An estimated 1,000 slaves traveled the Trail of Tears along with their Cherokee masters. A few used the opportunity to escape, but most did not. Many Cherokee who chose to evade removal and hide out high in the Smokies did so with their slaves.

Members of both the Western and Eastern Cherokee grew wealthy through slavery and came to side with fellow Southerners on such is-

sues as states' sovereignty and "property" rights. At the commencement of the Civil War, like other Carolinians and Tennesseans, many Eastern Cherokee took up arms in defense of their homeland. Out west in Oklahoma, the Western Cherokee—after much heated debate—also sided with the Confederacy. Some 7,000 Cherokee (approximately 25 to 33 percent of the fighting Cherokee population) would die in the war, most of them wearing Confederate gray. No state suffered a higher death rate than the Cherokee Nation.

Today, two miles north of Cherokee on U.S. 441, a plaque erected by the United Daughters of the Confederacy honors the Cherokee men who served in the Confederate army. You can also see a small display on Cherokee Confederates in the Museum of the Cherokee Indian in Cherokee.

CHEROKEE

Santa's Land Park and Zoo

Like Ghost Town in the Sky, Santa's Land Park and Zoo, 2.5 miles east of Cherokee on U.S. 19, tel. 828/497-9191, is something out of a simpler, less-cynical era. It's a Christmas-themed park featuring old-fashioned amusement park rides painted green and red. Young kids will love the kiddie Rudi Coaster (with antlers), the miniature steam train, the petting zoo (including "reindeer," of course), the juggling and magic-making elves over at the Jingle Bell Theater, and Santa's House, where they can get cheek-to-rosy-cheek with Saint Nick himself. The park also includes some nods to the mountain culture of the Smokies: a pre–Civil War cabin, a gristmill, and a moonshiner's still. If you're up here in October, you might want to take in the pleasant **Fall Harvest Festival.** The weekend event features mountain craft exhibits, fresh apple cider and apple butter, and more. Santa's Land is open May through October and Thanksgiving week Monday through Friday 9 A.M.–5 P.M., Saturday and Sunday 9 A.M.–6 P.M. November hours are Saturday and Sunday 9 A.M.–6 P.M. Starting in December, Santa's away—overseeing operations farther north, presumably. Admission runs around $14 for everyone 3 and up.

Old Pressley Sapphire Mine

Just east of Waynesville in Canton (Exit 33 off I-40) you'll find the Old Pressley Sapphire Mine, 240 Pressley Mine Rd., tel. 828/648-6320. The Old Pressley is a favorite of rock hounds and a storied source of one of the largest sapphires ever plucked from the earth, the 1,445-carat Star of the Carolina. Today you can mine a bit yourself ($10) or just enjoy the picnic area and browse the rock shop.

Lindsey Gardens and Miniature Village and Mini-Apolis Grand Prix Park

Popular with the younger set, this complex, at 1110 Soco Road, tel. 828/926-1685 or 828/926-6277, features miniature racecar tracks, bumper boats, miniature golf, a gem mine, and a diminutive train that meanders through the gardens and a village of over 90 miniature buildings.

ENTERTAINMENT

People come to the Smokies with a lot of different agendas, and your agenda will probably determine what sort of entertainment—if any—you seek out during your visit.

Maggie Valley Opry House

If you're here to experience Appalachian folk culture and music, be sure to catch the Maggie Valley Opry House, 3605 Soco Rd., tel. 828/926-9336, featuring Maggie Valley's unqualified bluegrass star, Raymond Fairchild, considered by aficionados to be among the best living banjo pickers. Cherokee-born (and part Cherokee) Fairchild, famed for a deadpan concentration as he picks, recorded his first albums in the early 1960s. Nowadays, after 40 years of festivals and different touring bands—including his famed Maggie Valley Boys with son Zane on lead guitar—Fairchild runs his Opry House and plays for appreciative fans with a backup band. If at all possible, get over to the Opry House at 8 P.M. any

The Strand Theatre in Waynesville

night April through October and catch this man in action. To get familiar with his work before you arrive, pick up his classic *31 Banjo Favorites* CD on the Rhythm label. It's a great trove of Smoky Mountain music.

Stompin' Ground

And speaking of mountain music, the Stompin' Ground, tel. 828/926-1288, may look like a big old barn on Highway 19 but it's ground zero for clogging. It throws open its doors nightly from May to October. Stomp inside, and you'll find some topnotch clogging afoot. And if you get the itch, you can give it a go yourself.

Diamond K Dance Ranch

This family-oriented nightspot (1 Playhouse Dr., Maggie Valley, tel. 828-926-7735) offers classic and contemporary country music (live and not), teen nights, Friday night fish fries

Dance on over to the Stompin' Ground.

© MIKE SIGALAS

($5.95), and award-winning chili. No alcohol is allowed on the premises.

Smoky Mountain Jamboree

In the same vein, the Smoky Mountain Jamboree, located on Acquoni Road opposite the Best Western, tel. 828/497-5521, boasts an alcohol-free "country music extravaganza" for $12.50 a ticket. Children 12 and under enter free with a paying adult. The show starts nightly at 8 P.M. June through October and on weekends only in April, May, and November (closed the rest of the year).

Unto These Hills Outdoor Drama

Of course, to fully grasp Appalachian culture, one needs to have an understanding of the history and contributions of its original inhabitants. Over at the Qualla Reservation you'll find the stirring *Unto These Hills,* with a cast of 130, many of them direct descendants of the men and women they portray. The show depicts the history of the Cherokee people from the point of first contact with Europeans to their 1828 deportation along the Trail of Tears. The script was written by Kermit Hunter, author of *Horn in the West,* the outdoor drama in Boone. Contact the Mountainside Theatre, 441 N. Drama Rd., tel. 866/554-4557 or 828/497-2111, website: www.untothesehills.com.

"Unto" saw its first performance here way back in 1950, and over 6 million folks have experienced the show in the half-century since. Like *The Lost Colony* out at Roanoke Island, *Unto These Hills* contains a compelling combination of elements: a powerful historical story; a powerful script; a beautiful, enigmatic theater; a strong, devoted cast; and the fact that the events on stage took place right here, on this soil, under these stars, with the same scent of pines and hemlock in the air. Shows run mid-June through late August, 8:30 P.M. nightly, except Sundays. Pre-show entertainment begins at 7:45 P.M. Reserved seats at the front of the theater run $16—and there's no discount for children. General admission seats in the rear of the theater run only a couple of bucks shorter for adults, but kids 6–13 pay only $6. Children under 6 get in

CHEROKEE

free with a paid adult. Group discounts are available for 20 or more.

Incidentally, if you're buying a combination ticket for the Oconaluftee Indian Village and Museum of the Cherokee, you'll receive a discount for *Unto These Hills* tickets.

Harrah's Cherokee Pavilion Theatre

While some see a visit to the Smokies as a chance to enjoy nature or explore different cultures, others see the region as a resort area, and they want to see some big-name stars. If this is you, your best bet on this side of the park is to head over to Harrah's Casino. The casino's 1,500-seat Cherokee Pavilion Theatre offers the strongest lineup this side of Dollywood. Performers have included Loretta Lynn, BB King, Charlie Daniels, Wynonna Judd, Bill Cosby, Brooks and Dunn, Kenny Rogers, and that patron saint of pit bosses, Mr. Wayne Newton.

Carolina Nights

After the casino, the next best bet for the "resorters" is the 300-seat Carolina Nights on Highway 19 across from Microtel in Maggie Valley, tel. 828/926-8822. The theater offers a prime-rib dinner and a show that stakes a claim somewhere between Nashville and Vegas; count on Blues Brothers imitators and a magic act along with your country and homespun comedy.

HART: Haywood Arts Repertory Theatre

Beside the Shelton House in Waynesville stands the 250-seat **Performing Arts Center,** 250 Pigeon St., where the Haywood Arts Repertory Theatre (HART) produces two main stage musicals, five main stage plays, and up to six studio theater shows every season. This means that they'll probably be performing something when you're here. The main stage plays and musicals tend toward mainstream classics: A recent season included *Our Town, The Sound of Music,* and *Antigone*. Tickets for plays and musicals run $12–15 for adults. The box office is located at the **Mast General Store** on Main Street, or call 828/456-6322 for show information and reservations.

OUTDOOR RECREATION

Let the Tennessee side keep Dolly and the Ripley's Aquarium—the North Carolina side of the park features the best rafting and skiing in the Smokies, as well as some of the best waterfalls.

Rafting the Nantahala Gorge

Southwest of Bryson City, the Nantahala River flows parallel to Highway 19 from Topton to Wesser, about 10 miles from Robbinsville. The gorge walls vary in height from 500 to 1,500 feet and offer excellent opportunities for white-water rafting, canoeing, and kayaking. Along the road you'll find several picnic areas and access to the rushing water. Guided white-water trips are offered by **Wildwater Ltd. Rafting,** 12 miles west of Bryson City on Highway 19, tel. 800/451-9972; **Nantahala Outdoor Center,** another mile along at 13077 Highway 19, tel. 800/232-7238 or 828/488-6900, website: www.noc.com; and **Nantahala Rafts,** 14260 Hwy. 19, tel. 828/488-2325. Of the three, Nantahala Outdoor Center, founded in 1972, is the largest. Rates to run the Nantahala with a guide—a fairly mild, family-friendly run—range from $22–28 per person. If you're looking for whiter water, the center also leads trips of various lengths and skill levels on the Ocoee, Nolichucky, Pigeon, and Chattooga Rivers. (On most of these rivers, be prepared to see a lot of other rafts as you go along.)

If you'd like to stay close to the river, the Nantahala Outdoor Center has a large lodge that includes simple motel rooms ($55–65), coed bunkhouse-style beds ($14 a person), and 2-to 10-bedroom cabins starting at $110 a night. Across from Wildwater Ltd. Rafting, you'll find the 22-acre **Falling Waters Adventure Resort,** 10345 Hwy. 74 W., tel. 800/451-9972, with roomy elegant yurts featur-

> *"That Nantahala is a master shut-in, just a plumb gorge."*
>
> —A mountaineer's description of the Nantahala Gorge, recorded by Horace Kephart in the early 1900s

ing French doors, tongue-and-groove pine floors, decks, and skylights. Rates are $64–79 a night.

Cataloochee Ski Area

If you've come to North Carolina in search of the world's best ski slopes, you have been criminally misled. However, Cataloochee, 1080 Ski Lodge Rd., tel. 828/926-0285, website: www.Cataloochee.com, has nine slopes (seven with snowmaking equipment), three ski lifts, and a rope tow. At publication, the park is in the midst of a three-year, $2.1 million infrastructure-improvement project. Rates run roughly $23 for adults on weekdays, $36 on weekends, with discounts for kids, teens, seniors, students, and members of the military. If you're coming here during the week, ask about the Kids Ski Free arrangement with various local lodgings, which can save parents considerable amounts of money. Night skiing is available too.

SHOPPING

Across Drama Road from the Museum of the Cherokee, **Qualla Arts and Crafts,** Hwy. 441 at Drama Rd., tel. 828/497-3103, ranks as arguably the best market in the world for authentic Cherokee crafts. First opened in 1946, the cooperative features the baskets, masks, pottery, finger weaving, woodcarving and other crafts of more than 300 Cherokee artists. Open year-round: 8 A.M.–8 P.M. June through August; 8 A.M.–6 P.M. September through October, 8 A.M.–4:30 P.M. November through May.

Dillsboro's Front Street and Haywood Road (Business 19) feature a number of shops worth a browse. Front Street's **Mountain Pottery** is a working studio where you can watch artisans creating raku pottery, handmade porcelain, and stoneware. Up on Haywood Road you'll find a handful of other shops, including the countrified **Corn Crib,** tel. 828/586-9626. And "quiltophiles" won't want to miss the **Apron Shop** between Haywood and Front on Webster Street, tel. 828/586-9391. It features locally handmade quilts, as well as aprons, pillows, and baskets.

In Waynesville, as in any good mountain town, you'll find just about everything there is to do on Main Street. For instance, you'll find the Waynesville location of the **Mast General Store,** 63 N. Main, tel. 828/452-2101, website: www.mastgeneralstore.com. Though this store opened only in 1991, both the Mast business and the building itself are much older. In fact, the first Mast store opened in Valle Crucis back in 1883. With its old oak floors and early-20th-century tin ceilings and fixtures, the Waynesville store feels as though it dates from the same era. It also still offers the sort of product diversity that led to the name general store in the first place. A 1923 advertisement for the old Boone Mast store even boasted of "Goods for the Living, Coffins and Caskets for the Dead." Today, Mast no longer caters to the departed, but the living can still buy Squirrel Nut Zippers, Charleston Chews, and Licorice Bullseyes from wooden barrels. You'll also find sturdy traditional clothing and outdoor wear and an assortment of such mercantile essentials as rosebud salves, stone ground meal, "courtin' candles," porch swings, rocking chairs, handmade crafts and baskets, goat's milk, lye soap, and, of course, Radio Flyer wagons. To get to the Waynesville store, take U.S. 276 south to Main Street, turn right, and then turn right into the parking lot.

Open on Main Street since 1945, **Whitman's Bakery and Sandwich Shop,** 18 N. Main, tel., 828/456-8271, serves luscious breads, pies, pastries, cookies, and cakes. They make sandwiches, too—so it's a good spot for lunch. Open Tuesday through Saturday at 6 A.M.

The **T. Pennington Art Gallery** features the drawings of Teresa Pennington, a self-taught artist whose personal takes on western North Carolina (including a recent series on the Blue Ridge Parkway) have won her national acclaim.

The **Open Air Market** on Main Street strikes an interesting balance between a newsstand and a grocery store. At the **Twigs & Leaves Gallery** in the center of town you'll find nature-related handcrafts, photography, and paintings, as well as a pottery studio.

Every Wednesday and Saturday during summer, you'll find local farmers arriving on the north end of Main Street for the **Farmers Tailgate Market.** This is a great place to pick up fresh mountain produce, including berries, new

CHEROKEE

potatoes, cucumbers, green beans, tomatoes, squash, onions, and carrots.

EVENTS

In May, Waynesville's **Ramp Festival** celebrates the tarnation out of Appalachia's favorite leek, something of a cross between the onion and the garlic clove. As with most celebrations in this neck of the mountains, the festival includes live bluegrass music, clogging in the streets, and lots of food for the sampling—including various manifestations of the ramp. For information on this festival, founded in 1931, call 828/456-8691. For 10 days in July, Waynesville hosts the **North Carolina International Folk Festival.** Call 828/452-2997 for information.

In late August, Cherokee's Ceremonial Grounds, beside the tribal office on U.S. 441, host the **Intertribal Traditional Dances,** with various tribes from around the United States arriving for dance competitions and demonstrations. For information call 800/438-1601.

Early October brings the **Cherokee Indian Fall Festival** at the Cherokee Ceremonial Grounds. The festival includes ceremonial dancing, blowgun demonstrations, archery, stickball games, and beauty pageants. For information call 800/438-1601.

Santa's Land Park and Zoo, east of Cherokee hosts, a **Fall Harvest Festival** on weekends in October, with mountain craft exhibits, fresh apple cider and apple butter, and more. Call 828/497-9191 for information.

The first two Fridays and Saturdays in December, Dillsboro's shops stay open late and lit for the picturesque **Christmas Lights and Luminaries** festival. Thousands of Christmas lights and candles brighten the evening, and brass ensembles and carolers fill the cold night air with music. It's a memorable atmosphere for some Christmas shopping. Call 828/586-2155 for information.

Where to Stay

Maggie Valley, with just around 350 full-time residents, offers lots of rooms. Cherokee's bed numbers shot up with the addition of the Harrah's Hotel across from the casino.

RANCH ACCOMMODATIONS

Cataloochee Ranch, 119 Ranch Dr., Maggie Valley, tel. 800/868-1401 or 828/926-1401, website: www.cataloochee-ranch.com, was founded in 1933 on an old Cataloochee Valley farm inside the national park. In 1938, fleeing the stringent land-use limitations within the park proper, founders Tom and Judy Alexander relocated the ranch to its current location bordering the park at the top of Fie Top Mountain, elevation 5,000 feet.

The Alexanders' children and grandchildren continue to run the ranch, which can host up to 65 guests in its cabins, suites, and rooms. Meals, as you might guess, come filling and family-style. Activities at the thousand-acre spread include horseback riding (for an extra fee), pack trips (ditto), hikes, sing-alongs, fishing, wagon rides, swimming, tennis, and the time-honored marshmallow roast. Three private entrances to the park provide ranch guests with another very significant amenity, and if you're here in winter (open holidays and weekends only) you're as close to the Cataloochee Ski Area (also owned by the Alexander family) as you can get.

Rooms in the ranch's big lodge run $145–275 April through November. The big breakfasts and dinners (often grill-outs when weather permits) come with your room fee. Lunches are available at an extra charge.

You'll find Fie Top Road off Highway 19 at Ghost Town in the Sky. Drive up the road for three miles, and you're there.

Interested in horseback riding but staying elsewhere? You can still book a horse at the Cataloochee for only a bit more than ranch guests pay.

Olde Town Inn

BED-AND-BREAKFASTS AND INNS

In Maggie Valley you'll find the **Timberwolf Creek Bed & Breakfast,** 391 Johnson Branch, tel. 828/926-2608, a large gray and white building folded into the side of the mountain. It features three rooms. The Timberwolf Retreat is a suite with a king-sized bed, vaulted red oak ceilings, a spa tub for two, and a balcony overlooking the stream outside. The other two rooms are the Woodland and the Streamsong—and the names pretty much tell you what view each provides. Both feature queen beds, whirlpool tubs for two, private decks, and private entrances. The Streamsong's double French doors open to a private deck over the stream.

Hosts Sandee and Larry Wright serve up a full gourmet fireside breakfast (sometimes featuring baked omelets and French custard toast with spiked apples)-or you can take your breakfast outside by the waterwheel. In the evenings the Wrights dish up some fresh baked goods and mugs of steaming hot cider in front of the fireplace—just the sort of treat that makes you feel like a well-loved nine-year-old. However, no actual nine-year-olds are allowed to stay here —kids, like pets, are officially deemed "inappropriate" at the Timberwolf. Smokers will need to practice their craft outside on the porch. Rooms run $195–245 a night. Wednesday is Dinner and Jazz Night. Contact innkeeper@ timberwolfcreek.com for more information.

For sheer tradition and pretense-free mountain hospitality, **The Jarrett House,** tel. 800/972-5623 or 828/586-0265, is hard to beat. It has been renting rooms and feeding hungry visitors since 1884, when it was opened by no less than Mr. Dills himself—founder of the town of Dillsboro—just two years after the coming of the Western North Carolina Railway.

Dills christened the inn the Mount Beulah Hotel, named after his daughter. Some may tell you that the hotel's original name came from the fact that it faces Mount Beulah, and that's true too. Dills, you see, also named the *mountain* after his daughter. Ah, the privileges of founderhood. Beulah's daughter still lives next door to the hotel.

A significant portion of the town's income used to derive from the passengers who piled out of the daily train up from Asheville for a noontime dinner at the hotel. Within a couple of years—beginning in 1884 with a pair of scandalously cigarette-wielding women from Edenton—outlanders had begun to come up and stay for the summer.

The hotel's second owners were Frank and Sallie Jarrett, who changed the name to Jarrett Springs Hotel to take advantage of a sulfur spring out back. They operated it from the 1890s through the 1950s—an amazing run. Sallie's country cured ham, red-eye gravy, and hot biscuits became the stuff of legend and a definite Jarrett House tradition. You can still pick up a ham dinner here—even if you're not a hotel guest—for $12.50. With the hot springs craze abated, the next owners changed the name to its current one. Though the hotel changed owners a number of times in the 1950s, all told it has had only four owners for 110 of its 120 years. The current owners, the Hartbargers, have been here since 1975 and clearly honor the mantle they've assumed. No pets, kids under 11, or credit cards are welcome here.

Also in Dillsboro, Lera Chitwood's **Olde Towne Inn,** 300 Haywood Rd. (Hwy. 23/74), tel. 888/528-8840 or 828/586-3461, is of the friendlier sort. It's located just across from the Great Smoky Mountain Railroad depot. The five rooms in the 1878 home are named after colors, and they run $75–135. All but the least expensive—the Yellow Room—have their own baths. Yellow Room occupants share with Mrs. Chitwood.

Nearby, in Sylva, Patrick and Mary Ellen Montague's 1914 bungalow, the **Freeze House,** 71 Sylvan Heights, tel. 828/586-8161, fax 828/631-0714, offers three rooms from $75–100. The house was built by Patrick's maternal grandfather (Mr. Freeze) during the First World War. Initially it was a private home that doubled during summers as a guesthouse for outlanders seeking the cool mountain air. When the train stopped bringing up guests after World War II, the Freeze family took in boarders year-round, and eventually it became a fully private home. In the mid-1990s, Patrick's son refurbished the two private guesthouses—equipped with kitchens and great for large families or groups. They are available for $400 and $600 a week.

Over in Waynesville, if you're looking to experience the sort of down-to-earth, agrarian lifestyle that existed up here before the tourists came, you'll find a good semblance outside of town at the five-bedroom **Ketner Inn & Farm,** 1954 Jonathan Creek Rd., tel. 800/714-1397 or 828/926-1511. Built in 1898, the inn rests on 27 acres of rolling farmland. You'll find country and Victorian antiques throughout, with porches and full country breakfasts. Children are welcome; rates run $55–75.

If you're looking for a B&B within walking distance of the shops on Waynesville's Main Street, take a look at Judith and Dennis Framptons' **Prospect Hill Inn,** 274 S. Main St., 800/219-6147 or 828/456-5980, website: www.prospecthillnc.com. This turn-of-the-last-century, seven-bedroom Victorian stands right on Main Street at the top of Prospect Hill at the edge of downtown. It provides a pleasant stay, with an enormous front porch manned with rockers and wicker furniture. Breakfasts are upscale—served on the porch with fine china and silver—and gourmet. The living room provides a good view of the Smokies. Rates run $95–135. Though they discourage kids in the house proper, the Framptons offer two efficiency apartments in the old carriage house behind the main house for $450 a week. The apartments overlook a quiet street and face Eagle's Nest Mountain.

CABINS AND LODGES

Sitting on the porch of your cabin at **Twinbrook Resort,** 230 Twinbrook Ln., tel. 800/305-8946 or 828/926-1388, website: www.twinbrookresort.com, you'd never guess that you're just 500 yards from U.S. 19. The 20-acre property features 16 one-, two-, three-, and four-bedroom cottages tucked beneath the hemlocks. Each cabin offers a fireplace, kitchen, cable TV, and phone. Members of the Henry family—who have owned Twinbrook since just after World War II—also provide all the little niceties of home, from toasters and coffeemakers to linens and firewood, all furnished at no extra charge. Twinbrook also features an indoor pool and hot tub, dressing rooms, and a recreation room with a pool table and game area. There are also mountain brooks to wade in, trails to hike, horseshoes, basketball, volleyball, barbecue grills, picnic tables, and a playground for the kids. Rates run from $100–270.

Country Cabins, 171 Bradley St., tel. 828/926-0612, are the same sort of cute, hand-hewn cabins you see at Cades Cove in the park. Located beside a quiet creek, they, like Twinbrook, seem much more out of the way than they are, just off Maggie's main drag. Each of the log cabins offers a wood-burning fireplace, a kitchen, and a porch, and you can walk to a number of shops and restaurants. Cabins run $105–120 a night for two people.

The Swag, 2300 Swag Rd., tel. 828/926-0430, website: www.theswag.com, really *is* out of the way—by design. Built of hand-hewn logs and sitting on 250 acres bordering the national park, the Swag is expensive, but it's popular with hikers who appreciate the private entrance to the park. First opened in 1981, the Swag offers 12 guest rooms furnished with antiques and patchwork quilts. Six of the rooms have fireplaces, and all have private baths. This is one of the few inns in the region to offer a racquetball court. The five-star dining room serves three meals a day to guests and the public.

The name, incidentally, refers to the dip in the mountains here—the private, 2.5-mile driveway to the lodge begins at the bottom of the swag and rises 1,100 feet to the inn's location at the peak. Consequently, the folks at the lodge will tell you, spring arrives at the bottom of the driveway three weeks before it reaches the lodge at the top. Open from Memorial Day to the end of October, the Swag is located off I-40 at Exit 20; head 2.8 miles south on U.S. 276 to Hemphill Road and follow the signs. Rates run $265–510 a night. If you're coming up only for a meal, lunch runs $16.50 per person, and dinner ranges from $30–45.

To rent an individually owned cabin (or vacation home) in the Maggie Valley/Cherokee region, call **Vacation Rental Cabins,** tel. 800/338-8228,828/926-3164.

HOTELS

Here's the big news in the Maggie/Cherokee region—the new 15-story **Harrah's Hotel and Conference Center,** located on Highway 19, is scheduled to open in fall 2001 across from the casino on the other side of Soco Creek.

Yes, you read that correctly—*15 stories.*

But don't worry—Harrah's assures us that this charming Smoky Mountain skyscraper will "*highlight* the beautiful mountain setting" (italics mine), which is a little like a doctor saying that a two-inch scar will hereafter "highlight" your child's face. Not that a towering casino hotel is bad, in its place. But whether its place is the middle of one of the lushest wilderness areas in North America is another question.

But with all of Harrah's money and all the Smokies beauty, no doubt Harrah's will have its charms, including an elevated walkway, high over a creek, connecting the casino with the hotel. When it's snowy outside, the views will be phenomenal.

Harrah's also pledges that the hotel's main lobby will incorporate traditional Cherokee art as well as other vestiges of ancient Cherokee ways: an indoor pool, spa, and workout room; a 15,000-square-foot conference center; a 24-hour restaurant; and Club Cappuccino, a coffee bar.

Certainly, Cherokee will benefit financially from this huge boost to its bed count. And the casino and nearby restaurants and shops will make more money as people linger longer in the immediate vicinity.

And it could be much worse: Imagine a 15-story cement tepee.

MOTELS

Up 1,000 feet above the town proper, clinging to the side of Setzer Mountain, you'll find the **Abbey Inn,** tel. 800/545-5853, a friendly, non-chain motor court with separated rooms, great views, and cheap prices:$39–79. See them online at website: www.abbeyinn.com. They also allow dogs for a small fee.

The 21-unit **Riverlet Motel & Restaurant,** 4102 Soco Rd./Hwy. 19, tel. 800/691-9952 or

CHEROKEE

828/926-1900, is a humble little motor inn beside the creek. To the right of the motel you'll find a little picnic area that narrows to a spot where two little riverlets rejoin each other. Here, Joe Sigalas, brother to the coauthor, proposed to his wife, Susan, in 1994. Joe says the coffee shop's pretty good, too—breakfast only. The Riverlet's open April through October; rooms run $27–99. Close by you'll find a **Comfort Inn,** 3282 Soco Rd., tel. 828/926-9106, hugging the same creek.

Maggie Valley's **Microtel,** 3777 Soco Rd./Hwy. 19, tel. 828/926-8554, a 58-unit motel, feels almost European—or shiplike—in its utilitarian classiness. Rooms run $35–109. The Micro features a picnic area, mountain views, and a covered pool. It's open year-round, unlike some of its competitors. Visit www.microtel maggie.com for more information.

CAMPING

Cherokee offers no less than 13 different campgrounds. **Indian Creek Campground,** nine miles north of town on Big Cove Road, 828/497-4361, is a favorite with tent campers, who appreciate the secluded sites. The 75 sites go for $16–17 a night. Other options include the cartoon-related **Yogi in the Smokies,** eight miles north of town on Big Cove Road, tel. 828/497-9151, with more than 200 sites for tents or RVs, three rental cabins, and programs for the kids.

Maggie Valley offers over 600 campsites, all of them with electricity and water, and some with sewers as well. The biggest is **Presley's Campground,** 1786 Soco Rd., tel. 828/926-1904, which features about 30 tent sites and more than 200 RV sites. Prices run $17–20 a night. The campground is open April through October only. Other choices include **Creekwood Farm RV Park,** 40 Happy Valley Circle, tel. 828/926-7977 ($18–20) and the tidy **Hillbilly Campground and RV Park,** 4115 Soco Rd., tel. 828/926-3353 (also $18–20).

Just east of Dillsboro, Sylva offers a number of pleasant cafés. For camping in the area, the privately owned **Fort Tatham Campsites,** 175 Tatham's Creek Rd., tel. 828/586-6662, offer shaded sites on a stream. You'll find the campground six miles south of the junction of U.S. 441, U.S. 23, and U.S. 74. Sites—most with hookups—run $15–18 a night. The campground is open between May and October.

Camping near Waynesville comes cheap at the **Sunburst** public campground, tel. 828/877-3265, adjacent to the Shining Rock Wilderness Area. Head seven miles east of town on U.S. 276, then six miles south on State Road 215. None of the 14 sites have hookups, but the area offers flush toilets. Campsites run just $4 a night.

FOOD

BARBECUE

Don't let the name keep you away. **Butts on the Creek,** 1584 Soco Rd., Maggie Valley, tel. 828/926-7885, may sound like a waterfront smokers club, but it provides arguably the best barbecue in the area. Inarguably, it offers the nicest location, with lots of windows and a deck looking out over Jonathan Creek. Butts dishes up great smoked pork and chicken ($6.25 for a sandwich), as well as full dinners—St. Louis ribs, chicken, Texas beef brisket—with two sides and hushpuppies for $7.95–16.95. They also offer some fine desserts made from scratch, including a great key lime pie and some tasty cobblers. Closed Mondays.

A lot of local folks prefer the **Bar-B-Que Shak,** located on Highway 19 below Ghost Town in the Sky, 828/926-0560. Here, the waitresses still call you "Hon," and you can still pick up a great pork sandwich for $2.50.

Over toward Waynesville you'll find **Eddie's Bar-B-Que,** 3028 Jonathan Creek Rd., tel. 828/926-5353, a very friendly, down-home spot with a mascot who looks not a little like our friend Piggly Wiggly. Here, a pork sandwich will run you $4.25; a platter with hushpuppies, coleslaw, and fried apples costs $7.45. Combo rib platters

candy store window, Mast's General Store

run up to $11.45. You'll find all-you-can-eat chicken on Thursday night and prime rib on Saturday. Closed Monday through Wednesday.

East of Waynesville on Highway 74, you'll come upon the town of Canton, home to **Skeeter's Barbecue,** tel. 828/648-8595. Skeeter's doesn't look like much from the outside, but it's the real thing. The barbecue comes down-eastern pit smoked in hickory; tangy vinegar red pepper; or traditional Southern tomato-based sauce. Unlike most barbecue joints, Skeeter's serves breakfast, lunch, and dinner, and you can find grilled chicken salads and sandwiches here as well. It's open Monday through Saturday, 7 A.M.–9 P.M.

MORE FOOD

For country ham, Southern fried chicken, or hand-battered mountain trout, head over to the **The Jarrett House** in Dillsboro, tel. 800/972-5623 or 828/586-0265, where they've been serv-

ing huge platters of good cooking family-style since 1884. You will not leave here hungry; your meal comes with coleslaw, candied apples, buttered potatoes, green beans, pickled beets, hot biscuits, and a drink. Dinners run $12.50. Kids eat for $5. It's open Monday through Saturday, 4–8 p.m., Sunday 11:30 a.m.–2:30 p.m. and 4–8 p.m. No credit cards accepted.

Over at Harrah's Casino in Cherokee, **Seven Sisters** serves up steaks, seafood, pasta dishes and desserts. **Mountaineer Buffet,** 6490 Soco Rd., tel. 828/926-1730, offers all-you-can-eat comfort food, outdoor dining on a large screened porch, and beautiful views.

Saratoga's Café, owned since 1988 by Jeff and Sarah Crider, serves both lunch (mainly sandwiches and salads) and dinners, which include mountain trout, rib-eye steaks, grilled tuna steak, and chicken. Saturday night features prime rib. Desserts include homemade pecan pie. You'll hear live music on Friday and Saturday nights. Wednesday is Jazz Night, when Sarah doubles as the resident torch singer and her father accompanies her on the clarinet. Also here is the **Rose Room Lounge.**

Set in a rustic cedar cabin, **J Arthur's,** 2843 Soco Rd., tel. 828/926-1817, offers fresh local mountain trout ($15.50), prime rib ($15.95), and a great gorgonzola salad ($7.50). The "Left Bank–style" French onion soup makes a great appetizer on a cool mountain night. The restaurant is family friendly—it offers a better-than-average kids menu ($6.95) and a toy-equipped Kids Corner for tykes. Open for dinner only.

If you're looking for Italian, Maggie Valley's **Snappy's Italian Restaurant and Pizzeria,** 2769 Soco Rd., tel. 828/926-6126, provides worthwhile Italian fare, as does Waynesville's **Antipasto's,** located in the Waynesville Shopping Plaza, tel. 828/452-0218 (closed Monday).

And you can't visit these parts without eating at least one big country breakfast, the kind with checkered tablecloths, stacks of pancakes, and apron-wearing waitresses and such. Some argue that the best is **Joey's Pancake House,** 4309 Soco Rd., tel. 828/926-0212, where you can pile on Belgian waffles, cinnamon French toast, eggs Benedict, slow-cooked oatmeal, creamy chipped

CHEROKEE

beef, and blueberry, chocolate chip, and banana nut pancakes beneath wagon wheel chandeliers. The pancakes are the true stars here—you can buy Joey's pancake batter by the sackful at the checkout. **Country Vittles,** 3589 Soco Rd., tel. 828/926-1820, also gets good reviews.

THE BATTLE FOR DUPONT STATE FOREST

DuPont State Forest, off Highway 64 between Brevard and Hendersonville, North Carolina, offers visitors 10,400 acres of forest featuring four major waterfalls on the Little River and several on Grassy Creek. But it was not always so. People visited this spectacular, formerly corporate-owned land for generations (by permission and not) and wondered why it wasn't protected and made more accessible to the citizenry. In 1995, after much legal wrangling, threats of development and the invocation of eminent domain, and the timely intercessions of the nonprofit Conservation Fund and state government, it was finally accomplished.

The forest was named for the corporation that made the initial 7,600 acres available to the Conservation Fund at bargain prices in 1996. For a time, the now-central 2,200-acre section encompassing High Falls, Triple Falls, and Bridal Veil Falls seemed doomed to become yet another exclusive, 100- to 200-home golf paradise at the hands of developer Jim "the Cliffs" Anthony—he of "The Cliffs of Glassy" fame. Fortunately, in late October 2000, Governor Jim Hunt and the elected Council of State voted 9-0 to use the law of eminent domain to preserve this area for all North Carolinians—and for all visitors to the state.

What with all the headlines over the months, the general public couldn't wait to explore the land once it was theirs. From the very start, hikers and bikers enjoyed the broad gravel roads laid out by The Cliffs to bring in the construction trucks that never came. In November, volunteers swept in to prepare the would-be fairways and golf cart paths for hikers, bikers, and equestrians.

The property features over 90 trails, most of them set on DuPont's old gravel roads; mountain bikes are welcome on several. Fishing and horseback riding are also permitted here. Thus far, camping is not. Hunting is, so be sure to wear fluorescent colors in season.

The elevation here ranges from 2,300 feet (below Hooker Falls on the Little River) to the 3,600-foot, exposed granite dome of Stone Mountain. The land includes the smallish Lake Julia. Most of it is forested with young to middle-aged hardwoods and white pine dating back to the middle 1900s.

Besides the beautiful waterfalls—several of which appeared in the 1990s film version of *Last of the Mohicans*—it's the eight or so miles of unpaved roads on the property that have kept DuPont's popularity growing. Most of the roads are closed to motor vehicles but provide tremendous opportunities for hikers, cyclists, and equestrians.

You can get to the DuPont State Forest from Hendersonville via Kanuga/Crab Creek Road, from Asheville and Brevard via Highway 64 and Little River Road, or from Greenville, South Carolina, via Cedar Mountain and Cascade Lake Road.

CHEROKEE

Outside Cherokee

CULLOWHEE

Home to a campus of Western Carolina University, Cullowhee (pop. 5,700) is a good place for students of Smoky Mountain culture. For travelers, one possible destination here is the **Mountain Heritage Center** in the H. F. Robinson Administration Building on campus. It tells the story of the Scotch-Irish, the principal settlers in this region. The center is open Monday through Friday 8 A.M.–5 P.M., Sunday 2–5 P.M.

Outside of town is **Judaculla Rock,** a huge soapstone carved with ancient Native American images. Call 828/586-2155 for directions.

For more information, contact the **Jackson County Travel and Tourism Authority,** 116 Central St., Sylva, tel. 800/962-1911 or 828/586-2155.

SOUTH ON 19: NANTAHALA NATIONAL FOREST

Visitors often confuse the purposes of national parks and national forests and are horrified when they see logging, hunting, and private building going on in the latter. Whereas a national park is set aside for preservation and recreation, a national forest encompasses recreation, forestry, hunting, and various other uses of the land. National forests are often bigger than national parks, and islands of private land may exist within them.

Perhaps due to a lack of publicity, many travelers in search of natural beauty zoom through national forests on their way to national parks. In the parks they often find clogged roads, crowded campgrounds and picnic areas, and too many other people. Many national forests offer the same wild beauty, hiking trails, and campsites, but with smaller crowds.

Case in point is the Nantahala National Forest, which at 515,000 acres is almost as large as the better-known Great Smoky Mountains National Park. Nantahala offers many more camping areas than the national park, and it includes the most rugged section of the entire Appalachian Trail—80 miles in all. Here also is the *Joyce*

Kilmer Memorial Forest, an awe-inspiring 3,800-acre tract of virgin forest with trees that tower over 100 feet high. Above the town of Sapphire, Whitewater Falls drops 3,411 feet in a horizontal distance of 500 feet. It's the highest waterfall in the eastern United States, and the national park has nothing like it.

You'll find the central administrative offices for the Nantahala National Forest at 50 South French Broad Avenue in Asheville, tel. 828/258-2850. Call or stop by for maps and other information.

The forest is formally divided into four districts. The **Cheoah Ranger District,** just south of the national park, contains the Joyce Kilmer Memorial Forest. No camping is permitted in the Kilmer area, but other campgrounds are close by. The **Highlands Ranger District** is the one with the most waterfalls, and it's an excellent place for picnicking. It runs from the Sylva area to the border with Georgia and South Carolina. The **Tusquitee Ranger District** extends all the way to the western tip of North Carolina and includes some small TVA-born lakes nestled in the mountains. It's a good place for fishing and camping. The **Wayah Ranger District** reaches from the Cowee Bald to the Georgia border. It includes the *Wayah Bald,* a mountaintop covered with wild azaleas that bloom spectacularly in May and June.

SOUTH ON 441: FRANKLIN

Franklin, the seat of Macon County, rests on an old Cherokee settlement. It also sits over some of the more unusual geological deposits in the United States.

North Carolina is the only state where all four "major" gems—diamonds, rubies, sapphires, and emeralds—have been found. Though the diamonds have been few and far between (maybe a dozen in recorded history), the area around Franklin (pop. 3,000) abounds in emeralds, rubies, and sapphires, as well as garnets and amethysts. Some call Franklin "the Gem Capital of the World." Tiffany's once owned an emerald mine in

LAND OF THE WATERFALLS

Not everyone can raft a river or hike to the top of a mountain, but everyone can enjoy a waterfall. If you do nothing else in the Nantahala, be sure to visit a few of the falls.

The town of Highlands is the center of the North Carolina waterfall country. From west to east, here are the major falls. From Franklin to Highlands, Hwy. 64 follows the Cullasaja River, which offers more falls than a *Dick Van Dyke Show* marathon. The first is **Lower Cullasaja Falls,** more of a cascade, really, in which the river falls for more than 300 feet in a quarter of a mile. Next comes **Dry Falls,** so named because visitors can walk behind the deluge and view the backside of water without getting wet. Then comes **Bridal Veil Falls,** which splash down 120 feet, landing partly on the road. You can get a free car wash here. (How did they ever get the asphalt to set?)

Once you get to Highlands, take NC 106 south for two miles to the **Glen Falls Scenic Area,** where the water plummets 50 feet. Or you can continue east on Hwy. 64 through **Cashiers,** then take State Road 107 south into South Carolina. Turn left on Wigington Road (SC 37/413), then when it tees two miles later, turn left on SC 130, which will rename itself NC 281 on the other side of the line. Once this happens, keep an eye on your right for the developed viewing area for **Whitewater Falls.**

Whitewater Falls is the tallest waterfall in the eastern United States. It is actually a pair of falls that fall sequentially on either side of the North Carolina/South Carolina state line. North Carolina claims the upper falls, which cascade 411 feet; South Carolina's lower falls come in at an even 400 feet.

Whichever falls you visit, be careful: people injure themselves, and sometimes die, due to the slippery rocks and long drops.

the area, and rock hounds from novice to expert flock here to see what the earth brings forth. Nearly all of the mines hereabouts are located in the Cowee Valley, north of town off NC 28.

Here's how it usually works. For a set fee—often around $10—mine proprietors provide you with a bucket of mud alleged to contain wondrous stones (some places allow the independent-minded to dig their own bucket's worth). Then you'll head over to the flume and have at it. Do it long enough and you'll probably find gemstones—possibly one that's worth more than you paid for the bucket of mud. Obviously, if the mines paid off all that well, the owners would be sifting through their own mud. But you knew that.

And you probably also know that this would be a memorable afternoon for kids. If you want to better your odds, pay extra for a "concentrated" bucket. In fact, most of the mines are "enriched" to begin with.

About a mile north of Franklin on Highway 441, you'll come across **Gem City Mine,** tel. 828/524-3967, which includes a sheltered flume line, allowing you to mine even if the rain's coming down in sheets. It's open May 15 through October 15. Call for hours. **Gold City Gem Mine,** 9410 Sylva Rd., 828/369-3905, includes a large covered area for rainy-day mining, wheelchair access, and even special kid-sized mining buckets. The **Jackson Hole,** tel. 828/524-5850, also with a covered flume, sits on Highway 28 and U.S. 64, halfway between Franklin and Highlands. It offers an on-site snack bar and gem shop. The **Jacobs Ruby Mine,** 269 DeForest Ln., tel. 828/524-7022, features only native stones. Or try the **Rose Creek Mine,** 115 Terrace Ridge Dr., tel. 828/349-3774. Camping is available there.

In Franklin, a lot of people like to shop for local arts and crafts at such shops as **Cowee Creek Pottery,** 20 West Mills Rd., tel. 828/524-3324, the **MACO Crafts Co-Op,** 2846 Georgia Rd., tel. 828/524-7878, and Michael M. Rogers Gallery, 18 W. Palmer St., tel. 828/524-6709.

If you'd like to stay in Franklin, you might consider the **Summit Inn,** 210 E. Rogers St., tel. 828/524-2006, a 14-room 1898 house atop Franklin's highest hill. Ornately carved highboys, armoires, and other antiques warm the rooms. Rates vary based on rooms, occupancy, and season, ranging from $59 to $99. Only 6 of the 14 have private bathrooms, so if privacy is important to you, be sure to ask when you make reservations. Children and infants are welcome; the inn even offers a special children's room. Children under 6 stay free in their parents' room; $10 extra for children 7 to 16. Cribs and rollaway beds are available.

The Summit also serves some of the best meals in Franklin—which can include lobster, steak, trout, and baked chicken. The soup and bread are homemade. Dinners are served family-style on tables lit by kerosene lamps. And this inn offers one amenity lacking from most proper B&Bs: pool tables. The inn is open year-round; in winter the dining room is open only on weekends.

FARTHER SOUTH ON 28: HIGHLANDS

At 3,835 feet, Highlands is North Carolina's second highest town, and it's in many ways the perfect resort town. In fact, it was originally planned in 1875 (by two natives of Kansas) as a resort community. The tale goes that the two Jayhawkers drew one line on a map from Baltimore to New Orleans and another from Chicago to Savannah. They built Highlands at the point where the lines intersected. In the 1920s, with the development of the Highlands Country Club, the prestige factor reached new heights. Today the town supports just 2,000 year-round residents and upward of 25,000 residents in summer.

As evidenced by the marker on Main Street, Spanish explorers under Juan Pardo passed through this area back in 1567 as part of Spain's aborted conquest of North America. Had Spain kept its grasp on this continent, Pardo's name would no doubt be as well known as those of Lewis and Clark. He and his men walked all the way up here from Fort San Felipe on modern-day

Parris Island, South Carolina, near Beaufort. Pardo's job was both to explore Spain's new dominion and to establish an overland route to the silver mines of western Mexico. He and his 300 men built blockhouses along the way and left small detachments to hold them and evangelize the local Indians. After passing through here, Pardo and his men tramped all the way to Alabama before finally heading back to San Felipe.

The Highlands area is the wettest in the eastern United States. It gets 80 inches of precipitation in an average year—and its plant life, from trees to lichens, is splendid. When the French botanist Andre Michaux came through in 1788, he noted the *shortia,* a plant whose only other known habitat was Japan. Asa Gray rediscovered the plant a hundred years later, and botanists still drive up to research it in Highlands.

Most people, however, come to relax. Highlands has a fine collection of houses belonging to summer people and retirees. The quaint houses in town start at around $500,000, so it's no wonder that the small grocery store here carries caviar along with bacon and eggs. Travelers delight in the lake at the west end of town and the waterfalls along U.S. 64 from Highlands to Franklin.

The most popular thing to do in Highlands is to walk the small town, browsing into the many downtown shops and galleries as you go. But you may also want to drive out to the **Highlands Biological Station** on Horse Cove Road, founded in 1927. If you were visiting the Smokies primarily to understand its plant life, you probably couldn't find a better place to start your journey. Now overseen by the University of North Carolina, this 16-acre research center offers facilities for qualified scientists researching Southern Appalachian biota and environments. Facilities include the kid-friendly **Highlands Nature Center,** tel. 828/526-2623, located in the chestnut Clark Foreman Museum Building. Here, kids and grownups can view a live beehive, peer through a microscope, and examine the rings of a pre-Columbian hemlock.

Back outside, you'll find a number of trails threading the station's **Highlands Botanical Garden,** which borders Lake Ravenel. Along these trails, you'll find an incredible real-life

CHEROKEE

primer on Southern Appalachian plant life—so far, researchers here have labeled some 450 plants native to the region.

The Biological Station is open from late May through Labor Day, Monday through Friday from 10 A.M. to 5 P.M. and on Sundays from 1–5 P.M. No admission is charged. The garden is open year-round.

Highlands Playhouse Highlands, NC 28741, tel. 828/526-2695, has presented dramas and musicals to summertime audiences since before World War II. Call for information and tickets.

For theater with a lighter touch, the **Highlands Studio for the Arts,** 828/526-9482, may be the way to go. Improvisational acting and one-act plays are the specialties, offered from July through September with performances on Tuesday, Thursday, and Friday nights.

Events

Highlands has enough seasonal visitors with enough free time on their hands to carry out and support quite a summer arts community. The **Chamber Music Festival,** held during July, offers chamber music concerts at the Episcopal church (a High Church in Highlands). Performances take place Tuesday nights and Sunday afternoons. For details, call or visit the Highlands Chamber of Commerce, 396 Oak St., tel. 828/526-2112. The **High Country Arts and Crafts Fair** in early June features a hundred or so craftspeople who gather at Mountain Hillbilly Crafts, seven miles south of Highlands on Highway 106. Call the chamber of commerce for more details. **Helen's Barn** on West Main Street is the place where locals and visitors meet on Friday and Saturday nights for a hoedown. Beginning and expert cloggers and square dancers send the hay a-flyin'. Food and drinks are available. Call 828/526-2790 for information.

Where to Stay and Eat

The **Highlands Inn,** on the corner of Fourth and Main Street, tel. 828/526-9380, website: www.highlandsinn-nc.com, was built in 1881. Today, the inn and its eatery—the **Kelsey Place Restaurant**-are the prime spots to stay and eat in Highlands. The inn offers 46 guestrooms from

May through October. Standard double rooms run from $94 to $134 a night. An "extended continental breakfast" is included.

Frank Lloyd Wright and Associates designed the **Skyline Lodge and Restaurant,** tel. 800/575-9546 or 828/526-2121, as a casino in the 1920s. Construction began in the 1930s, but the Depression turned more depressing than the project's backers had anticipated, and work halted. For decades the building remained unfinished until it was finally completed in the 1960s as a lodge. Located four miles east of Highlands on Flat Mountain Road, Skyline sits atop a 4,300-foot mountain on 55 acres that include old-growth conifers, a pond, a 30-foot waterfall, tennis courts, and a swimming pool. Rooms run $79 to $169 a night, including continental breakfast. The lodge also has new rental cabins. Call for prices and availability.

If you know about Wright, you know that this is no rustic hand-hewn log cabin tucked into the trees. The rooms are modern, with telephones and in some cases king-sized beds. Rooms on one side of the lodge look out on the waterfall; rooms on the other side offer a mountain view.

The lodge also offers fine dining; non-guests are welcome for dinner. Plates include locally raised trout sautéed with lemon, white wine, and butter ($18.95) and jumbo sea scallops tossed with fresh spinach, ginger root, and garlic in Jamaican tomato sauce ($19.95). Take note: Here across the Macon County Line, you're in a dry county, so you'll need to bring your own wine or hard liquor; the restaurant will charge a set up and/or corkage fee. The lodge is open May through October. To get there from Highlands, take Highway 64 east to Flat Mountain Road. Turn left and follow the signs.

A budget-friendlier stay inside town is the **Mountain High Inn** at Second Avenue and Main Street, tel. 800/445-7293 or 828/526-2790, website: www.mountainhighinn.com. Rates run $48–119.

The **Central House** at Fourth and Main Streets, tel. 828/526-9319, is a traditional, moderately priced country restaurant set in an 1878 inn. Dinners run around $19; you may want to start off with the inn's beloved blue crab soup.

The grounds include a waterfall and a pond. For something down-home and easy on the pocketbook, try some barbecue at the **Carolina Smokehouse,** on Route 64 northeast of town in Cashiers, tel. 828/743-3200, or a sandwich and chocolate malt at **Brigitte's Soda Fountain** on East Main Street in the Blue Ridge Pharmacy Building, tel. 828/526-9451.

In honor of sore-footed Juan Pardo, you might choose to eat at **Pescado's Highland Burrito** on North Fourth Street, tel. 828/526-9313. Pescado's offers fresh health-conscious Mexican food that's more Century City than Mexico City. But if you've been overdoing the barbecue, here's a great place to take a break.

WEST OF BRYSON CITY
Pisgah National Forest

"Get thee up to the top of Pisgah, and lift up thine eyes westward, and northward, and southward, and eastward, and behold it with thine eyes." Moses received these words as a divine command in the Old Testament, but they're worthy advice for anyone who wants to experience the sublime natural beauty of the Southern Appalachians without facing the crowds of Great Smoky Mountains National Park. Pisgah National Forest (PNF) covers 478,000 acres in two separate tracts that include some of the highest peaks in the eastern United States.

Although not as large as neighboring Great Smoky Mountains National Park, PNF has higher peaks, more waterfalls, and wildflower areas that surpass anything in the Smokies. It offers myriad hiking trails, campgrounds, picnic areas, and wilderness areas. All of these, however, are scattered between towns, and you may find a scenic wonder just down the road from a fast-food joint. This can be a blessing or a curse, depending on how hungry you are. Bottom line: For a big chunk of mostly uninterrupted, sometimes congested wilderness, head for the national park. For more solitude and a wider variety of things to see and do, stay in the Pisgah National Forest.

Like Nantahala to the south, Pisgah National Forest is divided into four administrative areas. The Toecane, Grandfather, and French Broad Ranger Districts lie north of Asheville, while the Pisgah Ranger District sits beside the Nantahala National Forest farther south. Though each will be briefly described here, for further general information about the forest and its many campsites and picnic areas, call 704/258-2850.

Physically disconnected from the forest's other three districts, the **Pisgah Ranger District** lies southwest of Asheville. It was once part of the immense landholdings accumulated by George Vanderbilt in his Biltmore Estate and was later transferred to public stewardship. The district includes several waterfalls as well as the Cradle of Forestry museum north of Brevard. Also notable is the Shining Rock Wilderness Area, a 13,400-acre preserve that's delightful for hiking. You'll need a permit to camp in the wilderness; you can pick one up free from the ranger's office two miles north of Brevard on U.S. 276. Call 828/877-3265 for information.

The **Toecane Ranger District** is located to the north and east of Asheville and extends to the Tennessee state line. It includes Mount Mitchell State Park, home of the highest peak in the eastern United States, a popular hike. You'll see large bursts of rhododendrons in the area in spring. Craggy Mountain Scenic Area is located near Craggy Gardens, a stop on the Blue Ridge Parkway. Roan Mountain is on the Tennessee state line. The district office is located in Burnsville on the U.S. 19E bypass. Contact the district ranger at 828/682-6146.

The **Grandfather Ranger District** is the northernmost part of the Pisgah National Forest. It includes Grandfather Mountain, the only private park in the world designated as a United Nations international biosphere reserve. For information call 800/468-7325 or visit www.grandfather.com. Here too are the Linville Gorge Wilderness Area and a handful of uncrowded campgrounds. The district office is located in the public library in Marion. Contact the district ranger at 828/652-4841.

The **French Broad Ranger District** is located on the French Broad River northwest of Asheville. The district office is located on the main street in downtown Hot Springs. Contact the district ranger at 828/622-3202.

Brevard

Famous for white squirrels, waterfalls, and music, Brevard was incorporated in 1867 with just seven residents—all of whom held public office. Now some 5,400 people live here, and Brevard often shows up on various lists of "Best Places to Live in the United States." This is some accomplishment, considering that the town serves as the seat for (cue eerie music) Transylvania County. The name merely means over (trans) the woods (sylvan). At least that's what they want us to believe.

The squirrels you'll see scuttling across the lawns and up the trees of the local parks. As for the waterfalls (there are more than 250 of them hereabouts), a good starting point is the 85-foot **Looking Glass Falls,** eight miles north of Brevard on Highway 276. Farther up Highway 276 you'll find the very popular **Sliding Rock,** a smooth 60-foot-long rock, over which pours a bone-chilling cascade sure to cool you down on the hottest of summer days. The slide is open from Memorial Day to Labor Day, and you'll find lifeguards and bathhouses at the ready.

The folks at the **Transylvania County Tourism Development Authority,** 35 W. Main St., tel. 800/648-4523, website: www.visitwaterfalls.com, have come up with a handy guide to many of the county's most popular falls. Stop by or call to get a copy.

The Brevard area is also home to the **Cradle of Forestry,** a school founded in 1895 to study the then-new science of forestry. Though the school closed in 1913, you can view the reconstructed campus about three miles south of the Blue Ridge Parkway on U.S. 276. It's open daily from 9 A.M.–5 P.M. and consists of a classroom, ranger's dwelling, and Black Forest–style lodge. No admission is charged.

Every summer, Brevard hosts 200 to 300 young folks for the **Transylvania Music Camp.** Big-name performers and conductors join these young musicians, and the combination attracts music lovers for daily concerts over a two-month period. For details about performances, call 828/884-2019.

For more information on Brevard in general, call the **Brevard Chamber of Commerce,** 35 W. Main St., tel. 800/648-4523 or 828/883-3700.

If you'd like to stay in Brevard, the you couldn't do much better than the **Inn at Brevard,** 410 E. Main St., 828/884-2105, website: www.innatbrevard.8m.com. Built in 1885, the inn offers five antique-laden rooms in the main house, as well as 10 cabin-style rooms with private showers in an adjacent annex. A full breakfast is included with the room charge, which runs $110–150 in high season, lower in the off-season. For something more economical, try the **Sunset Motel,** 415 S. Broad St., tel. 828/884-9106, where rooms run $40–70. Be sure to request a nonsmoking room.

Information and Transportation

TOURIST OFFICES AND CHAMBERS OF COMMERCE

For more information, contact the **Maggie Valley Area Chamber of Commerce,** 2487 Soco Rd., tel. 800/785-8259 or 828/926-1686. In Cherokee, stop by the **Cherokee Visitor Center,** tel. 800/438-1601. For more information about Dillsboro, contact the **Jackson County Chamber of Commerce** at 828/586-2155. Call the **Swain County Chamber of Commerce,** tel. 800/867-9246 or 828/488-3681, for more information on Bryson City and vicinity.

HOSPITALS, POLICE, EMERGENCIES

Call 911 for any emergency in this region.

Hospitals include the **Cherokee Indian Hospital** on Hospital Road, tel. 828/497-9163; **Harris Regional Hospital,** 68 Hospital Rd., Sylva, tel. 828/586-7000; and **Haywood Regional Medical Center,** 262 Leroy George Dr., Clyde, tel.

828/452-8559. To access the biggest hospital in the region, call the **Mission St. Joseph's Hospital Health Line,** tel. 800/321-6877 or 828/255-3000.

The **Rape Crisis Center of Asheville,** 50 S. French Broad, can be reached at 828/255-7576.

GETTING THERE
By Car
The biggest road in these parts is I-40, which from the west leads from Knoxville over the top of the national park, skirting its eastern edge. Take Highway 276 south, then get on Highway 19 and head west. From the Raleigh area or Wilmington, simply head west on I-40 to Asheville, then take Highway 19/23 west.

From Greenville, South Carolina, take Highway 25 north to Highway 74, then continue on to Asheville, where you can catch I-40 and Highway 19/23 west.

Visitors from Chattanooga usually enter this region on U.S. 65, one of the more scenic highways in the area. It crosses the lower portion of southwestern North Carolina, passing through towns such as Franklin, Highlands, and Hendersonville. The road is very pretty, but plan on a long trip and bring the Dramamine.

If you're starting from Atlanta, a favorite route is the Atlanta Highway (U.S. 78) to Athens, Georgia (a great stopover), then north on Highway 441 off the loop highway and all the way to Franklin.

By Air
The closest airports to the Cherokee region are in Asheville, Chattanooga, and Knoxville. Greenville, South Carolina, isn't much farther, so if you find a cheap flight there, take it.

By Bus
Driving on these mountain roads in the back of a huge bus sounds gut wrenching, but it is technically possible to get to Waynesville via Greyhound. Of course, routes are everything. While it'll cost only $21 and take an hour and a half to get from Knoxville to Waynesville (it's a direct route), it'll take you far longer to bus from Atlanta (the first thing your driver will do after leaving Atlanta is head toward Knoxville, where you'll have to transfer to the Knoxville-Waynesville line). The moral of the story? If you're going to let the dog do the driving, fly into Knoxville or Asheville. Of course, when you get to Waynesville, you'll be without transportation to the park or nearby towns. But if the bus is your best option, call 800/229-9424.

CAR RENTALS
If you're flying into the area and need to rent a car, you'll want to rent it at the airport. Call Alamo at 800/327-9633, Avis at 800/831-2847, Budget at 800/353-0600, Enterprise at 800/325-8007, and Hertz at 800/654-3131.

CHEROKEE

Chattanooga

Introduction

For visitors approaching Great Smoky Mountains National Park from the South, Chattanooga, Tennessee's fourth-largest city, is a great place to spend a couple of days. Downtown has a variety of attractions, all within walking distance of each other, and the **Tennessee Aquarium** is head and shoulders above the one in Gatlinburg.

Until country music staked out Nashville and Elvis laid claim to Memphis, Chattanooga was Tennessee's music town. The composer of "Chattanooga Choo Choo" used the name of the city only because it fit the needed number of syllables, but the song, recorded dozens of times by a variety of artists, put Chattanooga on the musical map.

The city also produced Adolph Ochs, who made the *New York Times* into the nation's best newspaper, and Bessie Smith, a blues singer famous around the world. It is also the home of some classic Southern junk food: Moon Pies and, in nearby Collegedale, Little Debbie snack cakes.

Chattanooga got its name from a Creek Indian word for Lookout Mountain, which dominates the city's skyline. The mountain was the scene of a bloody Civil War battle, and in the 20th century it became the site of legendary

© CHATTANOOGA AREA CONVENTION AND VISITORS BUREAU

Southern Belle Riverboat

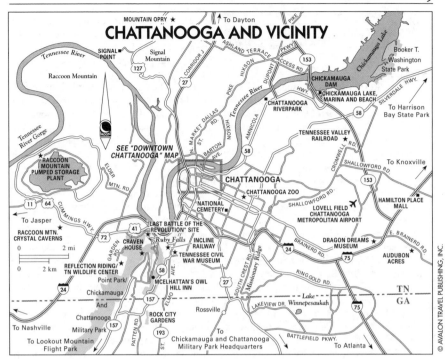

CHATTANOOGA AND VICINITY

MOUNTAIN OPRY ★   ↑ To Dayton

Tennessee River

SIGNAL POINT ■
Signal Mountain
127

Raccoon Mountain

Booker T. Washington State Park

ASHLAND TERRACE

CHICKAMAUGA DAM
153

CHICKAMAUGA LAKE, MARINA AND BEACH

SILVERDALE HWY.

Tennessee River Gorge

Raccoon Mountain

SEE "DOWNTOWN CHATTANOOGA" MAP

CHATTANOOGA RIVERPARK

58

To Harrison Bay State Park

RACCOON MOUNTAIN PUMPED STORAGE PLANT

TENNESSEE VALLEY RAILROAD ★

CROMWELL RD.

SHALLOWFORD RD.

To Knoxville

CHATTANOOGA

11 64

To Jasper

RACCOON MTN. CRYSTAL CAVERNS

CHATTANOOGA ZOO

153

HAMILTON PLACE MALL

NATIONAL CEMETERY

SHALLOWFORD RD.

LOVELL FIELD CHATTANOOGA METROPOLITAN AIRPORT ✈

0   2 mi

0   2 km

72

LAST BATTLE OF THE "REVOLUTION" SITE

CRAVEN HOUSE

Ruby Falls

INCLINE RAILWAY

41

E. BRAINERD RD.

DRAGON DREAMS MUSEUM

BRAINERD RD.

24

75

AUDUBON ACRES

REFLECTION RIDING/ TN WILDLIFE CENTER

TENNESSEE CIVIL WAR MUSEUM

58

RING GOLD RD.

24

Point Park/

MCELHATTAN'S OWL HILL INN

27

TN
GA

Chickamauga And Chattanooga Military Park

157

ROCK CITY GARDENS

Rossville

Lake Winnepesaukah

LAKEVIEW DR.

75

To Nashville

157

193

To Chickamauga and Chattanooga Military Park Headquarters

BATTLEFIELD PKWY.

To Atlanta

To Lookout Mountain Flight Park

© AVALON TRAVEL PUBLISHING, INC.

---

tourist attractions. Rock City and Ruby Falls still manage to compete with modern-day theme parks and the frenetic activity around the Smoky Mountains.

Note to visitors: The name of this city has four syllables. It's not "Chatnooga," as sometimes mispronounced by persons from points north.

HISTORY

Chattanooga sits just upstream from what used to be the wildest section of the Tennessee River. After flowing peacefully down the Great Valley, the river turns west, confronting two prongs of the Cumberland Plateau and cutting gorges so deep that they've been called "the Grand Canyon of the Tennessee River." Though the nickname is an exaggeration, the terror that flatboats faced in these waters was not. The worst of the obstacles to navigation here was a whirlpool called The Suck.

Dragging Canoe

Flatboats faced other hazards as well. In 1777, Dragging Canoe, a Cherokee who was opposed to the sale of his people's land, led more than 1,000 renegade followers to this part of Tennessee, where they called themselves the Chickamauga and continued to wage war on settlers. They allied themselves with British forces and did whatever they could to make life difficult for the colonists.

When the women and children of the Donelson Party came floating down from Long Island in upper East Tennessee in1779 on their way to the site of Nashville, the wild waters caused a boat in their flotilla to wreck. While trying to save it, the group came under fire from the Chickamauga. One of the survivors was 15-year-old Rachel Donelson, the future wife of Andrew Jackson.

John Sevier's militia led a raid in 1782 on Dragging Canoe's villages and destroyed them. Since Dragging Canoe was allied with the British, local boosters have seized upon this attack as "the Last

CHATTANOOGA HIGHLIGHTS

Often lost in the rush to the Tennessee Aquarium, **Ross's Landing** is a superb piece of landscape art that deserves a visitor's full attention.

The **Chattanooga Choo Choo** gives a glimpse of railroading's importance in this town, celebrated wherever big bands still play.

Rock City, heralded for decades by barns and birdhouses, remains much the same as in the days when people traveled on blue highways to see its wonders.

Point Park, at the tip of Lookout Mountain, provides a vista of Chattanooga and admiration for the brave troops who fought their way up the mountain slopes.

Raccoon Mountain Pumped-Storage Project, with a lake that fills by night and empties by day, shows TVA's ingenuity in producing electric power.

The **Mountain Opry,** up on Signal Mountain outside of town, offers live acoustic music that can't be beat.

The **Tennessee Aquarium** has to be on every visitor's list.

Visitors will delight in the cultural and culinary offerings at the **Bluff View Art District.**

One of the best depictions of an aspect of Tennessee history is the **Chattanooga African-American Museum.** The exhibits on Bessie Smith are a must for music lovers.

between the settlers and Indians improved. The Cherokee owned the south side of the Tennessee River, and about 1815 Chief John Ross built Ross's Landing, a place to which traders from the neighboring United States came by ferry. After the Cherokee were rounded up and removed to Oklahoma, whites poured across the river and named the town Chattanooga. Increasing steamboat traffic helped the town grow, but the railroad put Chattanooga on the map. Tracks from Atlanta, Nashville, and Knoxville converged here, and when the Civil War broke out, the city became an immediate prize.

The war was bad enough, but in 1867 a severe flood, followed by another eight years later, crippled the city. The 1870s marked a turnaround in Chattanooga, however, as money from the North flowed in to exploit the area's coal and iron resources. Soon iron and steel mills rose to the extent that Chattanooga was called "the Pittsburgh of the South." The mills brought a lot of money and good jobs to the region, but they also belched forth clouds of pollution, which, because of the surrounding hills, tended to pool in Chattanooga. Anyone with any money built a house on the surrounding ridges—Lookout Mountain, Signal Mountain, and Missionary Ridge.

From their lofty perches, the citizens of Chattanooga took great pride in their city. The Chickamauga and Chattanooga battlefields became the first national military parks. Residents ate Moon Pies, which were invented in Chattanooga, and happily drank Coca-Cola ("KO-ko-la") from the first bottler franchised by the Atlanta company. It had bought the rights to bottle the new soft drink for only $2.

Battle of the Revolutionary War," occurring as it did after Yorktown and before the Americans and English signed a peace treaty. Knowing that they were a part of this larger effort would no doubt have been news to Dragging Canoe and John Sevier, whose mutual detestation would probably have led to the battle, war or no war. Dragging Canoe, after more raids, died in 1792 after an all-night party. He was 60 years old, a ripe old age for someone in his line of work.

Steam and Rail

Once the Chickamauga were defeated, relations

Arrival of the TVA

The Depression brought the Tennessee Valley Authority (website: www.tva.gov) to town and an increasing number of tourists who took the advice painted on scores of barns to "See Rock City." One reason for the founding of the TVA was flood control, and Chattanooga was perhaps the chief beneficiary of this aspect of the agency. It took over an existing utility, established a presence in the city, and now controls its immense power-producing plants from here.

Like the other main Tennessee cities, Chattanooga saw its downtown deteriorate after World War II and the decline of the railroads. The interstate highway system came through, following the paths of the railroads, and funneled lots of traffic through the city. But most of that traffic was not going downtown. And no wonder—in 1969 the federal government pronounced Chattanooga "the dirtiest city in America." This galvanized the city, which put teeth in pollution controls, and by 1989 Chattanooga was one of the few cities in the East that fully complied with air quality standards. But this improvement came with a price. For a variety of reasons, downtown lost 18,000 manufacturing jobs between 1973 and 1984. The city looked to its two strong points—the river and the stream of people passing through—and decided to do something that would get those people to stop and spend money.

Chattanooga Nowadays

The 1980s and 1990s have brought a dramatic revitalization to downtown Chattanooga. The Tennessee Aquarium and Ross's Landing Park and Plaza have breathed new life into the place. Chattanooga consistently ranks high in various magazine "best places to live" rankings. In 2001, for example, *Outside* magazine ranked the city as one of 10 "dream towns."

For the visitor to the Smokies, Chattanooga offers new hotels and attractions that make it a very family-friendly place. You can check into a motel, walk to a museum or the aquarium, have a nice lunch, and come back to the motel for a nap or a swim—all without getting in a car.

Lay of the Land

Downtown

Chattanooga's downtown seems custom-made for visitors. There's plenty of parking and not a great deal of traffic, and many attractions are clustered close together. The Chattanooga Visitors Center at 2 Broad Street is a great place to get oriented and perhaps dispatch segments of the traveling group in different directions.

One option is to head down Broad Street, which contains a variety of shops. A walk in the opposite direction, across the pedestrian/skater/bicyclist-only Walnut Street Bridge, leads to another collection of shops and restaurants. Another choice is the Tennessee Aquarium and IMAX Theater and Ross's Landing, which surge with tourists.

The Bluff View Art District

For a totally different experience, hike up Third Street and turn left onto High Street—or follow the Riverwalk from Ross's Landing Park under the Walnut Street Bridge to the **Bluff View Art District,** a small enclave with galleries, restaurants, and an overall European feel.

North Chattanooga

If things seem a little hectic around the Tennessee Aquarium, walk across the Walnut Street Bridge to this neighborhood. You'll feel less like a tourist in this eclectic place. Check out the carousel at Coolidge Park.

Lookout Mountain

Coming from downtown and heading south, Broad Street becomes Highway 58, which leads to Lookout Mountain, home of the Incline Railway, Rock City, Ruby Falls, and the site of the "Battle above the Clouds."

Signal Mountain and Raccoon Mountain

Signal Mountain, Raccoon Mountain, and the Tennessee River between them make up "the Grand Canyon of the Tennessee River." To get to the former, take the Highway 127 exit off Highway 27 North. To get to the latter, take the Cummings Highway exit off I-24 heading toward Nashville.

SEEING THE CIVIL WAR IN CHATTANOOGA

Chattanooga is perhaps the best place in Tennessee to take in the Civil War. Significant battles were fought here, and because of the lay of the land, the events are relatively easy to follow.

In the decades after the war, Union and Confederate veterans held reunions at the battlefields and saw a need to protect them from encroaching development. *Chattanooga Times* publisher Adolph Ochs lent his support, and in 1890 Congress approved creation of the **Chickamauga and Chattanooga National Military Park,** the nation's first national military park. It was dedicated September 18–20, 1895. Veterans carefully placed about 1,400 monuments and historical markers indicating which brigade fought where. Ochs, even after he moved to New York to run the *New York Times,* was instrumental in buying land on Lookout Mountain and donating it to the public.

The best place to begin a tour is park headquarters, across the state line in Georgia. To get there, take Highway 27 south or get off I-75 on Battlefield Parkway and follow the signs west. The visitor's center holds various artifacts, a collection of 355 weapons, and an excellent bookstore. A multimedia production gives an overview of the battle. During warm weather, the museum often demonstrates activities related to the Civil War. Visitors can drive a seven-mile tour of the battlefield. If the weather is nice, bicycles are the best way to get around.

The Chickamauga battle was fought in a forested area with visibility of about 100–150 yards, one reason commanders were confused and the casualties were so high. The present-day forest, which has much more underbrush, may prove frustrating to those expecting a wide vista. If visitors are pressed for time, they should see just the visitor's center and depart for Lookout Mountain.

The center, tel. 706/866-9241, is open 8 A.M.–4:30 P.M., although the battlefield stays open from dawn to dusk. The Battle of Chickamauga slide show costs $2.25 for adults, $1 for children 6 to 16, and $1 for seniors. Admission is free to the visitor's center and the park.

The **Gordon-Lee Mansion,** tel. 706/375-4728, south of the Chickamauga battlefield site, served as headquarters for Union General Rosecrans before the battle and as a hospital afterward. The mansion is now a bed-and-breakfast. To get there, drive south of the battlefield on Highway 27. Turn right on Lee/Gordon Mill Road and go 2.5 miles to the town of Chickamauga. The mansion is on the right. Visitors can tour it in the afternoon in groups of 15 or more. The cost is $4.50 per person; you must call ahead.

Known for years as Confederama, the **Battles for Chattanooga Museum** at 3742 Tennessee Avenue in the St. Elmo neighborhood, tel. 423/821-2812, now has a name likely to appeal to Yankees as well. The museum's centerpiece is a three-dimensional, 480-square-foot layout consisting of 5,000 miniature soldiers, 650 lights, and sound effects that illustrate the battles of Lookout Mountain and Missionary Ridge. The museum also features dioramas and Civil War artifacts. During the summer, Sergeant "Fox Jim" McKinney holds forth and answers questions about the war. At other times he can be summoned by phone call at no additional cost. Admission is $5 for adults and $3 for children 3 to 12, with discounts for seniors. The museum is open daily except Christmas.

Closer in, **Point Park** occupies the end of **Lookout Mountain.** The Park Service maintains a small visitor's center here. During summer, rangers offer walks, talks, and demonstrations of Civil War–related activities. Parking is limited, so if there's no room in the Park Service lot, keep an eye on the meters.

The entrance gate to the park is the world's largest replica of the Corps of Engineers insignia. It was erected in 1905, not surprisingly by the Corps. Various batteries contain different kinds of cannons used in the battle, and the Ochs Museum and Overlook offers a very good view of Chattanooga. The hike there descends 500 feet and may tax those not up to a good climb back.

Craven House, the Confederate headquarters during the early parts of the battle, lies off Highway 148, the scenic highway. The original house was pretty much shot up during the battle and demolished for firewood afterward. What visitors see has been rebuilt and furnished to reflect the life of the Craven family. Admission is $2 each for ages 16–62 or $4 for an entire family. Hours vary, according to the park budget, but usually Craven House is open weekends April and May, daily June through August, and weekends September and October.

The **National Cemetery,** 1200 Bailey Ave., tel. 423/855-6590, was established in December 1883 by Union General George Thomas, the famous "Rock of Chickamauga." Soldiers tended to be buried haphazardly after battles, and this was an effort to give them a final resting place with honor and dignity. More than 12,000 Union soldiers from various battles—half of them unknown—are buried here. Veterans of other American wars, including the Revolution, also rest here, making this the largest national cemetery in the state. No Confederates are buried here.

Oddly enough, Germans are buried here as well—some 186 prisoners of war from World War I and II. In fact, this is the only national cemetery containing prisoners of war from both world wars.

The most famous marker is for James Andrews' Raiders, a group of Union spies who slipped into Georgia, stole a locomotive named The General, and headed north. The daring Raiders were eventually caught by the Confederates and hanged for their activities. Eight of them rest beneath a marker topped by a replica of The General. Four of them were the first recipients of the newly created Medal of Honor. Andrews himself is not buried here, for he was not in the military.

Keep in mind that this cemetery still has funerals; behave accordingly. Admission is free.

The **Orchard Knob Reservation,** in downtown Chattanooga, marks the hill from which Grant directed the assault on Missionary Ridge. It contains a tall marker but little else to see.

From a preservation standpoint, **Missionary Ridge** did not fare as well as Lookout Mountain. During various real estate booms in the late 1800s, homeowners snapped up property along the ridge, and now most of it is in private hands. When the veterans came back in the 1890s, they found houses on many of the battle sites. Several significant sites lie along Crest Road, among them the **Bragg Reservation, Ohio Reservation, De Long Reservation,** and **Sherman Reservation.** From the south, you can get to Crest Road from Highway 27 in Rossville, Georgia. Several streets in Chattanooga, such as Shallowford Road, run up to the ridge.

Signal Mountain faces Lookout Mountain and was, as its name implies, a place for Union communications after the Confederates had cut telegraph lines. **Signal Point Reservation** commemorates the efforts of the U.S. Signal Corps and offers an imposing view of "the Grand Canyon of the Tennessee River."

Note: Visitors may notice a lively trade in Civil War artifacts—bullets, buttons, and the like—in local shops. These are supposed to have come from private lands; it is strictly against the law to dig for artifacts, remove them from government property, or damage them in any way. Visitors who observe any suspicious activity should notify park officials.

CHATTANOOGA

THE BATTLE FOR CHATTANOOGA: CHICKAMAUGA

By 1863 things were not looking good for the South. In July, Ulysses S. Grant took Vicksburg on the Mississippi River, and the Battle of Gettysburg marked an end to any chance of the Confederacy's attacking the North. The Union turned its attention toward Georgia, and to get there it had to come through the rail center of Chattanooga.

Braxton Bragg was commander of Southern forces numbering 43,000 in Chattanooga when a Union army of 60,000 commanded by William Rosecrans approached. Chattanooga, beside the looping Tennessee River and next to high mountain ridges, was a very good place to get penned, so the Confederates retreated into Georgia. Sensing the chance to catch and defeat Bragg, Rosecrans pursued him into the heavily wooded plains near Chickamauga Creek. He did not know that Confederate troops from Gettysburg and other places had come by train to reinforce Bragg, bringing his forces to 66,000. The armies skirmished on the night of September 18, and at dawn the next day clashed in one of the bloodiest battles of the war.

Unlike Gettysburg or other places where battles were fought out in the open, the land here was covered with trees and thick underbrush. Much of the fighting was hand-to-hand, and officers had no clear idea of what was happening. This situation—and a huge piece of luck—determined the outcome of the battle.

One Union officer erroneously reported to General Rosecrans that there was a gap in the lines, and the general ordered a division to shift over and fill it. It did so, thus creating a real gap at the exact place where General James Longstreet—who had roomed with Rosecrans at West Point—poured 11,000 soldiers, who broke through the Union lines.

Rosecrans took the advice of his chief of staff, future president James A. Garfield, and retreated toward Chattanooga. One Union commander was not so willing to go. George Thomas took a stand on Snodgrass Hill and held off the Southerners long enough for the Union to make an effective retreat. For this he became known as "the Rock of Chickamauga," while Rosecrans, in his retreat, was labeled a coward.

Despite the victory, Bragg didn't fare well either. He refused to pursue the fleeing Northerners, to the disgust of Nathan Bedford Forrest and other Confederates. The cost of the battle was appalling. Bragg lost an estimated 30 percent of his men, and Union and Confederate losses totaled 4,000 men dead—among them 10 Southern generals—and 35,000 wounded.

The Union forces stumbled into Chattanooga. Bragg, following them at last, took up positions high above the city on Lookout Mountain and Missionary Ridge. His guns commanded the rail and river approaches, and other troops were so placed that no one could supply the vanquished troops. Bragg meant to starve them into submission. The Union situation got so bad that a newly promoted general was summoned to help. His name was U.S. Grant, and his arrival set the scene for the battle of Lookout Mountain and Missionary Ridge.

Sights and Recreation

DOWNTOWN CHATTANOOGA

A good place to begin your visit is **Shuttle Park South,** adjacent to the Chattanooga Choo Choo on Market Street. A 500-space parking garage offers a safe place to leave the vehicle before you set out to explore downtown. The electric shuttle buses—free to all—run from here to the Tennessee Aquarium and all points in between. The schedule is as follows: Monday through Friday 6 A.M.–10 P.M., Saturday 9 A.M.–10 P.M., and Sunday 9 A.M.–8:30 P.M.

Ross's Landing

Ross's Landing at once provides open space and pays homage to Chattanooga's history. It uses landscaped bands of public art and native plantings to tell Chattanooga's story. With surfaces that are alternately paved, grassed, or covered with running water, the bands begin with the year 1992, the dedication date, and work back in time as they move toward the river. Commemorated subjects include Sequoyah and his Cherokee language syllabary, Chattanooga's railroad heritage, and Bessie Smith.

The **Chattanooga Visitors Center,** just off Ross's Landing at 2 Broad Street, tel. 423/756-8687 or 800/322-3344, is a great place for visitors to orient themselves and plan their sightseeing. In addition to a huge collection of brochures, the center offers a slide show about the city, a reservation service for local hostelries, and information about events soon to take place. The slide show costs $2 for adults and $1 for children 6 to 12.

Tennessee Aquarium

The $45 million aquarium, tel. 800/262-0695, website: www.tennesseeaquarium.com, smack in the middle of Ross's Landing Park and Plaza, was the first of its kind devoted to freshwater aquatic life. The displays replicate the habitats that water falling in an Appalachian mountain forest would go through on its way to the sea. Visitors can see plant life and animals—some 7,000 species of mammals, fish, reptiles, and amphibians—as different in location and evolution as mountain salamanders and Gulf Coast sharks. Life from rivers around the world is also included—South America's Amazon, Africa's Zaire, Japan's Shimanto, and Siberia's Yenisey.

The aquarium's **IMAX Theater** shows educational and entertaining films on a six-story-high screen backed with a state-of-the-art sound system. Anyone subject to motion sickness should sit near the aisle. The admission price changes depending on the length of the film but runs about $7.25 for adults and $4.95 for kids 3 to 12. A combination ticket to the IMAX and the aquarium costs $17 for adults and $10 for kids.

The aquarium has proven enormously popular and at times gets very crowded. Ordering tickets ahead of time by phone is a very good idea. Admission is $12.95 for adults, $6.95 for kids 3 to 12, and free for kids under 3. The gift shop is free and open to the public. To get to the aquarium, take I-24 to downtown Chattanooga to Highway 27 North. Take a right onto Fourth Street, then turn left at the second stoplight onto Broad Street. Go two blocks, and the aquarium will be in sight.

Coolidge Park

Located across the Tennessee River from the aquarium, eight-acre Coolidge Park contains open space, an open-air stage, an interactive fountain, and—best of all—a restored, hand-carved carousel. All the figures on the ride were carved by students at the Horsin' Around school for carvers. (The school and studios can be seen north of town in Soddy-Daisy.) This new park was named for Charles Coolidge, a World War II soldier who won the Congressional Medal of Honor. The park is a part of the 22-mile Riverwalk along the Tennessee River.

River Sights

The 2,370-foot-long **Walnut Street Bridge** was built over the Tennessee River in 1891. It has carried pedestrians, trolley cars, and motor traffic. It served the locals for 87 years before it was closed. Rather than let the bridge be demolished

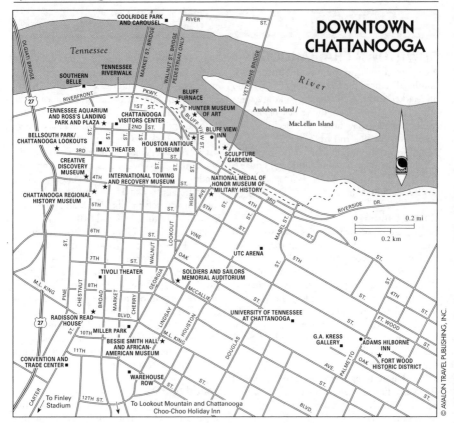

DOWNTOWN CHATTANOOGA

or left to decay, Chattanoogans had the vision to renovate it and dedicate it to human-powered traffic. Thus the visitor will see walkers, runners, bicyclists, and in-line skaters crossing what is billed as the longest pedestrian walkway bridge in the world. No fee is charged to use it.

Bluff Furnace Historical Park, located on the Riverwalk between the Walnut Street Bridge and the Hunter Museum, marks the site of the city's first heavy industrial plant. Completed in 1854, Bluff Furnace produced bars of pig iron. In 1859 the plant was leased by northern industrialists and began burning coke, a fuel used nowhere else in the South. Today the park features a stainless steel outline of the original furnace stack, a scale model of the complex, explanatory signs, and a multimedia, interactive

computer program highlighting the history of the riverfront. Admission is free.

Chattanooga Choo Choo

The Chattanooga Choo Choo, 1400 Market St., tel. 800/TRACK-29 or 423/266-5000, website: www.choochoo.com, is the latest incarnation of Chattanooga's 1909 Southern Railway Terminal, where in its heyday 68 trains arrived and departed daily on 14 tracks. The 85-foot dome is the highest freestanding such structure in the world. The last regularly scheduled train pulled out of Chattanooga in 1971, and the 61-year-old terminal was boarded up and all but abandoned. Twenty-four investors had other ideas, however, and after a year of renovation the station opened once more. It's been going strong ever since.

The 30-acre complex includes four restaurants (see below), a Holiday Inn, and shops. Guests can stay in railroad coaches that contain two complete rooms. Visitors can ride around the grounds in a 1930s New Orleans trolley, shop in 14 stores, and view an enormous 174-by-33-foot HO-gauge model train display that contains more than 3,000 feet of track, 1,000 freight cars, and model cities.

MUSEUMS

History

The **Chattanooga African-American Museum,** 200 E. Martin Luther King Blvd., tel. 423/266-8658, website: www.caamhistory.com, houses cultural and historical documents and artifacts pertaining to the city's black community. Admission is $5 for adults, $3 for seniors, $2 for students, and free for children under 12. The museum is located in **Bessie Smith Hall,** tel. 423/757-0020, which contains a 264-seat performance hall and exhibits relating to the blues singer. Blues and jazz concerts of national, regional, and local artists are presented here, and visitors can use a listening room to hear tapes of Bessie Smith and others. The exhibits are first class.

Two blocks from the Tennessee Aquarium, the **Chattanooga Regional History Museum,** 400 Chestnut St., tel. 423/265-3247, website: www.chattanoogahistory.com, interprets the various strands of local history—Native American, music, the Civil War, sports, and business—for all ages. *Chattanooga Country: Its Lands, Rivers, and Peoples,* is the museum's permanent exhibit, which includes hands-on activities for kids. This first-class museum is expanding and plans to construct a new building on its present site. Admission is $4 for adults, $3.50 for seniors, and $3 for children 5 to 18.

The **National Medal of Honor Museum of Military History,** 400 Georgia Ave., tel. 423/267-1737, has been put together by an all-volunteer staff. Here visitors will see collections of guns, knives, and sabers; uniforms from a variety of wars; enemy memorabilia; and displays that commemorate wars from the Revolution to Operation Desert Storm. Admission is free, but donations are appreciated. This museum is located close to the intersection of Georgia Avenue and Riverfront Parkway—not far from the aquarium.

Art and Antiques

The **George Ayer Kress Gallery,** at the corner of Vine and Palmetto Streets, tel. 423/755-4371, is part of the University Fine Arts Center and features exhibits of contemporary art in two galleries. Admission is free.

The **Houston Museum of Decorative Arts,** 201 High St., tel. 423/267-7176, website: www.chattanooga.net/Houston, is the legacy of one Anna Safely Houston, who had 10 siblings and managed to get married nine times. She opened an antiques shop in 1920 and built up a collection of more than 10,000 pieces of art glass, pressed glass, and furniture. She was partial to pitchers, and the collection contains several thousand of them. Hard times in the Depression caused her to close the shop, sell her house, and move into an old barn. She piled glassware from floor to ceiling, with pitchers hanging on ropes. For years she wouldn't let anyone see the collection, but she willed it to the city of Chattanooga in 1951. In 1957 a group of citizens established a museum to house it. However eccentric its founder, the collection is world class, containing Peachblow, Tiffany, and Steuben pieces, as well as cruets and miniature lamps. The collection is at home in a turn-of-the-last century house; admission is $6.

The **Hunter Museum of Art,** 10 Bluff St., tel. 423/267-0968, sits on a 90-foot limestone cliff overlooking the city and the Tennessee River. It consists of two buildings: a 1904 mansion and a building erected in 1975. Inside resides a collection of 1,500 works, only a small part of which can be displayed at any one time. Here the visitor will find works by Mary Cassatt, Thomas Hart Benton, Ansel Adams, Albert Bierstadt, Willem de Kooning, and Alexander Calder, to name a few. The pieces are rotated every two to four years, although some favorites remain on display all the time. The museum hosts touring shows as well.

The museum takes a leading role in Chattanooga's cultural community and offers all man-

CHATTANOOGA

ner of programs and activities. Admission is $5 for adults, $4 for seniors, $3 for students, and $2.50 for children 3 to 12. See www.huntermuseum.org for more information.

Religious

The Messianic Museum, just north of Chattanooga off Highway 153 at 1928 Hamill Road in Hixson, tel. 423/876-8150, website: www.ibjm.org, is housed in the headquarters of the International Board of Jewish Missions (IBJM), whose purpose is to convert Jews to Christianity—very controversial in Jewish circles. The two-story museum focuses on Jews and Israel and the founder of the IBJM. Exhibits include dioramas depicting events such as Moses on Mount Sinai, large photos of Israel, 250-year-old Torahs, lamps, scrolls, and works of art. The museum is open Monday through Friday 9 A.M.–4:30 P.M. Admission is free.

The **Siskin Museum of Religious Artifacts,** 1101 Carter St., tel. 423/634-1700, resulted from a promise to God. In 1942, Garrison Siskin was badly injured in a train accident and promised God that if his life and injured leg were saved he would spend the rest of his life helping others. Siskin lived, and he and his family became prominent philanthropists in Chattanooga. The family dispatched its rabbi to Europe in the 1950s to find and buy significant Jewish religious artifacts. Over time the family acquired items from other faiths, and now visitors can see the collection at this museum. See www.siskinfoundation.org for more information.

Specialty

The **Creative Discovery Museum,** 321 Chestnut St., tel. 423/756-2738, is a wonderful $16.5 million place with four exhibit areas: an artist's studio, an inventor's workshop, a field scientist's lab, and a musician's studio. Exhibits are hands-on. For instance, in the inventor's workshop, kids can sit in the driver's seat and program a full-size electric car, experiment with mechanical devices on a discovery table, and make their own inventions. Admission is $7.95 for adults and $4.95 for kids 3 to 12. See the museum online at www.cdmfun.org.

Dragon Dreams Museum, 6724-A East Brainerd Rd., tel. 423/892-2384, occupies a house with eight rooms and more than 2,000 dragons. The curator says the museum sprang from a personal collection "that was making the house a little strange." Each room has a theme—Fun Room, Fantasy Room, Japanese Room, and so on. Admission is $6 for adults and $3 for children 14 and under. See www.dragonvet.com for more information.

When this book went to press, the **International Towing and Recovery Hall of Fame and Museum** was itself getting towed. It was at Fourth and Broad Streets, tel. 423/238-4171, a piece of property bought by the Chattanooga Regional History Museum for future expansion. Now the towing museum hopes to find a new home. Wherever it lands, its purpose is to improve the towing industry's negative image. Exhibits include antique wreckers and other vehicles and a 1930s filling station.

PARKS, ZOOS, AND SANCTUARIES

Chattanooga's **Riverpark** stretches for 22 miles from Chickamauga Dam downstream past the city to Moccasin Bend. This greenbelt includes walkways, playgrounds, a rowing center, fishing piers, and boat docks. Riverpark celebrates the Tennessee River.

Audubon Acres, tel. 423/892-1499, is a 120-acre wildlife sanctuary east of Chattanooga. Visitors can see a cabin built by the Cherokee, cross a swinging bridge, and take hikes on 10 miles of trails. To get there, take Exit 3A off I-75, then go right on Gunbarrel Road. From November to March, the closing time is 5 P.M. Admission is $2 for adults and $1 for children 5 to 12. Visit www.audubonchattanooga.org/acres.html online.

In the middle of the river near downtown lies **MacLellan Island,** an 18.8-acre wooded area also owned by the Audubon Society and operated as a wildlife sanctuary. Trips to the island are scheduled from time to time, or you can catch a ride with a visiting school group. For information call 423/892-1499 or see www.audubonchattanooga.org/island.html.

Chattanooga's Horsin' Around School for Carvers

© JEFF BRADLEY

Booker T. Washington State Park, 5801 Champion Rd., tel. 423/894-4955, comprising 353 acres on Chickamauga Lake, created from TVA land, offers a swimming pool, boating and fishing, and a group camp for 40 people, but no individual campsites.

Don't show up at **Reflection Riding** expecting to get back in the saddle. The 375-acre botanical garden, which snuggles up against the west side of Lookout Mountain, has nothing to do with horses. The "riding" in the name is an English affectation meaning "path of pleasure." A three-mile drive goes through the park and connects to more than 12 miles of trails. Here you'll see more than 300 kinds of wildflowers and more than 1,000 species of other plants, plus Civil War skirmish sites. The Great Indian Warpath runs through here and is maintained in its original condition. Hernando De Soto is alleged to have come this way as well. Joint admission for Reflection Riding and the Tennessee Wildlife Center is $6 for adults and $3 for seniors and kids 4 to 12. Call 423/821-1160 for more information or visit www.chattanooga.net/rriding.

The **Tennessee Wildlife Center,** tel. 423/821-1160, website: www.tnwildlifecenter.com, serves as an educational center, complete with exhibits and a 1,200-foot Wetland Walkway. The red wolf exhibit is a good one to see. Feeding time—when the wolves come out of their dens—takes place at 2 P.M. on weekdays and 3 P.M. on weekends. To get to the center, take I-24 Exit 175 south onto Lookout Mountain Road. Turn left on Highway 41, go 0.7 miles, turn right on Highway 318 South, then turn right again on Garden Road. Continue one more mile.

The 1,199-acre **Harrison Bay State Park** sits off Highway 58 on the Chickamauga Reservoir, a.k.a. the Tennessee River, just northeast of Chattanooga. With 39 miles of shoreline, water is the chief focus here, and the park has one of the most complete marinas on any TVA lake. It also has a restaurant (open March through October), camping, hiking trails, and stables. For more information, call 423/344-6214 or visit www.state.tn.us/environment/parks/Harrison.

CHATTANOOGA

A ONE-OF-A-KIND PLACE

Outside of Chattanooga, in the Soddy-Daisy community, you'll find the only carousel carving school in America. **Horsin' Around** attracts people from all over the country, who come to learn the art of carving figures for merry-go-rounds. They produce all manner of realistic and fantastic wooden figures: horses, dragons, frogs, elephants, and fish, to name a few.

Visitors are welcome to tour the studios. To get there, go north of Chattanooga on Highway 27. Take the Soddy-Daisy Exit. Horsin' Around is located behind the Wal-Mart, which is visible from the exit. No admission is charged, and the studios are open Monday through Saturday 9 A.M.–6 P.M. Call 423/332-1111 or visit www.carousel carvingschool.com.

Be careful. More than one individual has toured this place, gone home and pulled up stakes, and moved to join the studio. It is that appealing.

LOOKOUT MOUNTAIN

Lookout Mountain rises just outside of Chattanooga's city limits and extends southwest more than 50 miles into Georgia and Alabama. If the National Register had a category for "Historic Tourism Destinations," then surely Lookout Mountain would be on this list. Ruby Falls and Rock City have survived the days of tourist homes and blue highways, and the Incline Railway still goes up and down what's called the steepest track in the world. Because of the fancy neighborhoods at the top, however, there are not many places to eat, particularly of the fast-food persuasion. Visitors are advised to pack a picnic lunch or order takeout from restaurants in Chattanooga.

Lookout Mountain Incline Railway

The railway, 827 E. Brow Rd., tel. 423/821-4224, was built back in the 1890s, when Lookout Mountain had large hotels where people came and stayed for weeks at a time. The cars operate like San Francisco's cable cars, by grasping a moving cable that stretches from top to bottom between the tracks. At their steepest, the mile-long tracks climb a 72.7 percent grade, perhaps the

© TENNESSEE DEPARTMENT OF TOURISM DEVELOPMENT

The Incline Railway has been climbing some of the steepest tracks in the world since 1895. The grade reaches 72.7 percent.

steepest tracks in the world.

Once at the top, visitors who wish to see Ruby Falls or Rock City can take a shuttle bus during summer and walk the three blocks to Point Park. The Incline Railway is open every day but Christmas, and cars leave three or four times per hour. A round-trip ride takes 30 minutes. Admission is $9 for adults and $4.50 for children 3 to 12. Visit www.ngeorgia.com/tenn/theincline.html for more information.

Ruby Falls

Ruby Falls, on Lookout Mountain Scenic Highway, tel. 423/821-2544, is the latest incarnation of a cave with a long history. Local Indians long knew of a cavern extending under the north end of Lookout Mountain. During the Civil War it was used as a hospital; later, a railroad tunnel cut off the original entrance. In 1928, a man named Leo Lambert hired a crew to drill a shaft

CHATTANOOGA

peering through the Needles Eye at Rock City Gardens

down to the cave so that he could commercialize it. On the way down, the crew hit another, hitherto unknown cave. When Leo and his wife, Ruby, explored it, they discovered a 145-foot-high waterfall. Leo named it after his wife.

Visitors descend to the cave in an elevator, then stroll approximately 2,200 feet back to the waterfall. The walk is very flat, almost like walking along a mine. At the falls, visitors are greeted with a light show and music only slightly less portentous than that planned for the Second Coming. Back on top, kids can enjoy a "Fun Forest" consisting of various climbing structures. Admission is $11.50 for adults and $5.50 for children 3 to 12. See www.rubyfalls.com for more information.

Rock City Gardens

At Rock City, tel. 706/820-2531, paths wind through large rocks, steps lead over other rocks, bridges span chasms, and visitors walk through tight places with names such as Fat Man's Squeeze. The culmination is the highly promoted view of seven states. Given today's pollution,

SEE ROCK CITY

Those of a certain age who ever traveled through the South might recall "See Rock City" signs on barns and birdhouses. Though long associated with Chattanooga, **Rock City Gardens** is actually on the part of Lookout Mountain that extends into Georgia. No matter where it is, this is perhaps the South's most famous attraction.

Rock City began with Garnet and Frieda Carter, who owned 10 acres on the top of Lookout Mountain. The property was filled with enormous pieces of rock in odd shapes. In the depths of the Depression, the couple got the notion to charge admission to their "rock city." But it lay quite off the beaten path—not the kind of place that people would see while driving along.

The Carters had the inspiration to hire a paint crew and put them on the road painting enormous signs on barn roofs. The farmers got a few dollars and a new paint job, and Rock City gained invaluable publicity. If this weren't enough, the Carters designed birdhouses whose roofs read "See Rock City" and scattered them far and wide. At one time approximately 900 barns as far as Michigan, Texas, and Florida lured tourists and unforgettably brightened America's blue highways.

Garnet Carter further contributed to popular culture by inventing miniature golf. The story goes that a guest at Carter's Fairyland Inn, wishing that the golf course was open, jokingly suggested putting a putting green in front of the inn. Using the odd piece of pipe and other materials, Carter built the first miniature golf course. This archetype was such a hit that Carter franchised the idea all over the country. See www.seerockcity.com for more information.

CHATTANOOGA

THE BATTLE FOR CHATTANOOGA: LOOKOUT MOUNTAIN AND MISSIONARY RIDGE

After the defeat at Chickamauga, Abraham Lincoln's administration ordered Generals U.S. Grant, William T. Sherman, and Joseph Hooker to relieve the siege of Chattanooga. Grant was in charge, and by November 1, 1863, he had established a supply line that was out of reach of Confederate troops and artillery. The next step was to drive the Southerners from the heights that overlooked the city.

While the Union was beefing up its forces, Confederate generals argued about Braxton Bragg's competence, their squabble reaching such intensity that President Jefferson Davis came to personally work out an agreement. The upshot was that Nathan Bedford Forrest left, James Longstreet was dispatched with one-fourth of the troops to attack Knoxville, and Bragg remained in charge.

On November 24, Grant sent Hooker's troops up the side of Lookout Mountain—a 1,716-foot gain in elevation—to take out the artillery. Fog covered the mountain that day, and under its cover Union infantry fought their way with surprising ease over boulders and around trees to the top, suffering only 500 casualties. Later on, this event became known as the Battle above the Clouds (Battle in the Fog not having quite the right ring to it).

With a big American flag planted at the top of Lookout Mountain, the Union forces turned their attention the next day to Missionary Ridge. Fought six days after Lincoln's Gettysburg Address and involving Southerners who had fought at that battle, in many ways this engagement looked to be a mirror image of Gettysburg, with the Southerners waiting at the top of a ridge for the Union troops to charge. Unlike the Northerners at Gettysburg, however, the Confederates had been digging in on Missionary Ridge for two months, and the hill was wooded and much steeper—453 feet higher than downtown Chattanooga.

Grant thought that a direct assault would be suicidal, so he ordered attacks on each side. Neither was very effective, so to keep the Confederates from shifting troops to reinforce the ends, he commanded men under General George Thomas ("the Rock of Chickamauga") to attack the first row of defenders straight on.

The word to go was all these troops needed. Stung by their defeat five weeks before at Chickamauga, they overran the first row of trenches and kept going. From his headquarters Grant could see regimental colors climbing higher and higher on the ridge. Fearing for the men, he asked who had ordered the charge. Reportedly, he was told, "No one. They started up without orders. When those fellows get started, all hell can't stop them."

The Confederates certainly couldn't. The Union troops took the rifle pits, captured the artillery, and chased the Rebels down the back of Missionary Ridge, yelling, "Chickamauga! Chickamauga!" One of the victors was an 18-year-old lieutenant who carried his Wisconsin regiment's colors up the hill after three men had died doing the same thing. He won the Medal of Honor for this deed and went on to sire Douglas MacArthur.

Chattanooga was never again in Southern hands. Grant was named lieutenant general, a rank last held by George Washington, and moved east to act as general in chief. Sherman set his sights for Atlanta and the march to the sea that would bring the South to its knees.

---

seeing all seven is probably not possible anymore, but it's an impressive view nonetheless. Perhaps the oddest thing about Rock City are the Fairyland Caverns and other places filled with figures seemingly designed in the 1930s.

To get there, get on Highway 58 heading south up Lookout Mountain and follow the signs into Georgia. Admission is $11.95 for adults and $6.50 for children 3 to 12. Food and needless to say souvenirs are available here.

Lookout Mountain Natural Bridge

Not too far from Rock City is a rock arch that's 85 feet long and, at its highest, 15 feet off the ground. This little-publicized arch rises in a ravine between the Good Shepherd Episcopal Church and Bragg Avenue off Highway 148. A sign indicates the presence of the arch, but visitors must park several hundred feet south of the sign.

Lively times used to take place here. The Southern Association of Spiritualists bought this property and an adjacent hotel in 1883 and conducted séances and pseudo-Indian ceremonies on the arch, some of them lasting well into the night and complete with Indian chants. This is a good place for a picnic. Don't forget the Ouija board.

Lookout Mountain Flight Park

For those not content to just look off the mountain, the flight park, below Covenant College on Highway 189 in Georgia, tel. 706/398-3541 or 800/688-5637, offers the opportunity to fly off it. Claiming to be the number-one hang gliding school in the United States, it provides a variety of training/flight packages. The simplest is a tandem flight, in which the rider is buckled into a two-person hang glider with an experienced pilot, towed by an airplane to a height of 2,000 feet, and released. The flight down is about 20 minutes long and costs $129. For $60 more, the airplane will cut riders loose at 4,000 feet. If wind conditions are right, the school offers flights off the side of the mountain. Visitors can watch free of charge. Visit the school online at www.hanglide.com.

RACCOON MOUNTAIN AND SIGNAL MOUNTAIN

Downstream from Chattanooga, the Tennessee River cuts through the Cumberland Plateau. The mountains that face each other across the gorge are Signal Mountain on the north bank and Raccoon Mountain on the south side.

Signal Mountain got its name from the belief that Indians used it for signal fires, but it truly lived up to its name when the Union army was under siege in Chattanooga. The Confederates had cut the telegraph wires, forcing the brand new U.S. Signal Corps to send coded messages by flags and torches. The town of Signal Mountain developed in the years after 1910. Signal Point is an excellent place from which to gaze at "the

Grand Canyon of the Tennessee River."

Raccoon Mountain is home to TVA's most unusual source of electric power: the **Raccoon Mountain Pumped-Storage Project,** tel. 423/825-3100. Since it's impossible to store large amounts of electricity, utilities have to be able to produce or buy enough power to meet peak needs. Power plants that run flat out from 6 A.M. to 11 P.M., however, sit largely idle during off-peak time, when most power users are asleep.

The Pumped-Storage Project uses off-peak power to pump water from the Tennessee River 1,204 feet up tunnels to a 528-acre reservoir. When the TVA needs power, the water flows down a passageway to the same pumps, only this time turning them to generate electricity. It takes 27 hours to fill the reservoir and 20 hours to release the water used to generate power.

TVA provides escorted tours from a visitor's center at the top of the reservoir to the underground power plant. The tour begins with a 1,200-foot descent in an elevator—the equivalent of a 106-story building. Tours are given daily, and the last one begins at 4 P.M. Admission is free. This is a good place for picnics and other recreation. Because of the ups and downs of the reservoir, however, no boating or fishing is allowed.

Raccoon Mountain Caverns, one mile off I-24 Exit 174, tel. 423/821-9403 or 800/823-CAMP, offers tours of a cave full of formations. Visitors can choose from a 45-minute walk in the cave—$8.95 for adults, $4.50 for kids 5 to 12—or various "wild cave" tours, which go off the beaten path. These can run from two hours to overnight, costing $26 to $49 per person. Call ahead for reservations or contact www.raccoonmountain.com.

AMUSEMENT PARKS

The **Lake Winnepesaukah Amusement Park** is six miles from downtown Chattanooga at 1730 Lakeview Drive in Rossville, Georgia, tel. 706/866-5681 or toll-free 877/525-3946. The kids won't mind crossing the state line for the more than 30 rides and attractions. During the tourist season, this place offers concerts by big-name country and oldies entertainers. Admis-

CHATTANOOGA

sion to the park is $3 for adults and children. Rides cost extra. Preview the park online at www.lakewinnie.com.

EXCURSIONS AND CRUISES
By Rail

Chattanooga has more of a railroad legacy than any other Tennessee city, and here is the place to get on board. The largest operating historic railroad in the South, the **Tennessee Valley Railroad,** 4119 Cromwell Rd. and North Chamberlain St., tel. 423/894-8028, features steam- and diesel-powered trains. The 1911 steam locomotive 4501 is the gem of the collection, which among other rolling stock includes a 1917 office car, a 1926 dining car, and a 1929 caboose. The railroad owns 40 acres that include four bridges and the 986-foot Missionary Ridge Tunnel. Grand Junction Depot is a 1900-vintage station containing an orientation center, a deli, and a large gift shop. On the other end of the line is a replica of a small-town station.

The ride lasts about half an hour between stations. On weekends during summer, the trains go to the Chattanooga Choo Choo. Rides cost $10.50 for adults and $5 for kids 3 to 12. See the railroad online at www.tvrail.com.

Another option for train lovers is **Dixie Land Excursions,** tel. 423/894-8028, a ride on a restored train along the old Central Georgia main line. Trains leave April through October from the Tennessee Valley Railroad's Grand Junction Station at 4119 Cromwell Road and then chug along to one of several locations in northwest Georgia. The daylong excursions include lunch either on the train or at a depot. The fare is $39–69, depending on itinerary. The trips are not recommended for patrons in wheelchairs or anyone with difficulty walking or climbing stairs. Seats are limited, so reservations are essential. Find the TVR online at www.tvrail.com.

On the Water

The 500-passenger *Southern Belle,* tel. 423/266-4488 or 800/766-2784, offers visitors a variety of cruises departing from Ross's Landing at the foot of Chestnut Street. Trips include rides through "the Grand Canyon of the Tennessee River," dinner cruises, and even a gospel dinner cruise. Trips run from Valentines Day through New Year's Eve. Call for schedule information or visit www.chattanoogariverboat.com.

Entertainment and Events

Chattanooga boasts more than 60 art, cultural, and historic groups that put on a wide variety of events. The **Allied Arts** line, tel. 423/756-2787, supplies information on what's happening. Visit them online at www.alliedartschatt.org.

ON THE STAGE

Built in 1921, the **Tivoli Theatre,** 709 Broad St., tel. 423/757-5042, was known as "the Jewel of the South," and no wonder. With a high domed ceiling, crystal chandeliers, and grand lobby, it was a wonderful movie palace wherein the likes of Buster Keaton and Mary Pickford appeared on the silver screen. It was the first theater in the South to have air-conditioning, but times changed, and the theater almost slipped

into oblivion. In the 1980s, fortunately, it underwent a $7 million renovation and expansion to its current 1,762 seats, not to mention the hydraulic orchestra pit, dressing rooms for 70 performers, and state-of-the-art theatrical equipment. Here one can enjoy an eclectic mixture of blues, classical, and country music; opera; theatrical productions; and dance. Call to find out what's playing, or go to www.chattanooga.gov/showplaces/on the Web.

FESTIVALS AND EVENTS

In May, barbecue lovers flock to the **River Roast,** a barbecue cooking competition, volleyball tournament, and rowing regatta. Held at Ross's Landing, the event concludes

THE EMPRESS OF THE BLUES

Bessie Smith was born on April 15, 1894. As a little girl, she sang and danced on Chattanooga street corners. As a teenager, she joined the Moses Stokes group of performers. She was heavily influenced by Gertrude "Ma" Rainey, a great blues singer.

Smith stayed with Stokes for less than a year and then set out on her own to tour Southern theaters. Though renowned as a blues singer, she branched into jazz, and during the 1920s she was the highest-paid black performer in the country. In 1923 Columbia Records released her "Down Hearted Blues," which sold 750,000 copies in one month—an unprecedented number of sales. She was billed as the "Greatest and Highest Paid Race Star in the World" and the "190-Pound Favorite of Negroes Everywhere."

Smith succeeded because she was a brilliant lyricist, a captivating performer, and one of the wildest women of her era. She penned such classics as "Black Water Blues," "Preachin' the Blues," and "Wasted Life Blues," which singers still perform. Critics regard her as the first important jazz singer. She recorded "St. Louis Blues" and "Careless Love" with a young trumpet player named Louis Armstrong, who recalled, "Bessie used to thrill me at all times. It's the way she could phrase a note in her blues, a certain something in her voice that no other singer could get. She had real music in her soul and felt everything she did."

En route to a concert in Mississippi in 1937, she was injured in a car accident and bled to death. A famous myth contends that she died after being turned away from a whites-only hospital, but this is not true. Bessie Smith was only 43 years old when she died.

with a Saturday night fireworks display. Call 423/265-4397 for information.

The **Nightfall** series of concerts plays on summer Fridays at Miller Place, at the corner of Market Street and Martin Luther King Boulevard. Lasting 7 to 10 –p.m., Nightfall consists of blues, jazz, zydeco, country, or bluegrass music, along with various concession stands. Call 423/756-2787 for information.

Mid-June brings the **Riverbend Festival,** a nine-day salute to music. Each day a different kind of music takes center stage—classical, country, blues, rock, etc. Local, regional, and up-and-coming national performers hit the stages along with a daily headliner—always a big-name star. One of the events is the **Bessie Smith Strut.** For scheduling information and tickets, call 423/265-4112 or visit www.riverbendfestival.com.

The **Hamilton County Fair** takes place in September at Chester Frost Park on the west side of Chickamauga Lake. Call 423/842-6748 or visit www.hamiltontn.gov/fair for details.

The **Fall Color Cruise and Folk Festival** takes place at the height of the fall foliage season. It's held downstream from Chattanooga at the Shellmound Recreation Area. Participants can travel by riverboat, bus, or car. Music, dance, other entertainment, and food await. Call 423/892-0223 or 800/766-CRUISE or visit www.marioncountychamber.com/colorcruise2.htm.

Christmas on the River, held on the fourth Saturday in November, centers on a parade of lighted floats and a fleet of lighted boats that cruise past Ross's Landing. Local groups sing carols, and the event ends with a fireworks display. Call 423/265-0771 for information.

The Southern Brewers Association Beer Festival presents a sudsy salute to the rapidly growing craft of beer making. Live music, barbecue, and beer samples from various brewers round out the festival, which is held in August. For further information, call 423/267-BREW.

The **Chattanooga Conference on Southern Literature,** held in April, brings big-name Southern writers to town for lectures, panel discussions, and a chance to meet their readers. For information call 423/267-1218 or 800/267-4232 or visit www.artsedcouncil.org/literature.htm.

SPECTATOR SPORTS

The **University of Tennessee Arena** on Fourth Street at Mabel, tel. 423/755-4618, known hereabouts as the Roundhouse because of its shape, presents UT-Chattanooga's men's and women's basketball games as well as concerts, circuses, and other big events throughout the year. Call for schedules and ticket information. To buy tickets, call 423/266-6627.

The **Chattanooga Lookouts** play AA minor-league baseball every summer in the Southern League. A part of the Cincinnati Reds organization, the Lookouts play at the new BellSouth Park—an easy walk from downtown on Chestnut Street. For tickets, call 423/267-4849. Visit the team online at www.lookouts.com.

NIGHTLIFE

Chattanoogans have been tapping their toes to country music for years. But they like jazz, rock, and just about every other kind of music, too. Many restaurants feature live entertainment regularly. The Friday edition of the local newspaper offers a pretty good listing. The following reviews were compiled by Suzanne Hall, a travel and food writer who has been covering the restaurant scene in southeastern Tennessee and around the world for more than 20 years.

Nationally known comedians entertain at **Comedy Catch,** 3224 Brainerd Rd., tel. 423/622- 2233 (info line) or 423/629-2233 (reservations), Wednesday through Saturday nights. Sunday is open mike night.

Dancers can do the two-step, the 10-step, or any step they want Wednesday through Sunday at **Governor's Lounge & Restaurant,** 4251 Bonny Oaks Dr., tel. 423/624-2239. The music is live, and the dance floor is usually crowded. Occasionally, a top-of-the-charts group headlines or stops in to do a late set.

North of Signal Mountain, the **Mountain Opry** is a bit out of town but well worth the trip. Every Friday night from 8 to 11, local musicians gather for bluegrass picking sessions. To get there, take I-24 across the Tennessee River. Exit onto Signal Mountain Boulevard, which becomes Highway 127. Go to the top of Signal Mountain and through town past the shopping center. Go another 1.6 miles to Fairmont Road and turn right at the Fairmont Orchard sign. The civic center that houses the Opry is 0.4 miles ahead on the left. The Opry has no phone.

Boot scooters wanting to rockabilly their babies around the floor should head for

Southside's Jazz Junction, 114 W. Main St., tel. 423/267-9003. You find live jazz and an extensive tapas menu Wednesday through Saturday.

Where to Stay

BED-AND-BREAKFASTS AND INNS

The **Adams Hilborne,** 801 Vine St., tel. 423/265-5000, website: www.innjoy.com, occupies an 1886 home designed for a mayor of Chattanooga. The stone house is adorned with porches, balconies, gables, and balustrades built in the Victorian Romanesque style. Inside are hand-carved coffer ceilings, arched doorways, and Tiffany glass. Guests in the 15 rooms can lie in bed and gaze at 16-foot ceilings surrounded by fine antiques and original artwork. All rooms have private baths, televisions, and telephones; some have fireplaces. Rates range $150–175.

Alford House, 5515 Alford Hill Dr., tel. 423/821-7625, sits on the lower side of Lookout Mountain between I-24 and Ruby Falls. Adjacent to national park land, the house was built in the 1940s. It features two decks and a hot tub. The four rooms—one of them a three-room suite—all have private baths, and the breakfast here is "light and healthy." Rates run $75–95.

Housed in a 1928 Colonial Revival mansion overlooking the Tennessee River and the city, the **Bluff View Inn,** 411 E. Second St., tel. 423/265-5033, contains antiques and fine art throughout. The nine rooms all have private baths, and the inn serves a full gourmet breakfast of items such as lobster hash with poached eggs. Rates are $95–225.

Charlet House Bed & Breakfast, 111 River Point Rd., tel. 423/886-4880, sits in the Olde Towne section of Signal Mountain. It's a quiet place that backs up to woods. The house was built in the 1930s and has a heated pool. The large rooms inside are decorated with antiques. All three suites have private baths, and one has a whirlpool bath. "The Retreat" comes with a full-sized kitchen, fireplace, and screened porch. Smokers are welcome. Breakfast is "homemade continental." Rates run $120–210.

McElhattan's Owl Hill Bed & Breakfast, 617 Scenic Hwy., tel. 423/821-2040, sits on four secluded acres near the top of Lookout Mountain. Decorated with antiques and oriental rugs, the house has two guest rooms, each with a private bath. Guest amenities include a pool table, fireplace, and cable TV, as well as games and books. Breakfast is cooked to order. Rates run $95–125.

HOTELS AND MOTELS

The **Radisson Read House,** 827 Broad St., tel. 423/266-4121 or 800/333-3333, is to Chattanooga what the Peabody is to Memphis—serving as the city's grande dame since 1872. Five U.S. presidents and Winston Churchill have all stayed here. The hotel fell on hard times as Chattanooga's downtown declined, but new owners have brought the old girl back with a complete renovation. In an inspired touch, each of the 13 floors features a different battle of the Civil War through framed illustrations. Rates are $79–149. Visit www.readhouse.com for information.

The more budget-minded can try the **Cascades Motel,** 3625 Ringgold Rd., tel. 423/698-1571, with rates at $28–50, or **Kings Lodge,** I-24 Exit 181, 2400 Westside Dr., tel. 423/698-8944 or 800/251-7702, with rates at $38–55.

Chanticleer Inn at 1300 Mockingbird Lane on Lookout Mountain, tel. 706/820-2015, occupies a series of stone cottages. A pool is open seasonally. The 16 rooms have individual entrances and private baths. The inn serves a Southern-style breakfast; rates run $40–86.

The Chattanooga Choo Choo offers some of the more unusual accommodations in the state. Guests can stay in one of 48 suites on board sleeping cars or in a Holiday Inn on the premises. There's a lot to see and do on the Choo Choo grounds—especially for kids. Rates are $89–115 for rooms in the hotel and $150 for a room on the rails. Call 800/TRACK-29 or 423/266-5000 or see the Choo Choo online at www.choochoo.com.

CAMPING

The **Best Holiday Trav-L-Park of Chattanooga,** tel. 706/891-9766, has 170 sites with full amenities. It's open year-round. Take East Ridge Exit 1 and follow the signs.

Chester Frost Park (Hamilton County Park), tel. 423/842-0177, has 188 sites. It's open all year, offering lake swimming, boating, and fishing. From I-75 take Highway 153. Exit at Hixson Park and follow the signs.

Harrison Bay State Park, 11 miles northeast on Highway 58, tel. 423/344-6214, has 164 sites. It's open all year and offers a pool, canoeing, and hiking trails.

Raccoon Mountain Campground, one mile north of I-24 at Exit 174, tel. 423/821-9403, has 123 sites. It's open all year and features lots of amenities, including the Raccoon Mountain Caverns' Crystal Palace Tour.

Shipp's RV Center and Campground, 100 yards east off I-75 Exit 1, tel. 423/892-8275, offers 100 shady sites with full amenities. It's open all year, but reservations are recommended.

Food

Visitors to Chattanooga will have no problem finding something good to eat. In the major tourist areas around the Tennessee Aquarium and the Chattanooga Choo Choo, and the North Chattanooga shopping district, there are dozens of places for a quick lunch. Menus range from submarine sandwiches and burgers to soups, salads, and complete meals.

When it comes time for dinner, the options are a little less numerous but equally varied. Long known as a steak and baked potato town, Chattanooga today offers a much wider selection of dinner options, created by imaginative chefs specializing in contemporary dishes from across the country and around the world. Of course, you can still get a steak or some down-home country cooking. Those with a hankering for a truly Southern dish can pay a visit to one of the city's many barbecue joints. The following restaurants were reviewed by Suzanne Hall.

BARBECUE

Looking for a great place for barbecue in Chattanooga? Ask 10 people and you'll get 10 different recommendations. Everyone has a favorite—that's because there's plenty of good barbecue in town. This list below is just the beginning. If one place doesn't suit your fancy, just go a mile or two down the road and try another. The main event at each spot is pork, but most serve chicken and some beef as well. All are open daily for lunch and dinner.

Buck's Pit Barbeque, 3147 Broad St., tel. 423/267-1390

Rib & Loin, 5946 Brainerd Rd., tel. 423/499-6465

Shuford's Smokehouse, 924 Signal Mountain Rd., tel. 423/267-0080

Smokey's Barbecue, 3850 Brainerd Rd., tel. 423/622-8996

Sportsman's Bar-B-Q, 231 Signal Mountain Rd., tel. 423/265-1680

TOP OF THE HEAP

Reservations are strongly suggested for dining in the authentic Victorian railway car at **Dinner on the Diner,** 1400 Market St., tel. 423/266-5000. Lobster bisque is a specialty and precedes dishes such as filet mignon with béarnaise sauce, salmon en croûte, and sautéed veal chops. The setting is elegant but the atmosphere relaxed at the **Chattanooga Choo Choo** complex restaurant, which serves dinner Monday through Saturday. The complex also includes the less expensive **Station House,** where singing waiters and waitresses serve chicken, steaks, and ribs Monday through Saturday for dinner only. The well-stocked salad bar includes all-you-can-eat boiled shrimp. The Choo Choo's **Gardens** restaurant offers Southern specialties like fried chicken, cat-

Looking for a great place for barbecue in Chattanooga? Ask 10 people and you'll get 10 different recommendations.

MOON PIES

The scene: Two Southerners and someone else in Cambridge, Massachusetts, are deciding where to eat lunch. Amid the various options, one Southerner suggests "a Moon Pie and an R.C. Cola." The second Southerner bursts out laughing, but the other person doesn't get it, not recognizing a longtime favorite lunch for working-class Southerners.

Moon Pies were invented at the Chattanooga Bakery in 1919. The originals consisted of a marshmallow-type filling between two four-inch-wide cookies. The whole thing—at least the classic version—is covered with a chocolate coating. These "pies" became enormously popular throughout the South. For some people, a Moon Pie and a Royal Crown Cola was as good a snack as one could get.

Because of vending machine requirements, today's Moon Pies are smaller and thicker than the original, but now they have *three* cookies separated by filling. They also come in a low-fat version and, seasonally, with vanilla, banana, strawberry, and other flavored icings and fillings.

The Chattanooga Bakery turns out about 300,000 Moon Pies a day and sells them as far away as Japan, where they are known as Massi Pie. The epicenter of Moon Piedom, however, is the annual Moon Pie Festival in the Middle Tennessee village of Bell Buckle in June.

fish, and rainbow trout. New Orleans–style bread pudding is a highlight on the dessert menu. Open seven days a week for breakfast, lunch, and dinner, the Gardens is a great place for families.

Chattanoogans have been marking special occasions in **Steaks at the Green Room,** 827 Broad St., tel. 423/266-4121, for decades. Housed in the historic Radisson Read House, the room is formal but not stuffy. The menu's focus is steak, but it also includes pasta, seafood, and other dishes. Dinner is served Monday through Saturday. Reservations are suggested. The **Read House** also has a great scotch and cigar bar.

In the Bluff View Inn, a bed-and-breakfast overlooking the Tennessee River, the **Back Inn Cafe** is an Italian bistro offering upscale Italian cuisine, gourmet pizzas, and other fare. Lunch and dinner are served seven days a week either in the mansion or on an outdoor terrace. Reservations are a good idea on Friday and Saturday. The inn is the centerpiece of the Bluff View Art District, a collection of museums, galleries, shops and an outdoor sculpture garden. For less expensive dining, the complex includes **Tony's Pasta Shop,** offering a menu of freshly made pastas and sauces, and **Rembrandt's Coffee House,** specializing in European breads, pastries, and fine coffee. Both offer indoor and outdoor dining and are open for lunch and dinner seven days a week. Sunday brunch is served at **Renaissance Commons.** The Bluff View Art District restaurants are on High Street across from the Hunter Museum of American Art. Call 423/265-5033.

Many Chattanooga shakers and movers are regulars at the **Southside Grill,** 1400 Cowart St., tel. 423/266-6511. The talented kitchen staff specializes in dishes of the New South, giving traditional ingredients like pork, chicken, fish and vegetables an upscale, contemporary flair. The kitchen also does wonderful things with portobello mushrooms. Set in a restored historic building near the Chattanooga Choo Choo, Southside serves dinner seven nights a week and lunch Monday through Saturday. The restaurant is totally nonsmoking except for the patio.

A consistently imaginative kitchen staff, led by a chef-owner, makes **212 Market Restaurant,** 212 Market St., tel. 423/265-1212, one of the most popular spots in town. The menu features pork, poultry, beef, fish, and lamb served with flair. The appetizers and pasta dishes are excellent. There's live music every Friday night and a great Sunday brunch, enhanced once a month by live jazz. Across from the Tennessee Aquarium, it's open for lunch and dinner seven days a week.

EASIER ON THE WALLET

The Greek, Italian, and American dishes are ample and well prepared at **Acropolis,** 2213 Hamilton Place Blvd., tel. 423/899-5341. It's adjacent to Hamilton Place, one of Tennessee's largest shopping malls, and open for lunch and dinner seven days a week.

Big River Grille & Brewing Works, 222 Broad St., tel. 423/267-2739, near the Tennessee Aquarium, has good food, a casual atmosphere, and beer, root beer, ginger ale, and cream soda made on the premises. The menu includes sandwiches, salads, and full meals. Lunch and dinner are served seven days a week.

The menu changes nightly and includes Caribbean, French, and American dishes at **Chef's Underground Cafe,** 720 Walnut St., tel. 423/266-3142. Down a flight of stairs from the street, this restaurant is owned by its chef, who serves lunch weekdays and dinner Tuesday through Saturday. Tuesday night's special is prime rib. On Wednesday, the featured item is a rib sampler. Thursday is Jamaican night. The chef will gladly prepare vegetarian dishes. The café also serves beer, and diners are welcome to bring their own wine. Reservations are advisable.

One of Chattanooga's most popular restaurants, **The Loft,** 328 Cherokee Blvd., tel. 423/266-3601, specializes in steaks, prime rib, seafood dishes, and indulgent desserts. Located just north of downtown, it serves dinner seven nights a week. Lunch is available Monday through Friday, and brunch is served on Sunday.

Don't pass up the amaretto crème pie at **Mount Vernon,** 1707 A. Cummings Hwy., tel. 423/266-6591. A favorite with Chattanoogans for more than 40 years, Mount Vernon serves top-quality Southern dishes in an attractive and friendly setting. Salad dressings are a specialty and available for purchase. Mount Vernon is open for lunch and dinner Monday through Friday and for dinner on Saturday.

Town and Country, 110 N. Market St., tel. 423/267-8544, has been dishing up steaks, prime rib, fish, and Southern-style entrées and vegetables since the 1940s. Located across the river from downtown in North Chattanooga, it's a good place for families. Dinner is served nightly Monday through Saturday and at midday on Sunday. Lunch is available Monday through Friday.

More Practicalities

SHOPPING

Across the street from the Hunter Museum, the **River Gallery,** 400 E. Second St., tel. 423/267-7353, offers original fine arts and high-end crafts. Visitors can peruse woodcarvings, jewelry, sculpture, basketry, studio art glass, handmade books, art furniture, and textiles. The gallery has a sculpture garden outside.

Eight of Chattanooga's old railroad warehouses make up **Warehouse Row,** 1110 Market St., tel. 423/267-1111, which offers outlet shopping in downtown Chattanooga. More than 40 shops of high-end merchandise, including Tommy Hilfiger, J. Peterman, and Danskin, are open daily.

North of Town

The area north of the river—across the Tennessee River from downtown—offers a collection of interesting shops. **Turner and Carver** offers art objects made from wood. **New Moon Gallery** sells New Age sorts of things. **Rock Creek Down Under** is a great outfitter. Nearby you'll find **The Clay Pot, Loafer's Glory, Garden Gallery,** and **Rising Fawn Folk Art Gallery.**

Hundreds of contemporary crafts workers sell their goods at **Plum Nelly,** 1101 Hixson Pike, tel. 423/266-0585. Offerings include functional pottery made by more than 150 potters and jewelry from more than 100 artists.

Mole Hill Pottery, at 1210 Taft Highway on Signal Mountain, tel. 423/886-5636, sells all kinds of pottery—dishes, objets d'art, and kitchen items.

TRANSPORTATION

Express Shuttle, tel. 800/896-9928 or 423/954-1400, offers van service between the Chattanooga Airport and the Nashville and Atlanta airports. Vans leave from 6:30 A.M. to 5 P.M. and cost $30 one-way to Nashville. Vans leave from the back of the Eastgate Mall at 5600 Brainerd Road or, for an extra $5, from the Chattanooga Airport itself. Visit www.TheExpressShuttle.com.

SERVICES AND INFORMATION

Chattanooga Area Convention & Visitor's Bureau, 1001 Market St., tel. 423/756-8687 or 800/322-3344, is open daily from 8:30 A.M. to 5:30 P.M. A larger visitor's center at 2 Broad Street is located just down from the Tennessee Aquarium. Access them online at www.chattanoogafun.net.

Resources

Suggested Reading

History

Corlew, Robert. *Tennessee, A Short History.* Knoxville: University of Tennessee Press, 1990. This condensation of a four-volume work is the definitive history book about the state.

Frome, Michael, *Strangers in High Places.* Knoxville: University of Tennessee Press, 1994. This book details the 40-year effort to bring the Great Smoky Mountains National Park into existence.

Kephart, Horace and Ralph Roberts, *Our Southern Highlanders: A Narrative of Adventure in the Southern Appalachians and a Study of Life Among the Mountaineers.* Knoxville: University of Tennessee Press, 1977. Originally published in 1913, this classic was the first ethnographic look at the people who lived in what is now the Great Smoky Mountains National Park.

Klebenow, Anne. *200 Years in 200 Stories.* Knoxville: University of Tennessee Press, 1997. Prepared for Tennessee's bicentennial, this book breaks history into enjoyable chunks.

Neely, Jack. *Knoxville's Secret History.* Knoxville: Scruffy City Publishing, 1995. Looking at topics as various as colonial days and the death of Hank Williams, this talented writer illuminates Tennessee's oldest city.

McPherson, James. *Battle Cry of Freedom.* Oxford: Oxford University Press, 1988. A one-volume history of the Civil War.

Pollard, Edward A. *The Southern History of the War.* New York: Charles B. Richardson Publishers, 1866. A revealing account of the War Between the States as it appeared to one contemporary Southerner.

Powell, William S. *North Carolina: A History.* Chapel Hill: University of North Carolina Press, 1988. A reprint of the 1976 book written as part of a series honoring the U.S. bicentennial. A good, well-balanced survey of the state's past.

Ward, Geoffrey. *The Civil War.* New York: Alfred A. Knopf, 1990. The companion volume to the Ken Burns Civil War documentary.

Description and Travel

Sakowski, Carolyn. *Touring the East Tennessee Backroads.* Winston-Salem: John F. Blair, 1993. This book should be on the front seat of any history buff driving though East Tennessee.

WPA Guide to North Carolina. Columbia: University of South Carolina Press, 1988. A reprint of the 1939 guide written by the Federal Writers' Project of the Work Projects Administration—a Depression effort aimed at putting writers to work and supplying guidebooks for states.

WPA Guide to Tennessee. Knoxville: University of Tennessee Press, 1986. A reprint of the Volunteer State's own 1939 guide. This book, full of the pride and prejudices of the time, gives a wonderful view of Tennessee—small towns and large.

Music

McCloud, Barry. *Definitive Country: The Ultimate Encyclopedia of Country Music and Its Performers.* New York: Berkley Publishing Group, 1995. Just what the title says.

Wolfe, Charles K. *Tennessee Strings.* Knoxville: University of Tennessee Press, 1977. A thin but authoritative book on country music.

Zimmerman, Peter Coats. *Tennessee Music*. San Francisco: Miller Freeman Books, 1998. This combination travel book and music guide to the state is must for roots music lovers.

Fiction and Literature

Agee, James. *A Death in the Family*. New York: Grossett and Dunlap, 1967. The best Knoxville novel.

Haley, Alex. *Roots*. New York: Doubleday, 1976. The fascinating tale of this writer's ancestors, slaves and otherwise.

Henry, O. *The Best of O. Henry*. Philadelphia: Courage Books, 1992. A good introduction to Asheville's most famous short story writer.

Marshall, Catherine. *Christy*. New York: Mc-Graw Hill, 1967. The inspiring story of a young woman who goes to teach school in a remote East Tennessee town. It later became a television show and a musical performed in the Smokies.

Wolfe, Thomas. *Look Homeward, Angel*. New York: Scribner's, 1929. The epic coming-of-age novel, first published in 1929, tells the story of a restless young man who longs to escape his chaotic family life in little Altamont (Asheville), NC.

Biography

Escott, Colin. *Hank Williams: the Biography*. Boston: Little, Brown and Company, 1994. A very good biography of one of country music's greatest.

Summitt, Pat Head. *Raise the Roof: the Inspiring Inside Story of the Tennessee Lady Vols Undefeated 1997–98 Season* New York: Broadway Books, 1999. The title says it all.

Summitt, Pat Head. *Reach for the Summit* New York: Broadway Books, 1998. The life story of

the second—so far—winningest basketball coach in America, the coach of the University of Tennessee Lady Vols.

Trefousse, Hans L. *Andrew Johnson: A Biography*. New York: Norton, 1989. A fine recounting of an underappreciated president.

Architecture

Moffett, Marian and Lawrence Woodhouse. *Tennessee's Cantilever Barns*. Knoxville: University of Tennessee Press, 1993. A study of the indigenous and ingenious structures found in the mountains of East Tennessee.

Neely, Jack. *The Marble City: A Photographic Tour of Knoxville's Graveyards*. Knoxville: University of Tennessee Press, 1999. Photographer Aaron Jay and East Tennessee's leading amateur historian take a fascinating look at their city's cemeteries.

West, Carroll Van. *Tennessee's Historic Landscapes*. Knoxville: University of Tennessee Press, 1995. With photos and astute commentary, this book leads the traveler though big cities and small towns in search of architectural treasures.

West, Carroll Van. *Tennessee's New Deal Landscapes*. Knoxville: University of Tennessee Press, 2001. This master of Tennessee architecture looks at the buildings that were built during the Depression.

The Outdoors

Camuto, Christopher. *Another Country: Journeying Toward the Cherokee Mountains*. Athens: UGA Press, 1997. Against the backdrop of the attempted reintroduction of the red wolf to the Great Smoky Mountains, the author mulls long and hard over humanity's impact upon, and estrangement from, the earth.

Moore, Harry H., *A Roadside Guide to the Geology of the Great Smoky Mountains National Park.* Knoxville: University of Tennessee Press, 1988. Even if in many places you can't see the rocks for the trees, this book will tell you what is there.

Smith, Richard, *Wildflowers of the Southern Mountains.* Knoxville: University of Tennessee Press, 2001. This filed guide to wildflowers is a delight, whether walking through a mountain meadow in May or sitting in front of a fire and wishing you were in the Smokies.

Wise, Kenneth. *Hiking Trails of the Great Smoky Mountains.* Knoxville: University of Tennessee Press, 1996. This guidebook, complete with maps, lists all the official trails and some very interesting off-the-beaten-path places.

Odds and Ends

Egerton, John, et al. *Southern Food.* Chapel Hill: University of North Carolina Press, 1987. Combining recipes, fine writing, and great photos, this book takes a satisfying look at country cooking.

Garner, Bob. *North Carolina Barbecue: Flavored by Time.* Winston-Salem: John F. Blair, 1996. Not so much a guidebook as a thoughtful look at the origins of and a celebration of the vinegary manna of the mountains. Other North Carolina regions (and barbecue styles) are covered as well.

Luther, Edward T. *Our Restless Earth.* Knoxville: University of Tennessee Press, 1977. A short and very readable guide to the geology of Tennessee.

West, Carroll Van. *The Tennessee Encyclopedia of History and Culture.* Nashville: Rutledge Hill Press, 1998. If readers like the historical bits in *Smokies Handbook,* they will love this 1,193-page volume, which is filled with fascinating short articles from a great many luminaries.

Wilson, Charles Reagan, and William Ferris, *Encyclopedia of Southern Culture.* Chapel Hill: University of North Carolina Press, 1989. This stupendous book—1,634 pages long—addresses mint juleps, sacred harp singing, kudzu, and other Southern items with scholarship and wit.

Accommodations Index

Restaurant Index

General Index

Festivals, Fairs, and Events

Hiking

Museums

General Index

Shopping

A Frame of Mind: 86
A Gardener's Place: 133
Alewine Pottery: 86
Appalachian Craft Center: 140
Apron Shop: 153
Armour House: 86
Arrowcraft Shop: 82, 88
Book Eddy: 109
Candy Factory, The: 109
Clay Pot, The: 191
Corn Crib: 153
Cowee Creek Pottery: 162
Deerfoot Quilts: 113
Earthtide School of Folk Art: 58
Farmers Tailgate Market: 153–154
Garden Gallery: 191
Great Smoky Arts and Crafts Community: 86
Halls Furniture and Auction: 59
Hanson Gallery Fine Art & Craft: 109
Happy Hiker, The: 86
Homespun Crafts and Antique Mall: 109
Jackson Antique Marketplace: 110
Jim Gray Gallery (Gatlinburg): 88
Jim Gray Gallery (Knoxville): 109
Jim Gray Gallery (Pigeon Forge): 77
Lee Roberson's Studio/Gallery: 58
Lee's World of Crafts: 59
Loafer's Glory: 191
MACO Crafts Co-Op: 162–163
Mast General Store (Asheville): 140

Mast General Store (Waynesville): 153
Michael M. Rogers Gallery: 163
Mole Hill Pottery: 191
Mountain Pottery: 153
Musicrafts: 112–113
Nancy's Art & Frame Shop: 58
Nawger Knob Craft Settlement: 58
New Moon Gallery: 191
Ogle's Broom Shop: 86
Open Air Market: 153
Pigeon Forge Pottery: 77–78
Pigeon River String Instruments: 77
Plum Nelly: 191
Qualla Arts and Crafts: 153
Rising Fawn Folk Art Gallery: 191
River Gallery: 191
Rock Creek Down Under: 191
Smoky Mountain Knife Works: 87
Smoky Mountain Woodcarvers Supply: 58
Stable Shops: 133
Stages West: 77
T. Pennington Art Gallery: 153
Three Blind Mice: 126
Turner and Carver: 191
Twigs & Leaves Gallery: 153
Vern Hippensteal Gallery: 88
Victorian Houses: 109
Warehouse Row: 191
Wood-N-Strings: 58
World Marketplace: 140
Yee-Haw Industries: 109

General Index

Acknowledgments

Thank you to my wife, Kristin Sigalas, for the encouragement and counsel. And to my co-writer Jeff, for being such an easy dog to hunt with.

A big thanks also for the help provided by Joel Young and the rest of the staff and volunteers at the Maggie Valley Chamber of Commerce & Visitors & Convention Bureau; to David Redman, director of the Cherokee Tribal Travel and Promotion Office; and to Marla Tambellini and Erin Guill of the Asheville Convention and Visitors Bureau. Thanks also to my brother, sometime research associate and photographer Joe Sigalas, PhD, whose involvement makes this perhaps the only guidebook to the Smokies whose barbecue reviews feature input from a recognized Renaissance scholar.

Thanks as always to Pauli Galin for her encouragement and advice, and to our affable and determined editor Ellen Cavalli, who got married during the production of this book, missed just one day's work for a honeymoon—and then apologized to us for the inconvenience. Thanks also for the professionalism of map editor Naomi Dancis, and to Sarah Coglianese and the rest of the crew in Avalon marketing.

Much is owned also to Tom and Cheryl, Nona, and Jen and Brian for watching the kids during deadline periods; to my sister Mary, brother George, and his wife Kristin N. Sigalas for their unfaltering foothills hospitality; to Leslie Anderson for the inspiration; to Pearl Sigalas, who will read this book cover-to-cover; and to Miss Sharon Hall.

And to my parents, who always pulled over to read the plaques.

—Mike Sigalas

Several on-the-scene Tennesseans made it possible for someone living in the shadow of the Rockies to write a book about Tennessee. Nathan Magness cheerfully called almost every phone number in this book and patiently explained that he wasn't trying to sell anything. Suzanne Hall ably selected and wrote up the restaurants and nightclubs in Chattanooga, and Adrienne Martini wittily did the same in Knoxville. Nancy Gray proofread the chapter on the Smokies, and Jack Neely generously shared his information and insight on Knoxville.

Mike Sigalas, who wrote the North Carolina portion of this book, served as a thoughtful sounding board for ideas and interpretations. I enjoyed working with him.

Thanks go to my family for the time this book has taken from them: Marta, who has hiked with me for three decades now, and Truman and Walker, who still vividly remember the time a bear strolled across the creek at the Chimneys picnic area and ate our lunch.

The spirit of Richard Marius, a dear friend who died all too soon in 1999, permeates this book. He brought me from Tennessee to teach at Harvard; he introduced me to my first publisher and enriched my life with his knowledge, wisdom, and endless stock of Tennessee tales. He was always proud to be a Tennessean, whether at the University of Tennessee or in the Harvard Faculty Club. Richard delighted in tramping along the trails of the Smokies, and I like to think that his spirit walks there still.

—Jeff Bradley

AVALON TRAVEL
publishing

How far will our travel guides take you? As far as you want.

Discover a rhumba-fueled nightspot in Old Havana, explore prehistoric tombs in Ireland, hike beneath California's centuries-old redwoods, or embark on a classic road trip along Route 66. Our guidebooks deliver solidly researched, trip-tested information—minus any generic froth—to help globetrotters or weekend warriors create an adventure uniquely their own.

And we're not just about the printed page. Public television viewers are tuning in to Rick Steves' new travel series, *Rick Steves' Europe*. On the Web, readers can cruise the virtual black top with *Road Trip USA* author Jamie Jensen and learn travel industry secrets from Edward Hasbrouck of *The Practical Nomad*.

In print. On TV. On the Internet.

We supply the information. The rest is up to you.

Avalon Travel Publishing

Something for everyone

www.travelmatters.com

Avalon Travel Publishing guides are available at your favorite book or travel store.

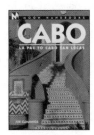

MOON HANDBOOKS provide comprehensive

coverage of a region's arts, history, land, people, and social
issues in addition to detailed practical listings for
accommodations, food, outdoor recreation, and
entertainment. Moon Handbooks allow complete immersion
in a region's culture—ideal for travelers who want to combine
sightseeing with insight for an extraordinary travel experience
in destinations throughout North America, Hawaii, Latin
America, the Caribbean, Asia, and the Pacific.

WWW.MOON.COM

Rick Steves shows you where to travel and how to travel—
all while getting the most value for your dollar. His Back
Door travel philosophy is about making friends, having fun,
and avoiding tourist rip-offs.

Rick has been traveling to Europe for more than 25
years and is the author of 22 guidebooks, which have sold
more than a million copies. He also hosts the award-winning
public television series *Rick Steves' Europe.*

WWW.RICKSTEVES.COM

ROAD TRIP USA

Getting there is half the fun, and Road Trip USA guides are your ticket to driving
adventure. Taking you off the interstates and onto
less-traveled, two-lane highways, each guide is filled with
fascinating trivia, historical information, photographs, facts
about regional writers, and details on where to sleep and
eat—all contributing to your exploration of the American
road.

*"[Books] so full of the pleasures of the American road,
you can smell the upholstery."*
~BBC radio

WWW.ROADTRIPUSA.COM

U.S.~METRIC CONVERSION

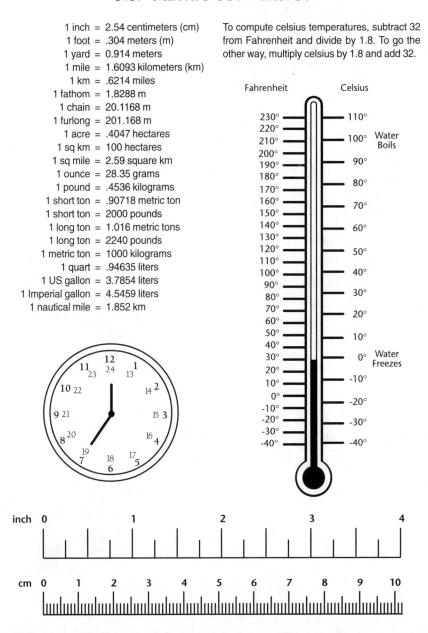

1 inch = 2.54 centimeters (cm)
1 foot = .304 meters (m)
1 yard = 0.914 meters
1 mile = 1.6093 kilometers (km)
1 km = .6214 miles
1 fathom = 1.8288 m
1 chain = 20.1168 m
1 furlong = 201.168 m
1 acre = .4047 hectares
1 sq km = 100 hectares
1 sq mile = 2.59 square km
1 ounce = 28.35 grams
1 pound = .4536 kilograms
1 short ton = .90718 metric ton
1 short ton = 2000 pounds
1 long ton = 1.016 metric tons
1 long ton = 2240 pounds
1 metric ton = 1000 kilograms
1 quart = .94635 liters
1 US gallon = 3.7854 liters
1 Imperial gallon = 4.5459 liters
1 nautical mile = 1.852 km

To compute celsius temperatures, subtract 32 from Fahrenheit and divide by 1.8. To go the other way, multiply celsius by 1.8 and add 32.

Fahrenheit   Celsius

230°   110°
220°
210°   100°   Water
200°   Boils
190°   90°
180°
170°   80°
160°
150°   70°
140°   60°
130°
120°   50°
110°
100°   40°
90°
80°   30°
70°
60°   20°
50°
40°   10°
30°   0°   Water
20°   Freezes
10°   -10°
0°
-10°   -20°
-20°   -30°
-30°
-40°   -40°

inch 0   1   2   3   4

cm 0 1 2 3 4 5 6 7 8 9 10

Will you have enough stories to tell your grandchildren?

Yahoo! Travel

DO YOU YAHOO!?